# Sex & God

## How Religion
## Distorts Sexuality

### Darrel W. Ray, Ed.D.

IPC Press
Bonner Springs, Kansas

Editors: Deborah Shouse, Kirsten McBride

Ray, Darrel W.
    Sex & God How Religion Distorts Sexuality
by Darrel W. Ray.
    Includes bibliographical references and index.
    LCCN 2011961234
    ISBN-13: 978-0-9709505-4-3
    ISBN-10: 0-9709505-4-3

Published by
IPC Press
15699 Kansas Avenue
Bonner Springs, Kansas 66012

Visit www.ipcpress.com for additional information.

Published 2012

Printed in the United States of America

Dedicated to
Julie

# ACKNOWLEDGEMENTS

I want to thank many friends who supported me during this intense process. First, Julie my love and partner who was involved every step, supporting and reading many of the early versions. My friend and travel companion Judy Roepke, who, for the second time in as many books, spent our European vacation time reading and critiquing a very rough draft. Thanks to Missy Andeel for her insights and critique of the manuscript. Some of her suggestions led me to change or refine several ideas.

Putting together this project required several special people that I have come to trust and rely on over my last three book projects. A big thank you to my editors, Deborah Shouse and to Kirsten McBride. Deborah also served as my psychologist and counselor during the most difficult parts of the writing. Kirsten's tough approach to editing kept me on the straight and narrow when I wanted to wander. Neither of them have any idea how many arguments I have had with them (in my mind) and they win almost all of them. Thanks to Micki Lubbers for her contributions to the final proofs.

Thanks to Shayne Schuldt whose ideas and support make him much more than a designer in this process. And to Adam Brown whose cover ideas made the design process easy. Finally, thanks to Amanda Brown for her help in the Sex and Secularism research in Chapter 16 and to Donald Wright for his help on Chapter 15 and Dr. Richard Carrier for his review and feedback on Chapter 4.

# CONTENTS

# INTRODUCTION

## My Journey

I have been a psychologist for over 35 years. Before I went into psychology, I thought I was destined to be a minister. I went to Scarritt College for Christian Workers for two years, and received a Master's degree in Church and Community. The result of this religious study convinced me that most religion was self-serving, but I remained a liberal Christian. Over the next 14 years, I helped train ministers, chaplains and other church officials in many protestant denominations and a few Catholic priests and nuns. I also trained army and civilian chaplains. Through my work, I saw layer upon layer of complicity in sexual scandals and financial fraud. The behavior of ministers and priests was clearly no better than the average behavior of their parishioners. I could see little positive effect of religion on behavior. In fact, it seemed that religion often was an excuse for bad behavior. Moreover, financial issues got quick response while sexual behavior was ignored or covered up.

Over time, I saw an astonishingly high incidence of sexual misconduct among the church leaders. Not all displayed this behavior, but almost all participated in hiding or ignoring it. This experience led me to a deeper study of how religion works and what allows such obviously inappropriate behavior to go on for years in all kinds of churches. No book or study I read seemed to address this question.

## Finding the Juicy Stuff

It is hard for me to remember a time when my sexual behavior was not influenced by Jesus watching or a god judging. By the time I became aware of sex, at about 8 or 9 years old, I knew it was dangerous, dirty, suspect and something I should not talk about. While my mom was pretty open about sexuality, she still thought Alfred Kinsey was a communist, Masters and Johnson were pornographers and that the books of D. H. Lawrence should be banned. My father did not seem interested in talking about sex except to make occasional obscure comments. As for my grandparents, I knew and loved all four of them but suspected that they had sex only four times, to produce their four children. The mention of sex could set any of them off on a religious rant.

I often sneaked the medical dictionary off the shelf and read all it said about sex, which, sadly, was very little. I asked questions my mother didn't want to answer, so she eventually took me to the library where we checked out books on sex. In the early 1960s, most of the books were "restricted." My mother had to check them out for me as I was only 12 years old. I came home from the library excited at the prospect of finally finding the answers. I read and read … for days. But much to my disappointment, I found few answers and many contradictions. The books were clinical and filled with biological "facts."

As I read, every so often a book would venture into the juicy stuff – like how to actually have sex – only to disappoint by saying, "You must communicate with your partner." or "Pray about your relationship and talk with your minister or priest." At the end of my research, I knew little more than when I started. Nevertheless, I became known throughout our school as *the* expert on sex, since I was the only one who had actually read the forbidden books. Boys had a hundred questions. I answered them with great authority and listened to their concerns. Despite all my reading, I knew little more than they did. For most it came down to, "My parents say that I will learn about sex some day and in the mean time I should read the Bible and pray for God's guidance."

Somehow I heard about the Kinsey Report.[1] In the interest of furthering my research, I asked my mom if she would check it out for me. She informed me that it was smut and that the library did not carry it.

Then one day a friend of mine, whose father was an elder in the church, revealed his father's stash of pornographic magazines. When his parents were not around, we both devoured first the pictures, then the articles. With this information, I soon became a true expert and began to answer questions much more intelligently. The main thing I noticed in these magazines was the lack of religious references. In fact, some even had anti-religious messages. I distinctly remember one photo spread that highlighted nuns in revealing habits and priests leering at them. Later I created my own collection of porn, and my brothers began collecting theirs as well. Ultimately, my mom found out and made a minor fuss. She threw everything away, so we got better at hiding it.

---

1  Alfred Kinsey's *Sexual Behavior in the Human Male* (1948) and *Sexual Behavior in the Human Female* (1953).

From then on, my sexual development involved pornography. Despite its bad reputation, it was one way to learn about sex. But everyone knows that porn is masturbatory material. As a young teenager, I noticed how many people acted like they did not masturbate or use porn. One preacher's son was famous for always having great sex photos in his pocket, yet he claimed he never masturbated. His father was caught three times having affairs with women in the church. It was an unwritten rule, "Do not admit to it or you will be labeled a 'homo.'" As I leered at friends' magazines in the shed behind my house, getting an erection under my jeans, I dared not admit the pictures had any effect on me, let alone admit that I masturbated later to the memory of those photos.

Reading *Catcher in the Rye* by J. D. Salinger (1951) was the first time I read a non-porn book that seemed to deal with the kind of sex and sexuality that I was experiencing in my own life. Of course, the fact that everyone thought it was a horrible book made me want to read it even more.

After getting married at age 20, I read *The Joy of Sex* by Alex Comfort (1972) and soon began thinking that everything the churches taught was wrong. But it wasn't until I was in graduate school and heard the great psychotherapist, sexologist and atheist Albert Ellis speak, that I began to recognize the whole religion and sex thing was a scam.[2] Ellis talked freely about sex and sexuality, using words I had almost never heard uttered publicly like "masturbation," "anal sex" and "blow job." It was an incredible experience. Unfortunately, living and working in a conservative community allowed for little discussion and exploration of his ideas. In the "goody two-shoes" world of church, no one would dare discuss how they used sex toys or a sexual position or technique. Even in liberal churches like Presbyterian U.S.A., Episcopalians and United Church of Christ, the language in marriage classes was so discreet and convoluted as to be useless. Many participants could not even use clinical descriptions of body parts without embarrassment.

Eventually I found places where people were comfortable with their sexuality. I met them at humanist meetings, secular book clubs, gay and lesbian groups, Pagan groups, atheist and deists meetings. Conversation and discussion about sex flowed easily. Whether sexual techniques or

---

2   Ellis' *Sex Without Guilt in the 21st Century* (2003) is an update of his ground-breaking 1958 book, *Sex Without Guilt.*

preferences, people seemed comfortable and open, nothing to hide or feel shameful about.

The contrast between these groups and church groups says volumes about religion's influence on our sexuality and led me to think: "What if we took religion out of sex? How would that look? How would it work? Why has religion gotten so tangled up in sex? How did that happen, and how does religion benefit from this arrangement? Do we benefit from having religion in our sex lives?" These are some of the questions that intrigued me and ultimately led to the research for this book.

## Viewpoint

Every author brings a viewpoint. While my personal views will undoubtedly influence the discussion, I will endeavor to stay close to the science and facts and give you resources to examine yourself. We will look at the science, the biology, the anthropology and much more to fully understand what human sexuality has been and still is. My hope is that this exploration will bring you closer to understanding yourself as a sexual creature so you can enjoy and celebrate your sexuality free of religious ideas and controls. I will also look at data collected from thousands of people who left religion to answer the question, "What happens to your sex life when you leave religion?"

If successful, you will learn more about you and your potential. You will gain greater understanding of the power religion has in distorting the lives of its adherents. I also hope you gain a sense of power and acceptance of who you are. My purpose is to challenge you, the reader, to look into the sexual training and indoctrination you received from childhood and make informed choices about how to conduct yourself as a sexual being. In many ways, we cannot understand ourselves unless we understand how religion has impacted us. Even if you were born to non-religious parents, the culture that surrounds you is replete with religious sexual messages. Religion has shaped our culture, our sexual development and our behavior. Examples of this include embarrassment over menstruation, taboos against masturbation and premarital sex, ideas that sex is sinful or somehow dirty. If we can eliminate religious sexual myths and learn to make rational choices, we can become more fulfilled and more informed. We can create our own value structure, free of dogma and based on ethical principles and acceptance of others, regardless of their sexual orientation.

Reading this book may be disturbing or confusing. After all, it looks at one of the most deeply ingrained areas of behavior and programming. If you find yourself disagreeing with something or feeling uncomfortable, take time to look at some of the source material listed. Examine the evidence for yourself. Then consider how it will inform you, change you, support you and give you new avenues and ideas for living your life.

I have given many talks on religion and sex and cannot count the number of times I have received emails and phone calls from people saying how liberated they felt after recognizing and challenging their religious programming. Sometimes it is almost miraculous. After one of my talks, a professional man emailed me this message:

> *My wife and I left your talk last night with our heads spinning.*
> *So many ideas applied to us as a couple. Things we had never*
> *thought to discuss or were afraid to tell each other. Let me just say*
> *that the discussion was beyond anything we have had in our 26*
> *years of marriage. I think our marriage was changed dramatically*
> *last night. No more reason to hide from one another.*

A young engaged couple attended one of my talks on a college campus. Later, they wrote to say they went home that night and talked until dawn with the result that they decided to break off the engagement. The ideas they heard made them examine their expectations of sex in marriage. In the end, they realized that their sexual styles were very different. They recognized that they were headed towards sexual misery, something they saw in their very religious parents. They parted good friends and felt like they had a much better idea of what their own sexual desires were.

I am sure the ideas presented here will not have that effect on everyone. But an honest reading, I believe, will find you challenging some closely held beliefs about your sexuality and give you a better understanding of others' sexuality.

In this book we will not only take a hard look at Western religious culture but also at other times and cultures. By examining how other cultures have dealt with sexuality, we will see how deeply restricted and programmed we have become by the religious environment of our time and our history.

## Organization of the Book

In Section I we will explore religion and sex broadly and identify some of the psychological methods all the major religions use to create shame and guilt about sex.

In Section II we will take a fun look at our biology and learn how evolution changes genitals and programs our behavior. In Section III we will examine how culture has impacted sex and religion over the last 10,000 years and ask the question, "How did so many cultures survive for thousands of years without Jesus looking into their bedroom?"

Section IV will examine the psychology of religion; specifically, how it distorts sexual ideas, body image, marriage, family and culture. Finally, in Section V we will look at what you can do about religiously taught sexual guilt and ask, "Do you really believe your religious mom or dad were virgins when they married?" We will break some romantic and religious myths about relationships.

With better knowledge, we can make better decisions and heal the damage of old decisions. This book will give you ideas and skills to question the religious programming of your family and culture and to empower you to blaze your own path without the chains of religion inhibiting and restricting you.

## Who Will Benefit from Reading This Book

This book will benefit anyone who wants to understand how religion impacts sexuality.

- If you are young and not yet experienced in marriage or relationships, this will show you the world of dating in a religious culture. You will learn about the unconscious games used by religious people to trap you into religion through marriage and relationships.
- If you are in a new relationship or newly married, you will learn about many hidden religious assumptions that directly impact your sex life. Examining these assumptions will give you the power to make informed decisions, free of dogma and indoctrination.
- If you have been married for 10 or 20 years or more, and want to know if your feelings and concerns are normal, this may give you some benchmarks to consider and ideas to further develop your relationship.

- Finally, if you are religious, you will be able to compare your particular religion with many others. You may want to explore such questions as, "Why do all major religions use shame and guilt, regardless of their theology or doctrine?" or "Why are women universally seen as second-class citizens in the major religions?"

# SECTION I:
# RELIGION IN PERSPECTIVE

## CHAPTER 1:
## RELIGIOUS FOREPLAY

Religion has the power to interfere with sex before it even gets started. This distorts sexuality and sexual expression and causes sexual dysfunction and acting-out behavior in many religious people, including leaders ....

*"... sex is great but the kingdom of heaven is better."*

**-City Bible Forum**

### Anna and Joe

Anna smiles at Joe as she unbuttons her blouse. They met in an adult singles Sunday School class four months ago and their relationship has really blossomed. She's ready to sleep with him and knows he will become her husband within the next year. Joe reaches toward Anna, watching her lovingly. But as he slips down her bra strap and kisses her shoulder, Anna realizes someone is watching her: Jesus. The crucifix Aunt Mary gave her eons ago glares at her from the wall. The Bible on the bed stand, unread for weeks, seems to bristle. Instead of tasting desire, the bitter taste of sin fills her mouth. Flooded with shame and guilt, Anna takes a step back. "I can't do this," she tells Joe.

Most adults feel they are making their own choices. But for adults like Anna who live in a religious culture, many of those choices have already been made for us. We're not even aware that our sexual identity is being throttled by a tyrannical set of impossible religious restrictions.

### Choices

This is a book about choices. Choices that were made for you and new choices you can make. You may be restricted in the choices you make about your sexuality by ideas you have never questioned, ideas that do not appear to have anything to do with religion. Some choices were made for you before you were even born. Some choices were cut off, some were prohibited, some were forced on you. Others felt like reasonable choices when you made them, but you now realize they were determined by the religious ideas and training you received. Even if you were not raised in a religious home, you were raised in a religious culture. From the way kids talked about sex in elementary school to the laws your legislators are passing today, sexual choices are being made for you based on religious assumptions.

How are your choices restricted? If you live in a Christian community, you will learn that god is always watching you. If you have impure thoughts, god knows. If you masturbate, god sees. If you have sex before you are married, god will punish you. You may be told you cannot marry someone you love because he or she is the same sex as you are. Preachers tell you that you don't need birth control because you shouldn't be having premarital sex. You also hear that masturbation will injure your marriage. You learn that the instant of conception is when some god plants a soul into the embryo and, therefore, it is a sin to stop the development in any way.

If you are female and living in a Muslim country, you may be prohibited from choices about mates or about control over your body. You may be forced to marry a man with other wives. You may have no choice about premarital sex; in fact, you might be killed for making that choice. As a Muslim boy you will be taught how to treat and control women, that they are subservient to you. You will read in the Koran that your wife is always supposed to be ready to have sex, even if she in the midst of cooking a meal.[3]

Unless you are in a more sex-positive minority religion, like Pagan, Wicca or Unitarian, you will never be taught the joys of sex. The religious messages from priest, minister, Sunday School teacher or imam are all focused on the role sex plays in god's plan. If you choose to have sex in any way that is not blessed by your particular god, you are sinning and subject to eternal punishment.

If you belong to one of the more liberal religions, you may not get the harsh messages, but the choices are still narrowed by your god. You may still feel guilty or uncomfortable about your son or daughter having a sex life in college. You may have difficulty understanding your nephew's choice to marry a man. And no matter how liberal your religion, the laws of your state may make you a felon whenever you have sex in anything but a missionary position. It may also be illegal for you and your spouse to use sex toys. Even liberal people may find it difficult to talk about their fantasies and sexual desires with their spouses. These inhibitions and ideas probably came from the many subtle signals that surround all of us in our religious culture.

All cultures have some rules and ideas about sex and sexuality, but the major religions have taken sex and sexuality as the strict purview of their god or gods. The major religions seek to restrict sexual expression for no apparent reason other than to propagate their particular dogma.

Human sexuality is vast in its expression. Even a cursory study of other cultures finds many different forms of sexual expression; if other cultures can survive for tens of thousands of years without the religious rules of Islam, Mormonism, Hinduism or Christianity, what purpose do religious restrictions and religious guilt serve? Why is masturbation a non-issue in

3  Some examples, from *Rights in Islam* by Ashraf 'Ali Thānawī (1863–1943): "When a man calls his wife for sexual intercourse, even if the woman is cooking at that moment, she should answer her husband's call." Or "If the woman performs nafilah (supererogatory) fasts without the permission of her husband and avoids meeting the desires of her husband, Allah loads the sin of three bad deeds over her." (Available online at http://www.darululoom-deoband.com/english/books/rightsinislam.htm).

modern secular Europe but still disapproved of by the Catholic Church? How is gay marriage a threat to marriage when Christian divorce rates in the United States are highest in the most evangelical and fundamentalist states? How is homosexuality destructive of a culture when many North American Native cultures and many ancient cultures, including Greece, celebrated homosexual relationships in song and legend?

Religion is about restricting sexual choices in the interest of the religion. Many beliefs and assumptions came from your religious upbringing and environment – assumptions that you may have unknowingly picked up from your devout grandmother, a prudish Sunday School teacher, or a religious gym coach. Religious sexual ideas can infect you, especially when you are young and unable to think critically. We hold many sexual myths as facts, and most come from religion.

Ironically, much of the evidence to dispute these myths can be found in our everyday lives. That is the power of religious myth; it can blind us to the obvious.

## Living a Lie

**Living a religious sexual lifestyle is tantamount to living a lie.** Religion distorts our sexuality when the majority of religious people live one life for the public and another in private. It can be as simple as living as a "happily married" couple when you are both miserable with your sex life. As a good Christian, Muslim, Buddhist or Mormon, you must deny and pretend that you don't masturbate, all the while "abusing yourself" regularly. You must condemn pornography even as you use it. You must preach against lustful thoughts even if you can't avoid them. You must condemn your spouse or others for certain sexual ideas, thoughts or preferences even when you have them as well. You must tell your children how bad premarital sex is even when you had several sexual partners before you were married.

In sum, most religious people live a double life. (When I refer to "religious people," I mean those who adhere to the mainstream ideas and beliefs of Christianity, Islam, Buddhism, Hinduism, Mormonism, etc.) We know from decades of research that the religious are no different from secular people when it comes to sexual behavior – they just feel more guilty about it. The result is a dishonest life. While secular people can live openly with their sexuality, negotiate ethically with partners about preferences and behaviors, enjoy fantasies and experimentation, religious people are constrained from being open and forthright because they view many things about sex as sinful. Nevertheless, they do it, hide it and deny it.

Religions of all kinds use our powerful sex drives to infect us with ideas that benefit the religion and hurt and inhibit our ability to be truly human. Religion's goal is to propagate religion. Sex is one powerful method for achieving this. That is the thesis of this book.

The social and psychological toll of living a lie includes emotional numbness to our own sexuality and often anger and aggression towards those who live a more open and honest sexuality.

Christopher Hitchens illustrated this best when he said:

> I always take it for granted that sexual moralizing by public figures is a sign of hypocrisy or worse, and most usually a desire to perform the very act that is most being condemned. This is why, whenever I hear some bigmouth in Washington or the Christian heartland banging on about the evils of sodomy or whatever, I mentally enter his name in my notebook and contentedly set my watch. Sooner rather than later he will be discovered down on his knees in some dreary motel or latrine, with an expired Visa card, having tried to pay well over the odds to be peed upon by some Apache transvestite.[4]

Hitchens' observation rings true for more than public figures. Average religious people may not make headlines, but their crises are as devastating to individuals and families. When a good Christian wife finds her husband harboring pornography, she may be appalled and find that she can't enjoy sex with him any more. When a good Christian man finds his wife having an on-line erotic exchange with another woman, he may be so hurt he eventually asks for a divorce. When Christian parents catch that their 14-year-old son kissing another boy, they may resort to incredibly cruel language and treatment, going as far as beating or ostracizing him. A Muslim father, learning that his daughter is secretly writing love letters to a boy, may go into a rage that results in severe beating or worse.

The list goes on, yet none of these offending behaviors is wrong or abnormal except in the light of religious insanity about sex. How can someone be honest about normal, harmless behavior when it leads to social sanctions and psychological abuse in the name of religion and religious beliefs? Sexual

---

4   From Hitchens' memoir, *Hitch-22* (2010).

beliefs are manufactured by religion and have no basis in reality. Believing and living according to these ideas leads to broken marriages, sexual dysfunction, child abuse and much more.

Without religion, none of these examples would come to such an end. Children would have no need to feel ashamed of perfectly normal behavior. Spouses would have room to negotiate sexual desires and needs in ways that respect both parties and lead to loving and sexually gratifying lives. Parents would have healthy ideas about normal sexual behavior and development and be able to teach their children skills for decision-making about their own bodies.

## Toxic Trio

Three key beliefs in "modern" religion lead to sexual distortions, sexual terror and support the many myths:

- Belief in an afterlife
- Belief in a voyeuristic, all-knowing god that determines your status in the afterlife
- Belief that the god dictates a specific kind of sexual behavior to the exclusion of all others, as a condition for entry into the afterlife

You must hold all three of these beliefs for religious distortions to truly impact your behavior.

Here is how this works. Simply believing in an afterlife does not necessarily create sex-negative behavior. For example, some New Age religions and most Pagans are quite sex positive and yet include some idea of an afterlife.

Believing in a voyeuristic god does not necessarily lead to sexual distortion either. You could believe in a god who wants you to masturbate and have joyful sex with your partner or partners, and watches you while you do it. This would not lead to celibacy or fear of eternal damnation.

The third belief combined with the first two creates sexual distortion. God expects you to adhere to a specific, narrow set of behaviors. Since he is watching you all the time, failure to comply will result in eternal damnation.

This unique combination of beliefs is what makes Islam, Christianity and other religions so powerful. These tenets provide a framework for understanding the behaviors of people in most of the major religions. This toxic trio creates a rigid system that prevents exploration outside arbitrary limits, ignoring patterns of attraction that are part of our genetic programming. The notion of specific sexual behaviors dictated by an all-knowing, voyeuristic and vengeful god can terrorize adherents into public compliance and private misery without leading to sexual self-actualization or fulfillment. This god inhabits your mind like a parasite ready to interrupt any improper behavior.

I have seen first-hand the destructive impact of these three beliefs. I once practiced as a clinical psychologist within an institution for adolescent boys and then in private practice for children and families, including marriage counseling. I then transitioned into organizational psychology working with executives, managers and employees.[5]

In this capacity, working with people who are having sexual difficulties, I asked, "What prevents you from communicating your concerns, desires or problems to your parents – wife – boyfriend, etc.?" Their first response was often one of terror as they answered: "I could never tell my husband what I really like. He would divorce me!" Or "I could never tell my parents my boyfriend and I are thinking about having sex. They would kill me." Or "I could never tell my parents that I am gay. They would disown me." These people were so afraid that they could not even imagine communicating openly with the most important people in their lives.

It took little probing to find religion at the root of this terror. Religion forces people into denying, avoiding, judging and hating themselves and others for their sexual desires and behavior.

As we will see in later chapters, people who are terrorized about sexuality do not make good decisions or lead sexually satisfying lives. They often perpetuate the cycle by terrorizing their children. People who learn sex without guilt make better decisions, talk and negotiate more openly with their partners and respect the sexual preferences and desires of others. They enjoy their own bodies and are less jealous, possessive and judgmental.

Religion seeks to control the uncontrollable, especially when control is the most difficult – in adolescence. What does religion gain by putting unnatural restrictions and perpetuating myths about sexuality? As I explored in my earlier book, *The God Virus: How Religion Infects Our Lives and*

---

5  I wrote two books in this field as well: *Teaming Up: Making the Transition to a Self-Directed Team Based Organization* (1995, McGraw-Hill), and *The Performance Culture: Maximizing the Power of Teams* (2001, IPC Press).

*Culture*, sex is only one of several channels to religious infection, but it is among the most effective.

### Religious Sexual Terrorism: Fear Is the Foreplay

If you were raised in North or South America, Europe, Australia, or India, China, the Middle East and Indonesia, you were very likely brought up in an environment dominated by one religion. In broad terms that means Christianity, Islam, Buddhism, Hinduism and Communism (yes, Communism acts like a religion where sex is concerned). These dominant religions tend to control and restrict sexual information, making their version of sex and sexuality the norm.

Most religions try to isolate people from alternative sexualities, persecute those who do not conform and teach that their behavior is immoral. The ability to control sexual information and induce guilt keeps people tied to the religion. How does a religion keep people coming back for forgiveness or feeling shame without controlling information and using sexual terror?

The sex drive is so powerful that only the most drastic psychological and physical means can control it. These means can be classified as religious sexual terror. Fear is the foreplay of religion. If done right, it interferes with all aspects of human sexual pleasure.

**Because of religious sexual terror:**
- An Iranian woman wears a dangerously hot burka in the desert.
- A priest prays for hours and hates himself every time he masturbates.
- A Christian father explodes on finding out his daughter had sex with her boyfriend.
- A minister and his wife can't enjoy interesting and creative sex.
- A woman can't tell her husband she would like to be spanked occasionally as part of a sexual ritual.
- A husband can't reveal he likes to dress in women's underwear.
- Two Christian teenagers can't openly negotiate condom use before they have sex.

## A Thought Experiment: Unbuttoning Religion

Imagine being taught from childhood that you and most of the people around you have a dangerous medical problem. But thankfully, it can be controlled, even prevented, with a simple button that lights up when pressed. You are given this button when you are 12 years old and told that it must be compressed frequently. If you ever neglect the button, the light will slowly dim, and at that point the medical condition will progress. If the light gets too dim, you will get a disease or have an accident.

To illustrate the dangers, you are shown photos and told stories of people who let go of their button and were destroyed. Adults, physicians, religious leaders and your peers all attest to the terrible things that happen when a person neglects his button. "Learn how to live with the button, then tell others how to live with it too," they admonish you. "Share the knowledge you gain from reading about your button." You learn that telling others makes the button glow longer, even brighter. You slowly learn to enjoy having a button. You feel proud of it as you tell others the joy of feeling safe and protected by the button.

This button impacts every aspect of your life. When you talk to someone, you feel compelled to tell them about button power, so you can take your finger off for a little longer. When you tell your children, the light stays on for several hours. You get into bed with your spouse and tell her about your button and she tells you about hers, and you both enjoy some lovemaking before the light gets too dim. Sure you have work to do, a lawn to mow, books to read, projects to complete, but ultimately, the button rules.

Years go by, and you get good at managing your button. Indeed, your button stays lit for days at a time with only the occasional push, because you are so skilled at working button praise into every conversation. Others are not as good at maintaining their button and they have family problems or physical problems. "Press your button. Talk to others," you urge. But they aren't as diligent as you and you see them pay the price. It saddens you that others don't take responsibility for their button and then complain that they are sick or in pain.

One day you meet a person who has no button yet seems perfectly healthy. "Where is your button?" you ask. "I threw it away decades ago. I have no idea where it is." This forthright and unhesitant answer shocks you, then creates a twinge of panic. First, you think, "He is in grave danger of some horrible illness or accident." Then another thought occurs. "Maybe buttons aren't necessary?" You toss that thought out. What is life worth if you don't have a button? You would feel emptiness, a true sense of loss. Even if someone could live without it, you can only imagine how miserable and lonely their life must be.

Occasionally, you hear that some of the richest or most successful people do not have buttons. Some people are even encouraging children to throw away their buttons. It terrorizes you to think that one of your children might stop pushing her button and come down with some terrible disease or disability. As a result, you redouble your efforts, telling more people about the joys of the button.

Even so, you find that your button does not glow as long as it used to. You continue faithfully pressing because you know that the warm comfort of a glowing button surpasses all understanding.

## Buttons in Your Life

While the button premise may seem ridiculous, it resembles many religious practices. For example, you may know Catholics, Muslims, Hindus, Buddhists, Sikhs or believers of any number of other religions that use prayer beads. Others clutch their Bibles and display them prominently at work, in their home or in their car. They may display religious symbols in their homes, their lawns and their webpage; others wear crosses, crucifixes or pendants. But it is not just prayer beads, Bibles or a prayer rug; religious people have almost identical beliefs to our button example. They believe that prayer prevents evil, heals illness, gives guidance and much more. They believe that going to church, mass or prayer meeting keeps their soul pure and clean. They believe that reading the Bible or religious material keeps evil thoughts at bay. Each of these is nothing more than a way to press the button. Praying presses the button. Reading the Bible, going to church, praying on a prayer rug, singing a hymn, all are ways to press the button and keep evil, illness or other problems at bay and ensure a reward in the afterlife.

It is the totality of the beliefs represented by these tokens that creates a deep dependency in the religious adherent. Tokens are just a reminder of the underlying belief. The token reinforces the belief and the belief reinforces the token. In our simple example, the belief in the inevitability of disease or accident was the driving belief behind the token. Without that belief, there would be no need for a token.

Religion has used tokens for thousands of years to reinforce beliefs. They are powerful psychological tools. They make soldiers feel invincible before battle, give mothers a sense of supernatural protection for their children and convince people god cured them of a disease.

But tokens are part of a network of conditioned responses. A conditioned response can be programmed into a rat, a dog or a person. Teach a creature that it must have a particular token to feel safe, and it will seek out the token whenever it feels threatened. Much like a child's security blanket or a dog's favorite toy, a token can be anything that we have learned to feel comfortable with or that we associate with protection and security.

Many cultures have tokens; it is a common behavior but one designed to make a person feel secure within a particular religious context. A Hindu would not feel comfortable or secure with Catholic prayer beads in his pocket. A Muslim woman would probably feel violated with a crucifix around her neck. A Buddhist wouldn't find a Baptist prayer meeting inspiring. Tokens are specific to a given religion and even a religious subset. For example, some tokens may only be worn by one gender, not by the other. Some may be used by Protestants and not by Catholics. Some may only be used at certain times of the year or during certain times in life. And most important, tokens are paired with specific beliefs. The crucifix is paired with belief in death and resurrection along with other ideas. A Bible or Koran represents a belief that the deity can and does communicate directly to you.

As humans we want to feel secure. We learn early in life to associate security with things and behaviors. We associate security with our home, with owning property, having money in the bank, going to work every day. In reality, these do not make us secure. We create them to feel more secure. When we feel insecure, we do things to increase security like save money, improve our home, install a security system or take a second job. In each case, these help us feel more secure.

In these examples, our sense of security has some basis in reality. And there is direct evidence that having money in the bank helps protect us from financial stress. Owning a home ensures we have a place to seek shelter when it rains or snows. Security systems can warn us of a fire or an intruder *and* there is direct evidence that they work.

On the other hand, tokens don't reduce the likelihood of burglary, put money in the bank or decide where to invest a tax refund. Tokens simply evoke a conditioned response that helps us relax and feel secure and reminds us of beliefs such as: "We will be rewarded in the afterlife," or "a god or angel is watching over us." Early childhood teaching and years of practice convince the religious that these actually work. "I prayed a hundred times and my son got well" – never mind that a hundred prayers were said to keep him from getting sick in the first place.

The rituals associated with a token are believed to be mandatory. You cannot just pray to Mary every few years or take your beads with you when you feel the need. "Pray without ceasing," St. Paul said (I Thessalonians 5:27, NIV).[6] The token takes on a life of its own. It must be attended to or it will not work. It demands attention. If you miss a prayer meeting or mass, forget to pray or read the Bible, you will feel anxious – you forgot to press the button. God may not protect or reward you.

## Sex and Pushing Buttons

What do buttons or tokens have to do with sex? Tokens keep the mind focused on religious requirements, ensuring that the person behaves according to the dictates of the deity. If the deity says masturbation is a sin, then having a set of prayer beads or a Bible next to your bed at night is a powerful reminder of what is and is not sinful. When the person eventually succumbs and masturbates or has sex, he will count two hundred beads for forgiveness. If a woman has the urge to bring a boyfriend to her apartment, she may take the picture of Jesus down before he comes over. If she leaves it up, she may not be able to reach orgasm because Jesus is watching her.

The more the person uses the tokens and prayer to resist sexual temptation, the more the behavior becomes ingrained. Powerful biological urges make the person want to masturbate or have sex, but the fear of hell impinges on her thoughts. She picks up the beads, reads the Bible or kneels and prays to resist temptation. Any number of physical actions may be used, but they all lead to the same result – deeper infection with religious sex.

The person may resist temptation successfully, in which case the biological need generally grows stronger. He may succumb immediately, but have to pray, kneel, count beads, read the Bible or something similar to assuage the guilt.

In other cases, a person may successfully redirect his attention and energy to other activities, often of a religious nature. He may become a

---

6   Unless otherwise noted, all quotations from the Bible are from the New International Version (NIV).

missionary, work for the poor or teach Sunday School. The redirection of energy often benefits the religion. The more a religion makes a person feel guilty and insecure, the harder the person works for the religion. This is especially effective for sexual guilt. Ultimately, a religion may so undermine a person's sexual confidence that he or she becomes a celibate nun or priest or stops having sex with a spouse in order to be able to channel energies into religious study and endeavors.[7]

The token keeps the person focused on the god to the exclusion of other more natural behaviors. People who don't pray, who don't sing god's praises, who don't read the Bible can't be trusted and are a threat to the comfort and security of the religious. Those without tokens are not a part of the "in group," which makes them suspect.

The token and the beliefs it represents takes on greater meaning and comfort than real sex. Here is what one religious leader said at the end of a long article on sex and god, "As we conclude our sex series we learn that sex is great, but the kingdom of heaven is better."[8]

Religious sexual foreplay often interferes with sex before it even gets started. For example, you dare not ask your spouse for a new kind of sex for fear that he or she will believe it is sinful, even in marriage.

Our culture teaches us to think of marriage as lifelong and exclusive. However, the biological and anthropological facts do not support this notion as we will see in later chapters. Most humans are too sexual to stay tied up in a single sexual style for decades. Of course, people can stay in committed relationships for decades, but they will only be happy if they keep the sexual energy properly channeled and not artificially dammed up by religious ideas.

Failing this, sexuality will express itself – sometimes in unusual or inappropriate places. That is why thousands of "happily married" religious leaders engage in illegal sexual behavior every year, to say nothing of the many Catholic priests "married" to the church. At the same time, millions of religious followers engage in sexual behavior that is legal but violates their

---

7   Some might call this psychological sublimation. That is, redirecting energy from a socially unacceptable urge or dangerous desire into something more socially acceptable and somewhat gratifying or rewarding. Without going into psychoanalytic theory, I think a cognitive-behavioral explanation is much simpler, and easier to understand as we see it working in the everyday world.

8   From the website of City Bible Forum, Melbourne, Australia. Available online at http://melbournecbf.wordpress.com/2011/05/27/ffl-27-may-sex-can-anything-be-better/.

religion's moral code, such as having heterosexual or homosexual affairs, masturbating or using porn. They can engage in extra prayers, confession, Bible reading or giving money – pushing the button – to gain forgiveness, then go back to doing it again. It keeps the vicious cycle alive.

# CHAPTER 2:

# YOU CAN TAKE RELIGION OUT OF SEX,

# BUT YOU CAN'T TAKE SEX OUT OF RELIGION

*Where do we get our sexual maps? Why is religion so interested in giving us the map? Why are sexual restrictions so important in the religious sexual map?*

*"Of all the delights of this world man cares most for sexual intercourse. He will go any length for it-risk fortune, character, reputation, life itself. and what do you think he has done? He has left it out of his heaven! Prayer takes its place."*

-Mark Twain, Notebook, 1906

### Putting the "Fun" Back in "Fundamental"

Religious sexual morality is fundamentally meaningless. Any instruction is largely negative. Where does the Koran instruct on the ethical way to have a fun and open sexual relationship? Where does the Bible teach a parent how to deal with a child's sexually oriented questions? How many sermons have been preached on the multitude of ways to give a woman an orgasm? Is there a chapter in the Book of Mormon on oral sex for males and females? Of the dozens of Scientology books, which ones teach about the joys of sex toys in masturbation? Do any of these religious documents teach people how to relate to one another respectfully and equally as sexual beings?

Sex is the weak spot of religion. What would happen if sexual restrictions were taken out of the equation? Can you imagine the Pope waking up one morning and saying, "Wow, I had the best wet dream last night. I think we will make masturbation legal in the Catholic Church." Could the president of the Mormon Church receive a revelation that women are allowed up to three lovers? Such a revelation was given to Joseph Smith, allowing him all the wives he wanted.[9] And a similar revelation came to Mormon Church President Welford Woodruff in 1890, eliminating the practice of polygamy in the church. God gave him the revelation just in time for Utah to be admitted to the Union.[10] Imagine such homophobic ministers and leaders (who have all been caught engaging in suspect acts) as Ted Haggard, Bishop Eddie Long, Senator Larry Craig or George Rekers saying homosexuality should be accepted by the church.

Let's explore where we get our sexual ideas and preferences. Then we can better understand how religion plugs into the development of sexuality to its own advantage.

### Our Limited Sexual Maps

We inherit a map of sexuality from our culture and religion just as we inherit a map of the food we eat. Our food map is small compared to the

---

9   Joseph Smith had a total of 34 wives in all, some as young as 14. Eleven of his wives were already married to other men when he essentially stole them under the command of his god (See http://www.wivesofjosephsmith.org/). Brigham Young, leader of Mormonism after Joseph Smith's death, went several steps further and married 55 women. At least six had living husbands before he stole them.

10   Congress made elimination of polygamy a condition for statehood.

global possibilities. Indeed, your food map is so limited that you might starve to death in the midst of plenty if you were transplanted to another time or place. How well would you fare if you were plunked down in the jungles of Brazil or the Kalahari desert in Africa? Local peoples survive, even thrive, but you would starve or get accidentally poisoned by eating the wrong food.

In modern society, we have expanded our local food map with a variety of ethnic foods and spices unheard of by our ancestors. As a result, we have far more interesting and varied foods than any culture in history. Yet, even with these amazing changes, some religions still try to control food selection: Jews and Muslims condemn pork and classify foods as Kosher, halāl (lawful) or harām (unlawful); Hindus condemn meat of any kind; some Buddhist traditions require a vegetarian diet, etc. Many religious people find the old rules ridiculous and simply ignore them in favor of more interesting and varied eating experiences.

The same is true of sex. The breadth of sexual behavior is enormously varied across cultures and time. Your individual sexual map is tiny compared to the knowledge, experiences and practices of other people and times. Unfortunately, because of religious interference, our sexual maps are not only restricted, they are inaccurate.

Just as some religions restrict foods or dictate their preparation, most religions restrict sexual practices and dictate holy and unholy, clean and unclean practices.

Religious sexual maps are based largely on Bronze- and Iron-Age tribal ideas, but for most of us, that's what we know. No one is born with an understanding of sex and sexuality. We learn it from explicit teaching and more important, from the myriad signals in our environment. Starting as infants and toddlers, we may get messages like, "Don't touch yourself down there!" or we feel the disapproving hand of a parent when we show curiosity about our own anatomy. Jokes from adults and peers instruct us on how to think about sex. We observe dress and absorb comments like, "She is dressed like a prostitute."

As a 19-year-old church camp counselor, I was asked to take a camper aside and read certain scriptures to warn him against masturbating. He'd been a little too enthusiastic the night before and one of the other campers had complained. It was a difficult assignment, since I masturbated regularly myself, to my great shame. In the same camp, I witnessed a young girl run crying across the campus after being told by the minister that she was dressed like a slut. Over the course of the next years, that same minister was caught twice having affairs with women in his church.

These kinds of experiences help us build our sexual map. Maps are somewhat different depending on whether you are a Muslim or Catholic, Orthodox Jew or Episcopalian, but they have one thing in common: They bear almost no relationship to the reality of who we are as sexual creatures. None is based on biological or evolutionary fact. None draws upon anthropological knowledge or neurological studies of brain development and sexuality.

These religion-based maps only get updated when the culture forces it. For example, birth control was considered sinful by virtually all religions just 100 years ago. Today, most religions say nothing about birth control for married people. Even the Catholic Church looks the other way while still disapproving. It was almost unthinkable for a woman to wear pants 100 years ago, especially inside a church. If all the women wearing pants were kicked out of church today, most churches would stand empty. Sex before marriage was very sinful 100 years ago. Today, 95% of all Americans have sex before marriage.[11] Churches still preach against it, but the statistics show most people aren't listening.

Religions are slowly modifying their maps of sexuality, but not without a fight. These modifications still have nothing to do with who we are. They are based on the Koran, Bible, Book of Mormon or some other obsolete text. Religion's success, for much of the last three thousand years, depended heavily on sexual myths. Today is no different. It's just more difficult to perpetuate such myths when so much contrary information is available on the Internet or from books in the library.

### Religious Maps

The sexual map we acquire in youth includes body image, masturbatory guilt, sexual preferences and more. From what turns us on to what turns us off. From attitudes about menstruation to the right of women to wear certain clothing. But using this guilt- and shame-ridden map as a guide to sexuality is like using a map of an ancient city sewer system to locate the fiber optic network.

11   Guttmacher Institute News Release, 19 Dec 2006, "Premarital Sex Is Nearly Universal Among Americans, And Has Been For Decades." Online at http://www.guttmacher.org/media/nr/2006/12/19/index.html.

What if the only map we had of a city was made 2,000 years ago? How useful would it be today? My city was an open prairie 2,000 years ago with no roads and maybe a few animal paths. A map of that reality would be of little use today.

An accurate map of a city or country requires measurement, constant adjustment and updating. No map can display every aspect of a particular landscape. Does a road map tell where the sewer pipes are? Does it show where the best soil for planting is? Maps are only an approximation of the territory.

Religion tries to give us maps of sexuality that are no better than a 2,000-year-old map of my hometown. In addition, each religion also tries to convince us that their map is never wrong or inaccurate. If you have trouble understanding or interpreting the map, you need only talk to your imam, priest or minister. They can show you the way.

If I were convinced that my 2,000-year-old home town map was god-inspired and totally accurate, I would ignore buildings, concrete, trees, cars and any other object that was not on my map. I would refuse to believe what was right before my eyes, and then very likely something terrible would happen – like crashing a car into a tree or a building. It seems like an absurd idea, but it is roughly the same as someone trying to use the Bible as a guide to sexuality. In the last 100 years, we've learned a lot of about human sexuality and sexual development.

There are hundreds of Christian books on marriage. One of the long-time bestsellers is *Sacred Marriage: What If God Designed Marriage to Make Us Holy More Than to Make Us Happy* by Gary Thomas (2000). Using this book as a map for sex and marriage teaches how to pray better, deal with conflicts through faith in Jesus and how to deny sexual appetite. Nowhere does the book discuss how to negotiate a fetish scene with your partner, nor does it contain information on fun, healthy sex. But it does have a lot of ideas about how wrong sex is in the eyes of god. The underlying message, repeated ad nauseam, is one of guilt couched in "spiritual" language. Sex is a minor part of god's plan and shouldn't be an important part of a faith-based marriage. It is not until Chapter 11, "Sexual Saints: Marital Sexuality Can Provide Spiritual Insights and Character Development," that Thomas discusses sex.

Thomas' book, as well as most Christian marriage books, is an excellent exercise in how to create huge amounts of guilt between two married people. The irony of groups that study books like this is that many, if not most, had sex before marriage, masturbate and peek at porn occasionally, all the while pretending they never do such things. In other words, they are behaving like human beings even as they pretend that some ethereal, spiritual entity inhabits their bodies and watches them day and night to keep them righteous.

The book is all about god. It is really a threesome, with an invisible man in the middle constantly meddling with the pleasure and bonding that ordinarily develops between married couples. This is a formula for disastrous sexual communication, and ultimately, divorce or a sexless marriage. Having talked to and witnessed uncounted Christian marriages, I have concluded the product of this kind of training is anxiety and guilt. Within a few years, sex loses meaning and fun, becomes perfunctory and may cease altogether.

### Don't Defile Yourself (or you will go blind)

All religions have something to say about sex, and it rarely coincides with scientific knowledge of sex and sexuality. How many times has a young person suffered through the night, praying and asking Jesus or Allah to help him not defile himself by masturbating? How many young lives have been destroyed in Iran, Pakistan or Saudi Arabia because religious parents caught their daughter kissing a boy? How many Baptists or Catholics have suffered through years of sexual deprivation because their religion prohibits premarital sex? How many pregnancies and sexually transmitted diseases have children of evangelicals contracted because their religion disapproves of sex education?

Many a person has been prohibited from exploring a possible relationship with a perfectly good partner only because of one or the other's religion. Many people have been discouraged from enjoying their own bodies in perfectly harmless yet enjoyable ways, because a priest or imam told them such actions would send them to hell or make them go blind.

Most deeply religious people will claim that sex is sacred. The "sacred rules" associated with a given religion invariably coincide with the interests of the religion in forwarding its own propagation. Rarely does a religion allow truly human sexual expression. Religions claim, "We are not animals. We should not behave like animals in our sexual expression." Yet, religions of all kinds prescribe sexual behavior that looks far more like those of animals than humans.

For example, the Pope's prescriptions for sex look remarkably like the way dogs, cows or cats express their species sexuality. A Muslim or Southern Baptist has views of sex that are more closely related to the reproductive strategies of insects. For example, most animals have sex only when they are in heat or sexually receptive – for procreation. Humans can have sex any time. Procreation is a small part of human sex. Recreation and bonding is far more important. Therefore, to have sex only for procreation is not human, but more like other animals. Humans may have sex thousands of times for every live birth. No dog or insect does that.

## Sexual Restriction

Sexual prohibition is in the DNA of all the major religions. Without it, the entire religion may collapse. The most successful religions depend on sexual restrictions and condemnation. They redirect the energy of sexual repression and guilt to drive growth and maintain power. Without sexual repression they lose their advantage.

It is not just Western religions that use this strategy. Eastern religions are as oppressive. Hinduism and Buddhism use sex in many ways; Buddhist monks and nuns cannot have sex. Boys at a very young age are put into training in monasteries.[12] The Dalai Lama says that homosexuality is wrong though he preaches tolerance. Most forms of Buddhism practiced in Asia sanction and disapprove of various forms of sexual expression from masturbation to homosexuality to anal sex. Japanese and Thai Buddhist practices and beliefs have followed the notion for centuries that women's aspirations toward Buddhahood are far weaker than men's. These traditions also hold that women pollute the earth every month with their blood. Western (read California) Buddhists have cleaned up Buddhism with modern ideas from feminism, but Buddhism is no more friendly to women than Islam or Christianity.

Hinduism has proscriptions on women, especially during menstruation. The caste system restricts who can have sex with whom. When confronted with the notion of sexual repression, Eastern religion apologists cite the many

---

12  A very informative editorial in the *Bangkok Post* decries the sexual corruption of the Buddhist clergy. If one simply substituted Catholic for Buddhist, the article would be virtually identical to any that might have been written in *The Boston Globe* or the *Irish Times*; (Sanitsuda Ekachai, "Sex in the monastery," available online at http://www.bangkokpost. com/blogs/index.php/2009/01/30/sex-in-the-monastery?blog=64).

Hindu scriptures that talk positively about sex and even offer instruction. Despite its scriptures, Hinduism is sexually repressive.

An examination of Hindu practice in India reveals bans against public kissing, sex during menstruation and pornography. In many ways, Hinduism is more Victorian than Victorian England. Some attribute this to the influence of England during Victorian times, but Hindu sexual restriction goes back thousands of years. A recent *Newsweek* report on the treatment of women placed India as 141 out of 165 countries, one of the worst countries in the world.[13] With an 80% Hindu population, much of the repression in India is related to Hinduism although Islam undoubtedly contributes its share. Sexual repression of women pervades Indian society in all castes. In a government response to the survey, the official quoted Hindu scripture that glorified women with no mention of the fact that religion was probably the root cause of much of the repression and restriction.

Further, Orthodox Jews prohibit sex during a woman's menstrual cycle and seven days after. The practice is based upon ancient ideas of female uncleanliness. What is the message to a woman if she is told she is unclean for one third of each month?

All religions say that sexual prohibitions are in the interest of greater enlightenment, salvation, freedom from sin and closer communion with god. If you take away the supernatural or spiritual, the whole scheme falls like a house of cards. Why would I deny myself one of the greatest pleasures in life? Without the promise of a great supernatural reward or greater punishment, such self-denial makes little sense. Plus, it is entirely possible that your sexual sacrifice will be in vain.

If the Muslim god is correct, then the Christians may as well enjoy themselves since they are going to Islamic Hell. If the Baptist god is correct, all the abstinence and celibacy by Catholic priests is a big waste of potential pleasure and a lot of suffering for nothing.

Once you recognize that sexual restriction is critical to religious propagation, you can construct a new sexual framework for yourself. To construct that new framework, to design a map that has some relationship to reality, we must understand biology, psychology, history and anthropology. It requires us to look at sex across many times and cultures, to understand the breadth

---

13   As reported online at http://www.dnaindia.com/india/report_india-ranks-as-low-as-141-in-condition-of-women- survey_1591332.

and depth of human sexual practices. Armed with this information, we can begin to make informed decisions about our sexuality. We can also learn the appropriate place of sex in creating and supporting the joy that comes from bonds formed in long-term committed relationships.

Removing religion from sex allows for an exploration that is unencumbered with dogma. Ethics become more important than religious notions of morality. In the following chapters we will look at religious sexual myths.

# CHAPTER 3:

# SCREWING WITH RELIGIOUS MYTHS

*Many common sexual beliefs are founded in religious indoctrination. They often impact us profoundly without our knowledge.*

## Common Myths

Many myths are built into our sexual ideas. Most people never question or examine them. In fact, to question the myths is to question the religion. How does one question the virgin birth without questioning Catholicism? How does one examine the pedophilia of Mohamed marrying a nine-year-old girl without questioning Islam? How does one talk about Joseph Smith's revelation in the 1840s that Mormon men can have many wives and President Wolford's "about face" revelation in 1890 that Mormons can only have one wife, without questioning the foundations of Mormonism? All of these are sexual myths.

The very first story in the book of Genesis is a sexual myth, "… then the eyes of both of them were opened, and they realized they were naked; so they sewed fig leaves together and made coverings for themselves" (Genesis 3:7). Exactly what Adam and Eve did is never stated, but it had something to do with sex!

In the Koran we learn the myth that women have an illness when menstruating:

> **The Cow 2:222,** They question thee (O Muhammad) concerning menstruation. Say: It is an illness, so let women alone at such times and go not in unto them till they are cleansed. And when they have purified themselves, then go in unto them as Allah hath enjoined upon you. Truly Allah loveth those who turn unto Him, and loveth those who have a care for cleanness.

In Romans 5:12, Paul is very clear that original sin came from Adam and has corrupted mankind ever since. "Wherefore, as by one man sin entered into the world, and death by sin; and so death passed upon all men, for that all have sinned." From this unfathomable idea come centuries of torture and deprivation for millions of humans. You were born imperfect and your very sexuality is living proof of that imperfection. It can and will damn you forever, especially if you are a woman. Woman tempted man and caused the "Fall," therefore she is the more sinful and suspect of the sexes.

Other myths are more specific to our sexual behavior. Masturbation is against god's commandment not to spill your seed. It was called Onanism for centuries after the poor fellow Onan in the book of Genesis who chose to spill his seed rather than father a child by his deceased brother's wife. A quaint practice of the day that modern religionists forget to include in their list of sins – failing to father children by your dead brother's wife. Modern religionists look at the spilling of seed as the crime, *not* screwing his brother's wife, probably against her will.

The list of myths we acquire about sex and sexuality is amazingly long. Here is a short sample:

- God is watching as you have sex.
- Jesus does not want you to masturbate.
- Homosexuality is a far greater sin than adultery.
- Women should cover themselves for modesty in the sight of the lord.
- Women should be sexually available to their husbands under almost any condition.
- Sex outside of marriage is always wrong.
- Pornography is harmful to women and children.
- Religious leaders are equipped to counsel you on sex and marriage.
- Menstruation is dirty; you should not have sex with a menstruating woman.
- Teaching children and adolescents about sex will encourage them to actually do it.
- Teaching children about Jesus' plan will help them resist sexual temptation.
- Fantasizing is wrong. If you lust in your heart, you have committed adultery.
- No one else feels the sexual feelings you feel, so you must be sinful.
- Premarital sex will damage your marriage.
- Too much sex in marriage is wrong.
- Women don't enjoy sex.
- All men want from women is sex. Women are Jesus' sexual gatekeepers.
- Premarital purity and abstinence will help you have a long and happy marriage.
- Women who have had a lot of sex partners are sluts.
- Men who have a lot of sex partners just use women.
- Women should be subservient to men.
- Anal sex is repulsive and wrong in the sight of god.
- Punishment for adultery is deserved.

- Women are the tempters and lead men astray.
- Oral sex is unnatural.
- God inserts the soul at the moment of conception.
- Sexual pleasure is dangerous.
- Ministers who go astray deserve forgiveness just as Jesus commands.

These myths and many more are part of the larger map of sex that we carry around in our heads. You may not believe most or any of these, but many people do. These myths have a direct impact on a person's ability to enjoy and develop sexually and influence how they relate to and teach their children *and* which politicians they vote for.

One of the most pernicious Christian myths is the myth of monogamy.

## Myth: Christians are Monogamous

Monogamy as the natural state is so deeply ingrained that most Christians and Jews are able to totally ignore the hundreds of wives and concubines of their god's most holy men – Solomon, David, Abraham and many others. Indeed, monogamy as Jesus defined it is not even practiced among most Christians.

Jesus defined monogamy as one sex partner for life:

**Matthew 5:31–32,** It was also said, "Whoever divorces his wife, let him give her a certificate of divorce." But I say to you that every one who divorces his wife, except on the ground of unchastity, makes her commit adultery; and whoever marries a divorced woman commits adultery.

Other passages also make it clear that divorce is not an option except in the most extreme case of adultery. For example, Paul says in

**1 Corinthians 7:10–11,** To the married I give this command (not I, but the Lord): A wife must not separate from her husband. ¹¹But if she does, she must remain unmarried or else be reconciled to her husband. And a husband must not divorce his wife. . . . **(39)** A woman is bound to her husband as long as he lives. But if her husband dies, she is free to marry anyone she wishes, but he must belong to the Lord.

Just to make the point as clear as possible, Jesus said

**Marhew 19:4-6,** "Haven't you read," he replied, "that at the beginning the Creator 'made them male and female,' and said,

'For this reason a man will leave his father and mother and be united to his wife, and the two will become one flesh'? So they are no longer two, but one flesh. Therefore what God has joined together, let no one separate."

Premarital sex was not an option for Jesus or Paul. Based on this, the Christian view of monogamy has been "one partner for life," with the only exception being death of the spouse. Even in the case of adultery, the wronged spouse is not supposed to remarry. How many Christians today would fit into that definition of monogamy? Every Mormon who had premarital sex, every Baptist who has had an affair, every Catholic who has received an annulment (except for adultery), every person who remarried after a divorce – all are living a non-monogamous lifestyle.

Newt Gingrich, former speaker of the U.S. House and very conservative Catholic, has had three wives and who knows how many other partners. He is anything but monogamous, according to this definition. Is Ted Haggard, former president of the National Association of Evangelicals, monogamous? He admittedly had sex with a male prostitute. Is Earl Paulk, mega-church evangelical minister, monogamous? It turns out, through DNA testing, that his "nephew" is really his son. He had sex with his sister-in-law to father the son. (The son, qua nephew, is now taking over the ministry.) Having sex with your dead brother's wife was a biblical commandment, but Earl evidently couldn't wait until his brother died.

Many members of Haggard and Paulk's congregations are as non-monogamous as their leaders.[14] Some would say that people like Newt Gingrich or the evangelist Joyce Meyer are serial monogamists. But the idea of "serial monogamy" makes no sense. Either one is monogamous or not according to the Christian tradition.

So monogamy is a myth among most Christians. At least the Muslim men don't have to deal with that problem. They are permitted up to four wives, though Mohammed allowed himself many more.

### Myth: Jesus Makes Marriage Better

Thousands of sermons have been preached on how to bring Jesus into your marriage. I've heard at least a dozen from ministers who eventually got

---

14 Barna Group, 2004. "Born Again Christians Just as Likely to Divorce as are Non-Christians." Available online at http://www.barna.org/barna-update/article/5-barna-update/194-born-again-christians-just-as- likely-to-divorce-as-are-non-christians?q=divorce.

caught in affairs or divorced themselves. A 2000 study by the evangelical researcher George Barna found that fundamentalists have the highest divorce rates.[15] The leaders in divorce were non-denominational, Episcopal, Baptist and Pentecostal. Not much evidence of Jesus present in those marriages.

The divorce rates among ministers is roughly equal to that of the general population.[16] If those who preach and teach about welcoming Jesus into their marriage show equal divorce rates, obviously the Jesus treatment isn't working.

Dr. Roy Austin, a religious therapist and graduate of Southwestern Seminary, made this observation about the Barna study:

> Magical thinking is often a factor among evangelical and fundamentalist couples and that leaves them less prepared for the rigors of marriage. The atheist doesn't believe in God and so doesn't depend on God to save or fix a marriage. It's just "the two of us," and that takes the magic aspect out of it.[17]

Gary Thomas, author of *Sacred Marriage* and director of the Center for Evangelical Spirituality in Bellingham, Washington, says, "Christians should use marriage to seek 'holiness, not happiness.'" Mr. Thomas believes that the Christian church contributes to divorce by being too tolerant. "Christians need to think of their marriage as a chance to serve Christ. A Christian who *gets divorced* puts their happiness before their devotion to Christ." It is pretty easy to see how following this guy's Jesus might lead to marital unhappiness and divorce.

These are just a few of the many myths religions perpetuate on their members. In the next chapters, many more will be explored in different contexts.

---

15   "Dumbfounded by divorce," a report by Christine Wicker on the Barna study. Available online at http://www.adherents.com/largecom/baptist_divorce.html.

16   As noted by Lisa Takeuchi Cullen, in "Pastors' Wives Come Together," *Time Magazine*, 29 March 2007. Available online at http://www.time.com/time/magazine/article/0,9171,1604902,00.html, and "Study Shows Average Divorce Rate Among Clergy," available online at http://articles.latimes.com/1995-07-01/local/me-19084_1_divorce-rate.

17   As reported by Wicker in "Dumbfounded by divorce."

# CHAPTER 4:

# DID JESUS MASTURBATE?

# AND OTHER INTERESTING THOUGHTS

*What happened to the symbols of sexuality in Christianity? Why does Christianity demand monogamy? Were all early Christians asexual?*

### Jesus: Married, Non-Existent, Female or Closeted Gay?

The idea that a god is watching you during sex, knows when you are masturbating and sees you when you look lustfully at another person comes from early Christian writings that are influenced by a strong antisexual mythology. The New Testament and the Ante-Nicene Fathers[18] advised avoiding sex to make sure you don't fall into temptation. Christian writings and tradition make Jesus a virtual eunuch.[19] Jesus was called rabbi. Throughout Jewish culture, a rabbi has been a married man, unless he is a widower. How could Jesus be a rabbi and not married? It's highly unlikely for him to be single at age 30. Any wife would automatically make Jesus a sexual creature, especially if he had children. Being married or having children would interfere with the Christian narrative of Jesus as an asexual creature.

Another possibility is that he was female but was thought to be male (see also the discussion of Androgen Insensitivity Syndrome in Chapter 10). If he was born of a virgin, that means he was conceived through parthenogenesis. Parthenogenesis is the ability of a female to reproduce without being fertilized by male sperm.[20] Unfortunately, the offspring of any parthenogenic human would be female since that is all parthenogenesis ever produces. Therefore, biologically speaking, Jesus would have been a female, if the virgin birth were true.

It is interesting to look at the whole virgin birth idea from a biological perspective. Sex as an unclean act is a theme throughout Christianity. How can the savior be born of an unclean act? Such a thing could not be allowed in the sex-negative worldview of early Christianity. For this reason, there was some editing going on by the early writers to eliminate inconvenient facts. Wives, children, sexual conception all would say that Jesus was a

---

18   The Ante-Nicene Fathers wrote about and defended Christianity from about 100 to 325 CE. Most Christians are not familiar with these writings, yet they are the basis for much of what Christians believe today. The Ante-Nicene Fathers include Clement, Ignatius, Polycarp, Justin Martyr, Irenaeus, Tertullian and others.

19   Jesus does discuss eunuchs and seems to say that making oneself a eunuch is a good idea, if you can do it: "For there are eunuchs who have been so from birth, and there are eunuchs who have been made eunuchs by others, and there are eunuchs who have made themselves eunuchs for the sake of the kingdom of heaven. Let anyone accept this who can" (Matthew 19:12).

20   Parthenogenesis does not naturally occur in humans or in mammals, although it has been induced in mice and rabbits and a few other animals. For more information on induced parthenogenesis, see Kawahara, M., Wu, Q., et al. (2007). "High- frequency generation of viable mice from engineered bi-maternal embryos." *Nature Biotechnology* 25 (9): 1045–50.

sexual creature, born of two other sexual creatures. But all this challenges the asexual perspective of the early church.

## What Happened to the Women and Children?

And what about those who followed Jesus? In the Jewish culture of the day, marriage was incredibly important, as it is today among most Jews, especially Orthodox. It is difficult to believe that most of Jesus' followers were not married. Peter certainly was (Luke 4:38). And Paul makes a clear reference to wives: "Don't we have the right to take a believing wife along with us, as do the other apostles and the Lord's brothers and Cephas?" (I Corinthians 9:5). Most authorities would concede that at least some of them were married.

But the wives were left out of the New Testament and so were any children. Is it possible for such a large group of apostles and disciples not to have children? It has been suggested that Jesus and his disciples were all gay, hence no need for wives or children. But that seems a bit far-fetched.

So what happened to the women and children? Ask a Christian biblical scholar, and he might say, "Women were not seen as important, so there was no need to refer to them." That answer has some validity, but male children were important. Where are the references to the sons of Peter or Paul or the grandsons of John?

Progeny are always a problem when there is a charismatic founder; just look at the problems Mohammed's children and grandchildren caused. The split between Sunni and Shi'a Islam is, in part, a result of the battle for spiritual succession between the children of Mohammed and his key followers. And what about the split in the Mormon Church between Joseph Smith's son and Brigham Young? In a patriarchal culture, sons have a claim to the property and reputation of their father, especially oldest sons. Just as Oral Roberts' son took over his empire and Billy Graham's son took on his father's ministry, early Christians would have revered the sons (and daughters) of apostles.

There can be no doubt that children and grandchildren existed. Paul would have known some of them, but his writings rarely mention the original apostles and never mention their children.

As for Paul, a well-educated Jewish official, it would have been imperative for him to be married. Did he abandon his wife and children to wander around the Mediterranean proselytizing for the new Christian cult? What happened to his children and grandchildren? Why were these people edited out? And how did they get edited out?

### Inconvenient Women and Children

I suggest two reasons: First, the political inconvenience of having children on the record, and the second, the importance of the asexual myth to Christianity. It is probable that some kind of struggle took place between the growing church hierarchy of the late first century and the grandchildren and great-grandchildren of the founders. Ultimately, the budding hierarchy won and did its best to erase the names of those who were descended from Jesus, Paul, Peter and other important figures. Once the non-related leaders gained the upper hand, history was rewritten without wives, children or grandchildren.

The subsequent church's suppression of female figures in the Jesus story is good evidence that women, in particular, were edited out. The Gospels of Phillip, Mary and Pistis Sophia all have stories of conflict between Mary and Peter. In each story, Peter is said to oppose what Mary says because she is a woman. Yet, these and many other writings show women played significant roles at one time. While several of these writings have been rediscovered in recent times, like the Gospel of Mary, all these manuscripts date from the 200s to the 500s CE. They were probably in wide circulation for the first 400-500 years of the church, and then eliminated.

Dr. Richard Carrier, a scholar of ancient history, says:

> Women were conspicuously important to the cult from day one. Paul has to thank several for providing funds and housing for his congregations and sets rules for their equal participation in the church. The Timothy letters and the anti-woman passage in Corinthians are forgeries, and represent later Christian misogyny, whereas Paul was nearly an egalitarian, and Acts makes a point of mentioning the role of numerous female converts. So the silence on disciples' wives/daughters/ mothers (and kids) is even more bizarre.[21]

Many early writers had motivation to edit out any inconvenient or powerful women. The strong patriarchal model of early Christianity did

---

21    Private communication with Richard Carrier. See his blog http://richardcarrier.blogspot. com/2011/06/pauline-interpolations.html and discussion of early Christian feminism in *Not the Impossible Faith*, pp. 110-11 (2009) and associated endnotes.

not allow for powerful women, so it was best to edit these women out than to have questions later. Others simply forged new documents that mention no women or children. Tertullian (160-220 CE), the "Father of Latin Christianity," has been revered and quoted by Christian scholars for centuries. He was amazingly misogynistic. With him setting the pace, it is no wonder that women were eliminated from the narrative where possible.

## Rewriting History

We have recent parallel examples of religion eliminating competing versions and rewriting the story while eliminating women. For example, the Mormon Church started rewriting its history before Joseph Smith's body was cold in the ground, and it continues to rewrite it today. Ask a devout Mormon how many wives Joseph Smith or Brigham Young had. He probably won't tell you 34 and 54, respectively (plus or minus a few). Church officials deny or downplay plural marriage. Even Joseph Smith's wife, Emma Smith, denied her husband was polygamous and campaigned against it after he died. Yet Brigham Young practiced polygamy and encouraged it among his followers in Utah. The Church does not celebrate these women and children, though they played a big part in the early Mormon Church.[22]

Catholicism has actively rewritten its history and that of others' versions of Christianity from the beginning. For example, those who opposed the winners at the Council of Nicaea in 325 CE were edited and eliminated from the writings shortly thereafter.[23] The heretic of the day was the bishop of Alexandria, Arius (ca 250-336). His so-called heresy had an enormous following, including two Roman Emperors, but the winners wrote the history. Constantine ordered Arius' writings burned and suppressed – and thus we know little of him except through the denunciations of Catholic

22   The Mormon church's official website answers the polygamy question as follows: "In this dispensation, the Lord commanded some of the early Saints to practice plural marriage. The Prophet Joseph Smith and those closest to him, including Brigham Young and Heber C. Kimball, were challenged by this command, but they obeyed it. Church leaders regulated the practice. Those entering into it had to be authorized to do so, and the marriages had to be performed through the sealing power of the priesthood. In 1890, President Wilford Woodruff received a revelation that the leaders of the Church should cease teaching the practice of plural marriage." Available online at http://mormon.org/faq/#Polygamy.

23   The Arian concept of Christ is that the son of God did not always exist, but was created by – and is therefore distinct from and inferior to – God the Father. This belief is grounded in John 14:28 "Ye have heard how I said unto you, I go away, and come again unto you. If ye loved me, ye would rejoice, because I said, I go unto the Father: for my Father is greater than I."

writers. Arian Christianity along with its writers and thinkers continued to thrive for another one hundred years in some parts of the empire, but their writings have largely disappeared.

## Christian Asexuality

The second reason to eliminate these "inconvenient" historical figures deals with sex and sexuality. In the Christian view, sex was an unclean act. Ask Christians, "Did Jesus have sex?" and watch their nonverbal response. Or ask, "Did Peter enjoy sex with his wife?" or "Did Mary and Martha, 'whom Jesus loved,' ever enjoy a good orgasm?" Such questions do not compute in the Christian mind. The Christian founders are seen as asexual.

Contrast these beliefs with Muslim beliefs about their founder's sexuality. Mohammed gives all sorts of advice on when to have sex, with whom to have sex, how to treat sexual slaves, etc. Mormon founders were also very sexual. In the Mormon pantheon, Jesus was even married. Mormonism started out as polygamous, but as Mormonism attempted to become more accepted within the greater Christian culture, it evolved into an asexual cult as well.

Unlike some other religions, asexuality is so important to Christianity that it has written and rewritten its history to reflect the non-sexual nature of its founders. The asexual ideal of Christianity allows it to assign guilt to anyone who falls short of this ideal.

## Mary Was a Virgin

The appearance of asexuality was so important that even the mother of Jesus had to be a virgin. The Catholic Church vehemently denies that Jesus had any brothers or sisters, despite the mention in Mark 6:3.[24] If Mary had other children, then she would have participated in the unclean act of sexual intercourse and would not be the pure and undefiled person of Catholic mythology. It is upon this mythology that entire components of the catechism are built. Mary was not married to Joseph. She was married to god, and a god impregnated her. Joseph was just a convenience to give cover for the potential embarrassment that Mary was really a sexually active adolescent

---

24  Mark 6:3, "'Isn't this the carpenter? Isn't this Mary's son and the brother of James, Joseph, Judas and Simon? Aren't his sisters here with us?'" And they took offense at him." No less than five other scriptures refer to Jesus' siblings: Matthew 12:46; John 2:12; John 7:3; Acts 1:14; and Galatians 1:19.

who got pregnant with her boyfriend. According to church doctrine, the marriage was never consummated, and Joseph didn't hang around long. Mary was a virgin before, during and after the birth of Christ (*Catechism of the Catholic Church, Second English Translation*, 496-511). No mention is made of Joseph after Jesus' incident in the temple when he was 12.

This plays out in current sexual distortion with respect to nuns. Nuns are celibate and are "married" to Jesus. They also practice a good deal of Mary worship. Many nuns and priests, as well as the Pope himself, worship Mary above Jesus. Although they would deny this, a look at their behavior says otherwise. When Pope John-Paul II was shot, during his ride to the hospital he kept repeating, "Mary, my mother." A year after he was shot, he made a pilgrimage to Fatima to give thanks to Mary for his recovery.

While we have focused on Catholic doctrine, ideas like the Virgin Birth also inform the Orthodox and Protestant branches. There may be nuances and differences, but the one thing they all hold on common is the asexuality of the founders. For example, the Nicene Creed is common to all and contains this fundamental concept:

> ...who for us men, and for our salvation, came down from
> heaven, and was incarnate by the Holy Ghost of the Virgin
> Mary, and was made man ....[25]

So does the Apostle's Creed which many Protestants use:

> I believe in God, the Father Almighty,
> Maker of heaven and earth,
> and in Jesus Christ,
> His only Son, our Lord:
> Who was conceived by the Holy Spirit,
> born of the Virgin Mary....[26]

There are other minor variations on the creeds, but all refer to the Virgin Mary. The creeds were originally designed to standardize beliefs and to persecute or eliminate those who did not adhere to key ideas.

---

25  Second Council of Constantinople (381 CE).

26  Book of Common Prayer (1662 CE).

Modern non-demoninationalists[27] claim they have no creed, but queried on the validity of a Virgin Birth, they will respond, "That is what the Bible says, so it must be true."

Knowing that early Christian founders were human, we can conclude that they masturbated, married, had sex, had children, had affairs occasionally and certainly lusted in their hearts. But in Christian scriptures, the founders seem untouched by human desires. There is only the slightest hint that Paul experienced a problem when, in Corinthians, he talks about a "thorn in the flesh." We can only guess what he is referring to. Maybe he masturbated too much, drank a little too much wine or had a mistress.[28] He wouldn't be the first religious leader to do so.

### Masturbation: The Single-Handed Sin

As with most religions, Christianity teaches that masturbating is wrong or at best questionable. Mark Driscoll, founder of the Seattle mega-church, Mars Hill, is only one among many religious leaders who preach against masturbation:

> "... Masturbation can be a form of homosexuality because it is a sexual act that does not involve a woman. If a man were to masturbate while engaged in other forms of sexual intimacy with his wife then he would not be doing so in a homosexual way. However, any man who does so without his wife in the room is bordering on homosexuality activity, particularly if he's watching himself in a mirror and being turned on by his own male body."[29]

Self-sex is the first sex a person has. To characterize it as abnormal is a distortion of natural sexuality. Sooner or later a child will hear that this most private and important sexual activity is unnatural and will likely cause problems in his or her spiritual growth, marriage or eye sight.

---

27   Non-denominationalism is a vague and confusing term applied to many mega-churches that have sprung up in much of the Christian world. They are often characterized by theological and political independence and a single charismatic leader. Examples include Willow Creek, Calvary Chapel, Cornerstone Fellowship and Christ's Commission Fellowship (Phillipines).

28   2 Corinthians 12:7-9, KJV: "And lest I should be exalted above measure through the abundance of the revelations, there was given to me a thorn in the flesh, the messenger of Satan to buffet me, lest I should be exalted above measure."

29   Driscoll's free online book is available at http://theresurgence.com/books/porn_again_christian.

Jesus' idea that lust in the heart is the same as adultery feeds right into the guilt around masturbation.[30] Masturbation generally involves some degree of imagination and visualization. Lucky for women, adultery as Jesus knew it was between a man and a married woman. A single woman could not commit adultery. Also, the Bible does not prohibit women from masturbating, though most Christian denominations would frown on it.

The idea of adultery was directly related to a man's property rights. The prohibition is to prevent one man from interfering with another's property, as in Exodus 20:14, "You shall not commit adultery." and 17, "You shall not covet your neighbor's house; you shall not covet your neighbor's wife, or male or female slave, or ox, or donkey, or anything that belongs to your neighbor."

## Why Are Jews Monogamous?

Interestingly, there is nothing in the Ten Commandments about the number of spouses you can have. At the time of the writing of Exodus and Deuteronomy, polygamy was well accepted and practiced by Judaism and surrounding cultures.

Under Rome in the first century CE, the monogamous Romans were tolerant of polygamous Jews. Herod the Great was allowed to have many wives because he was Jewish.[31] There was no outcry at that time against Herod's behavior because it was an acceptable practice. As with many cultures, polygamy was generally practiced by the upper classes since it required excess resources to support multiple wives. Even when polygamy was most widely practiced, most Jews would still have been monogamous as a practical matter.

Probably as a result of three hundred years of domination by the monogamous Greeks and Romans, polygamy slowly lost favor even in the upper classes. But polygamy was not formally outlawed in Judaism until the 11th century.[32]

---

30   Matthew 5:27-28, KJV: "Ye have heard that it was said by them of old time, Thou shalt not commit adultery: But I say unto you, That whosoever looketh on a woman to lust after her hath committed adultery with her already in his heart."

31   Flavius Josephus says Herod had 9 wives and at least 15 children. At least five names are known: Doris, Mariamne I, Mariamne II, Cleopatra of Jerusalem, Malthace. (*The Works of Flavius Josephus*, War of the Jews, Book 1, 28:4.)

32   Gershom ben Judah (c. 960 -1040), one of the most influential rabbis of his time, put the nail in the polygyny coffin with many rules and laws he advocated. Some sects of Judaism continued to practice polygyny until more recent times, but this was rare.

### Why Are Christians Monogamous?

Jesus said nothing against polygamy, even though he undoubtedly saw it practiced by his Jewish contemporaries. No later Christian author in the New Testament condemns the practice either.

A reference in 1 Timothy 3:12 indicates polygamy was practiced among Christians, "Deacons must be husbands of only one wife." Some Christians must have had more than one wife, otherwise why make that a requirement?

The world of early Christianity was a mix of monogamous and polygamous practices both inside and outside of Judaism. As Christianity spread to non-Jewish communities in the Roman world, many would already have been monogamous, so polygamy would not be an issue. But in polygamous North Africa and the Arabian Peninsula, accommodations had to be made. The Church may have disapproved of polygamy, but conversion was more important at that time. Once an area was converted, then the Church slowly went about forcing out polygamy. It was too much to ask that a wealthy polygamous convert give up two of his three wives, but the church could ask that his sons refrain from marrying more than one wife. As a result, the early church is largely silent on the issue so as not to alienate possible converts and gain access to wealth.

Christian views on monogamy are not based in scripture, and early church leaders had difficulty condemning polygamy. All the key players in the Old Testament were polygamous. Augustine (354-430 CE) did not condemn the patriarchs for their polygamous ways but said polygamy was no longer necessary. He created a tortured argument and taught that the reason why patriarchs had many wives was simply because they wanted more children. Therefore, he said that the need to produce many children was past, so monogamy was more acceptable. He never actually condemned polygamy. If you are confused by this argument, you are not alone.

Some Christians were probably polygamous for the first few centuries, but Christianity was more a movement of the lower classes who were monogamous already. Thus, from the beginning, monogamy would have been the norm simply because it was a lower class religion. It was not until the fifth century that the church formally outlawed it. Then it became a bedrock principle.

But the issue was still cropping up in Martin Luther's time a thousand years after Augustine. In a letter to Chancellor Gregor Brück, January 13,

1524, Luther stated, "I confess that I cannot forbid a person to marry several wives, for it does not contradict Scripture."[33]

Modern-day Christian culture ignores the fact that there is no prohibition on polygamy or more accurately, polygyny[34] (many wives), or for that matter polyandry (many husbands). In matters of marriage, the Bible is largely silent. The Mormons had no problem with polygyny. They believe that Jesus had three wives. Joseph Smith instituted polygyny from the very beginning.[35]

As we can see from the polygyny of Mormonism, Hinduism and Islam, religions can be quite successful with non-monogamous forms of marriage. Christian monogamy was a function of the cultural pressures of the first three centuries. At the same time, a severe type of monogamy evolved in Christianity.

Sexual pleasure within marriage is not discussed or encouraged in the New Testament. The Ante-Nicene Fathers are downright hostile to the notion of sexual pleasure. Their belief that Jesus may return any day to judge you meant that you had better be sexually pure at all times or you might end up in hell. The concept of an all-knowing, voyeuristic and vengeful god created a religion of strong guilt and fear around sex.

So to answer the question we began with in the title of this chapter, "Did Jesus Masturbate?" If he existed, he probably did at some point in his adolescence. It would be the rare boy who does not experiment with his own body. On the other hand, some people are born asexual. If Jesus was asexual, he might never have masturbated. Jesus said:

> **Matt. 19:12,** For some are eunuchs because they were born that way; others were made that way by men; and others have renounced marriage because of the kingdom of heaven. The one who can accept this should accept it.

Maybe he was a eunuch from birth. In that case how can a eunuch give advice about sex and marriage?

---

33  From De Wette's collection of Luther's Letters (1826).

34  Polygamy is the popular word for "many wives", but we will use the more accurate "polygyny" from here on so that we can contrast polygyny "many wives" with polyandry "many husbands."

35  See the *Journal of Discourses*, Volume 4, page 259. The Journal of Discourses is a collection of public sermons by early leaders of Mormon church.

Now let's turn to the mechanics of shame and guilt to help us understand why sex is so important to most religions and why they use it so much.

# CHAPTER 5:

# THE SHAME OF IT ALL

*How is shame different from guilt? How does shame work to keep people religiously infected and in line? How is shame different in Islam versus Christianity?*

## Shame vs. Guilt

Religious guilt and shame are the primary tools of most organized religions, but they are used to different degrees and ways. Why does Islam or Hinduism use one sexual system and Christianity another? Much of the answer to this question may be found in how these religions use shame and guilt.

For purposes of our discussion, let's define religious guilt as the feeling you get when you know you have violated a rule or moral principle. No one else may know of your action, but an all-voyeuristic god knows. Guilt is something that, once programmed, can function without anyone else knowing. If you are taught that masturbation is against god's law, then whenever you do it, you will feel guilt even though no one knows you did it.

Shame is a deeper emotion, one that incorporates one's identity as well as the judgment of other people. It is the idea that a certain behavior makes you a bad, damaged or diseased person. A Muslim woman is taught from birth that anyone who loses her virginity before marriage is eternally damaged. She becomes like a diseased and filthy person to god and her community. Such a belief creates both terror and focus on avoiding behavior that might lead to shame. She is told stories and shown examples of women who violated this law of god. In everyday conversation, the idea is associated with defilement, dirt, disease, as well as loss of social connection, status and support. A defiled woman is the target of social ostracism and abuse. It is remarkably parallel to the button story in Chapter 1.

This is an entirely different level of programming than guilt. With shame, the very thought of engaging in a given behavior evokes associations of disease and ostracism. Actually doing the behavior creates huge emotional turmoil. Feelings of filth and uncleanliness may overwhelm the person, making him or her feel worthless. In other words, shame leaves a deep psychological mark. Here is a story that illustrated this point from an American Muslim woman who is now an atheist:

> When I started maturing, my mother came into my room, sat down and said, 'Never touch yourself; it will ruin your marriage.' That was the extent of my sex education. I knew what she meant but had never had the urge to that point. Over the next year, I began to have urges and thoughts. I resisted doing anything for almost two years, then one night I succumbed and gave myself my first orgasm. The next morning I was so ashamed that I became

*sick. I stayed home from school. I cannot express the feelings of filth, disgust and horror that I experienced. I was afraid that I had already ruined my marriage at 14 years of age. I wondered if my future husband would be able to tell and would reject me. Not long after, I became very religious. I hoped to show my devotion to Allah and find a way out of my shame. While I mostly resisted, every so often I would succumb, and the whole process would start again with an even stronger devotion to Allah.*

Fortunately, this woman left Islam and happily masturbates or has sex with her boyfriend without any shame or guilt. Her ordeal, however, is shared by millions of women in Islam as well as Christianity, Hinduism, Mormonism and many other religions.

Due to its deep-rooted nature, shame is far harder to erase than guilt. The shamed person actually creates a new identity that incorporates a permanent condition of defilement. Guilt may be forgiven with a prayer or confession, but shame indelibly marks the identity. The shamed person may feel so defiled or diseased that she may engage in irrational, self-defeating behaviors.[36] Often she dives deeper into religion, hoping to get some relief.

Shame is often more destructive than guilt, which is why I will focus on it here.

## Shame and the Family

Shame invokes a stronger response from family and community than guilt. A girl may be guilty of disobeying her mother. She may feel guilt and her mother may be angry. She may do extra housework or cooking to get back in her mother's good graces and then move on. But for a person who violates a shame rule, no amount of penance or praying will wash the spot clean. No amount of forgiveness from mother or father will cleanse the shameful action. Additionally, other people in the community, especially the family, take on the dirt and filth identity. As a result, the girl or woman (and it is mostly focused on women in shaming cultures) is punished and isolated like a leper.

In ancient Greece, the word "aidos" (shame) applied to men and women but with a sexual meaning for women and a more "honor" meaning for men.

---

36  If you are thinking that guilt and shame sound a lot alike, especially in the extreme, you are correct. Entire books have been written trying to distinguish between the two. To keep the discussion from getting too academic, we are using these simple distinctions.

Men could be shamed on the battlefield. Women were shamed sexually. According to Greek legend, the goddess Aiskhyne gave people a sense of shame so they would avoid certain behaviors.

In the New Testament (which was originally written in Greek), "aidos" is only used twice, once in reference to female modesty so as not to bring shame on themselves or the community. The other reference is non-specific:

> 1 Timothy 2:9, KJV, "In like manner also, that women adorn
> themselves in modest apparel, with shamefacedness and sobriety;
> not with braided hair, or gold, or pearls, or costly array."

At different times in history, Christianity has used shame as an important tool, but the use of shame often requires a tight-knit community or tribe that can punish violators.

With the protestant reformation, the idea of the "priesthood of all believers" pushed Christianity away from shame and more toward guilt. Protestants were accountable directly to their god and must ask him for forgiveness, not a priest or church official. This idea reduced the emphasis on community and increased focus on the individual. That is probably why Christianity, especially Protestantism, places a stronger emphasis on guilt than on shame.

## Islam, the Shame Religion

In the West many people marvel at the power of Islam to control people and oppress women so completely that they will wear head-to-toe clothing in 100° F (38° C) heat. Islam has a very different approach to sexual control than Christianity and the two approaches are rooted in their beginnings. Islam began as a tribal religion, whereas Christianity began more as an individual or family religion. Christianity struck out from Palestine, converting one person or one family at a time. After the initial successes and conquests by Mohammed and his tribe, conversions were as much military as spiritual. Mohammed was both a political and military genius and used his success and charisma to convince the superstitious tribes around him that he had Allah on his side. As such, the sword was the instrument of persuasion.

Often an entire tribe converted to Islam. In the Arabian Peninsula there were Jewish, Christian and pagan tribes. The division and conflicts among the many tribes helped Mohammed gain ascendancy and ultimately control. Mohammed took his tribal customs and traditions and injected them into his new religion. Many of the ideas and traditions he implemented were already contained in the tribes he conquered, so in many cases, no major changes were required of his new followers. For example, most, if not all, of the tribes were polygamous. Women were seen primarily as chattel and under the complete control of their fathers or husbands. The communities of the new Islamic religion in the 600s CE often converted en masse. With minor modifications, they kept practicing their traditions. Mecca was already a major pagan religious shrine; Mohammed conveniently changed it to a place of worship and pilgrimage for Allah.

Practically speaking, Mohammed unified a fractured region under a single religion and did it with a superior military. Conquest, war and male dominance were the hallmarks of Islam. Despite political splits over the centuries, the tribal nature of Islam remains intact.

In contrast, Christianity started out as an underground movement. Christianity did not have the strong and solid tribal roots of Islam. While it may have originated in Judaism, it rapidly left those tribal roots behind. For more than three centuries it had to hide or run from Roman authorities and did not come into its own until the 400s.

In many ways, Islam looks much more like the tribes of ancient Israel than does Christianity. Reading the Old Testament and the Koran side by side, the rules and commandments are remarkably similar. Both allow, even command, the killing of those who do not bow to their god. Both allow sex slaves:

> **Exodus 21:7-11, NLT,** When a man sells his daughter as a slave, she will not be freed at the end of six years as the men are. If she does not please the man who bought her, he may allow her to be bought back again. But he is not allowed to sell her to foreigners, since he is the one who broke the contract with her. And if the slave girl's owner arranges for her to marry his son, he may no longer treat her as a slave girl, but he must treat her as his daughter. If he himself marries her and then takes another wife, he may not reduce her food or clothing or fail to sleep with her as his wife. If he fails in any of these three ways, she may leave as a free woman without making any payment.
> **Koran [viii] Sura 24 [The Light], Verse 31,** And say to the believing women that they cast down their looks and guard their private parts and do not display their ornaments except what appears thereof, and let them wear their head-coverings over their bosoms, and not display their ornaments except to

their husbands or their fathers, or the fathers of their husbands, or their sons, or the sons of their husbands, or their brothers, or their brothers' sons, or their sisters' sons, or their women, or those whom their right hands possess (female sex slaves), or the male servants not having need (of women) ....

Both give the male head of the family total control and treat women as property with economic and political value. Both are strongly patriarchal and punish women more than men for sexual transgressions. Both have a strong shame focus.

The modern approach of Christianity, based on individualistic guilt, does not allow it to stone people, chop off their heads or shame them into becoming suicide bombers. Were Christianity in a position to put women to death for wearing a bikini, or failing to fast during Lent, there would be far less secularism. That is the advantage of Islam. Fail to fast during Ramadan in Iran or Saudi Arabia or any number of other countries, and you risk bodily harm – to say nothing of wearing a bikini.

How does Islam accomplish this? From birth, its adherents are deeply infected with ideas of honor and shame. When communities of Muslims develop in new countries, they form tight communities that facilitate enforcement of religious principles. If possible, they even set up alternate courts to enforce Shari'a Law. How is this different from the Irish in New York or the Indians in London? The answer is that while such subcultures have their own customs and traditions, none ever successfully implemented separate systems of enforcement equal to Muslim communities. The murder of Theo Van Gogh, the fatwa on Salman Rushdie, the death threats to the former Dutch parliamentarian Ayaan Hirsi Ali,[37] the riots, death threats and killings over the Mohammed cartoons, the honor killings of young women in Holland, are all examples of the shame culture of Islam in action.

The simple psychology of shame uses early childhood terror and natural defensive mechanisms to ensure conformity. Sanctions do not need to occur often. As long as children see and hear of them occasionally, they will internalize them. Westerners are horrified at the public beheadings in Saudi Arabia or stories of young girls being killed by their own brothers

---

37 Theo Van Gogh was murdered by a Muslim man in Amsterdam for making a short film about women in Islam. His partner, Ayaan Hirsi Ali, was threatened and has been in hiding or guarded since. Similarly, Salman Rushdie is under threat of a fatwah for publishing his book *Satanic Verses*.

for running off with a boyfriend. A Muslim father in Toronto killed his daughter for defying him and writing her boyfriend.

Imagine what such stories do to Muslim children who live inside the culture and communities, even in Western countries. In the secular West, we know such things will not happen to us. Children in Muslim cultures have no such assurances. Even if they have kind, loving, less religious parents, they are still finely tuned to their religion. They easily internalize the terror that such a fate could befall them if they do not adhere to the dictates of Allah.

## Male Shame

While men may not suffer shame as much as women, it is still a constant force in the lives of Muslims. Males are responsible for the chastity of all women in their household, for defending the faith and for avenging insults to the religion. They must show courage in battle so as not to bring shame on their families or communities. The male side of Islamic shame requires punitive measures for anyone who would bring imagined filth upon Allah or Mohammed. Therefore, men are compelled to ensure purity within their family and community.

Today, Islam effectively resists secularization primarily because of its use of shame. Within the community, each person's sexuality is tied to his or her family and to the community. To violate the sexual rules of Allah violates both the family and the community. This powerful distortion allows Islam to remain isolated from secular sexual influences. The terror of social sanction or violence keeps young people from following their heart. It prevents healthy sexual exploration and development in men and women.

## Shame and Modern Cults

Modern cults like Mormonism, Jehovah's Witnesses and Scientology are more shame-based than mainstream Christian groups. Cults tend to create a closed community where members are isolated from the rest of the world through deep indoctrination. At the same time, the system requires members to watch one another and report violations of behavior or doctrine to an authority figure.

Shame can be brought upon the family for one person's behavior. For example, if a Jehovah's Witness sees another committing a sin, he is obligated to report it to the elders. Two elders then investigate the incident.

If they determine a violation has happened, a three-elder committee meets with the member in a disciplinary meeting. The discipline can be anything from a mild reproach, to a public announcement at the meeting, to being disfellowshipped.

During the discipline meeting, the person is encouraged to reveal if he or she has witnessed others committing sin. The idea is that a person cannot be guilt-free if he has seen others sinning and not reported it. Unlike Islam, Jehovah's Witnesses have to work in a culture that has competing religions and many secular influences. It is a major task to keep the members isolated from outside ideas. Guilt and shame are the main tools.

### Conclusion

Lest I overstate the case, shame is not limited to religion. It can be used without reference to religion or the supernatural, but religions have found shame to be a powerful tool for maintaining religious conformity and to control or limit sexual behavior. Building on our understanding of these psychological tools, let's look at how these come together to allow many of the abuses perpetuated by religion.

# CHAPTER 6:

# MIND POLICE AND THOUGHT CONTROL

Guilt is a key tool by which religion controls people. Guilt impedes effective communication and undermines sexual confidence and enjoyment.

"PORNOGRAPHY: The name given to any sexual literature somebody is trying to suppress."

-Alex Comfort, *The Joy of Sex*

### Religious Police

Saudi Arabia has religious police charged with maintaining the public morals. They arrest people who are in violation of the religious dress or behavior codes of the kingdom. Thus, if two people kiss in public, they are subject to arrest and prosecution by the religious authorities. If a woman is not properly covered in public, she is seen as a public danger and prosecuted for exposing an ankle or face. Consequences can be severe for both the individual and the family. As we discussed in Chapter 5, shame is an enormously effective tool because it brings communal pressure to bear on both the individual and the family.

While we may be horrified at the notion of religious police, there are ways to control by different means. The guilt cycle is an effective method of creating self-policing and self-censorship. It works like this.

### The Guilt Cycle, or the Police Officer in Your Head

Each religion has certain things that are forbidden or sinful. Children are taught these with many examples, stories and subtle signals as they grow up. In the area of sex, the secretiveness, subtle language and behavior of adults and occasional public examples all work to infect a child with fear of transgressing. Also, punishments, ostracism and humiliation often occur when sexual behavior is discovered or suspected, ensuring that these lessons are internalized. If a person violates the code, there is no way to hide, the god knows you did it, even if your parents do not, and the god will punish you unless you confess. These are powerful ideas for a child. Children are very susceptible to magical thinking at three to seven years of age, when they're being taught magical ideas about gods watching or punishing them. It is a pattern of thinking that is embedded in the child's mind and often continues in adulthood.

Fast forward to today. A child learns that you must pray for forgiveness when you do something bad. If you do not pray or do not confess, god will punish you. This scenario sets up the guilt cycle.[38]

When you transgress or sin, you must return to your personal religion for forgiveness. Catholics do not confess their sins to Baptist ministers. Baptists don't ask forgiveness from Muslim clerics. You must seek forgiveness from

---

38   For a full discussion of this concept, see Chapter 4 in my previous book, *The God Virus: How Religion Infects Our Lives and Culture,* "God Loves You – The Guilt that Binds," p. 83.

the place where you learned about sin. It is as if the religion infects you with the disease and then gives you a fake cure.

The former Muslim, now atheist, Ayaan Hirsi Ali gives a perfect example of the guilt cycle in her excellent book *Infidel* (2007). A popular local imam, Abshir, began spending time with her. In his sermons, he preached strongly against intimacy before marriage and sinful thoughts, but his behavior was somewhat different. Ali says,

> I was having more and more sinful thoughts. When we were alone Abshir would kiss me, and he could really kiss. It was long and gentle and thrilling and therefore sinful. Afterward I would tell him how bad I felt in the eyes of Allah, how much that bothered me. And Abshir would say, "If we were married, then it wouldn't be sinful. We must exercise willpower and not do it anymore." So for a day or so we would steel ourselves and refrain, and then the next day we would look at each other and just kiss again. He would say, "I'm too weak, I think of you all day long."

She concludes,

> In hindsight I don't think of Abshir as a creep at all. He was just as trapped in a mental cage as I was. Abshir and I and all the other young people who joined the Muslim Brotherhood movement wanted to live as much as possible like our beloved Prophet, but the rules of the last Messenger of Allah were too strict, and their very strictness led us to hypocrisy. At the time, though, I could see only that either Abshir or Islam was thoroughly flawed, and of course I assumed it was Abshir.

Sexual drive pushes a person one direction, religion uses the guilt cycle to push back. The internal conflict creates misery and self-blame, leading right back to the religion. An effectively infected person will learn from childhood the things that are sinful and develop an internal moral police force to keep watch on all thoughts and deeds. **This is not the same as a conscience.** People develop a conscience with or without religion. Our culture teaches murder and cheating are wrong; we don't need religion to know this.[39]

---

39  For an in-depth look, see Steven Pinker's essay, "The Moral Instinct," *New York Times Magazine*, 13 Jan 2008. Available online at http://www.nytimes.com/2008/01/13/magazine/13Psychology-t. html?pagewanted=all.

Guilt comes from a different place in our mental experience, a place that is independent of general cultural training and directly related to religious indoctrination. That is why two people may feel guilt about different things while being equally convinced that cheating and murder are wrong.

A simple mental experiment will illustrate this. Mary, a Catholic, was raised from birth to go to mass and pray each week. If she misses mass, she feels guilty. Sally, a Presbyterian from childhood, was taught that church attendance is good but not mandatory. If she misses church, she doesn't feel too guilty about it as long as she has a good excuse – like visiting her elderly grandmother. Judy, an atheist from birth, wouldn't dream of wasting a Sunday in church and feels no guilt whatsoever. All three women firmly believe that cheating and murder are wrong and abhor such behavior. This thought experiment shows how each religion imprints a unique guilt pattern on their adherents but has no bearing on whether a person is law abiding or moral.

Of course, there is also non-religious guilt. We usually feel it when we make a bad choice or mistreat someone. But non-religious guilt is directly related to widely held cultural expectations, whereas religious guilt is clearly related to a specific religion. Using this model, it is possible to learn what people feel guilty about and trace it directly back to religious childhood training.

Religious training may lead people to feel guilty when:

- I don't put money in the offering plate at church.
- I promise to pray for someone and then forget when I say my prayers.
- I use the Lord's name in vain.
- I think a lustful thought.
- I know someone needs to be saved and I don't witness to them.
- I walk by a beggar and don't put any money in his can.
- I forget to bring my Bible to church.
- I don't do what the Lord wants me to do, like go to the hospital to visit the sick.
- I don't spend enough time preparing my Sunday School lesson.
- I pray for selfish things.
- I put my loved ones above others.

- I feel conflicted over a decision, knowing that if I were a better Mormon (or Christian or Muslim) the answer would be very clear to me.

This list could go on and on. Religious guilt is a bottomless pit. The distinction between religious guilt and the more generic cultural guilt is important in understanding how religion impacts the mental life of religious people. Having a religious police officer in your head makes the job of keeping you infected with religion much easier. No religious police required.

## Sex and Guilt

Growing up in a religious environment, children learn what not to do sexually. They learn that some practices or ideas, such as homosexuality, lust, masturbation and pornography are sinful. These ideas are embedded in the minds of children years before they are ready for marriage, so it's no surprise that many religious people have little or no experience with sex and know little about their sexuality.

The guilt cycle that results from this training creates a form of self-censorship. Because so many sex acts and ideas are liable to lead to eternal damnation, people have a strong incentive to avoid expressing or discussing secretly held ideas and interests. Fear leads to hidden thoughts and activities and prevents normal, appropriately channeled sexual expression.

It is like damming a river. Sooner or later the water will flow around or over the dam. Controlled release allows for benefits like recreation and irrigation and less potential destruction downstream. Simply damming water leads to problems.

Sexually inhibited or frustrated people will eventually express sexual energy, but in ways that may be destructive of self or others. They may condemn those who express themselves freely and attempt to impose religious restrictions on them. They may become inappropriately aggressive toward others or have secret affairs that undermine their family and relationships. Worst of all, they may physically, verbally or sexually abuse those who are more vulnerable. Ignoring sexual drive and energy is a dam without a flood control plan.

Religious guilt can take a normal, straightforward drive and distort it into unrecognizable forms. Many a church has angry, gossipy women in the kitchen who have not had sex in years. Many a male church elder has been known to abuse his children or wife. The incidence of sexual acting-out on the part of important church members is not reflected in clergy abuse statistics. It seems reasonable that church members engage in at least as much sexual acting out as clergy. This is not to say that everyone in a church is acting-out sexual frustration, but there are many, as we might suspect from the divorce statistics discussed in Chapter 3 and the porn and child abuse statistics we will discuss next.

There is no way to quantify the sexual behavior of religious people because the behavior is so easily hidden. But if priests can get away with child sexual abuse for decades and ministers have illicit affairs for years, even fathering children[40] with church members, why wouldn't this be happening with many others in the church?

Over the course of 30 years, I saw dozens of quiet scandals among laity. The issue came to glaring clarity for me when three lay church officials from two different churches were caught in various forms of inappropriate or abusive behavior in the same week! One man was found to have abused his own children from a young age. A key woman had a child that was not fathered by her husband, but by one of the ministers. Another long-serving and upstanding "family-values" leader was "exposed" and pushed out of the church for homosexual behavior.

It is time to acknowledge that sex is happening all the time among church members, but it is hidden, secret and all too often exploitative or abusive. Three statistics bear this out:

1. In the United States, the most religious areas of the nation have the highest divorce rates.
2. One of the best predictors of child abuse and sexual abuse is the religiosity of the parents. The more religious the parents, the more likely they are to abuse their children.[41,]
3. The states with the highest porn use are Utah and Mississippi.[42]

---

40   See, for example, "Earl 'The Abomination' Paulk is the Father of his own Nephew," at *The Independent Conservative*, http://www.independentconservative.com/2007/10/24/earl_paulk_abomination/.

41   Overwhelming evidence suggests that religion is involved in abuse. See Jackson, et al. (1999). "Predicting abuse-prone parental attitudes and discipline practices in a nationally representative sample," in *Child Abuse & Neglect*, 23 (1); and John Hules' 2005 compilation of over 100 studies connecting religiosity of parents to child sexual abuse, available online at www.hules.us/SCI_SUM2.pdf.

42   "Red Light States: Who Buys Online Adult Entertainment?" by Benjamin Edelman, *Journal of Economic Perspectives*, 23 (1), Winter 2009.

Mormon Utah tops all states in Internet porn in each of four different measures. Generally speaking, the more religiously conservative U.S. states and zip codes have the highest porn use by a small margin. In the most religious areas, the only time porn use drops is on Sunday, but it more than catches up the rest of the week.

Could these three statistics be related to religiously dammed-up sexual desire? Could these be proxies for the effects of religious sexual repression? It seems to point in that direction.

Now let's look at how religious sexual guilt impacts women more stongly than men.

## Women, the Guilty Sex

Gender differences are evident in infants with respect to emotional expression, social interaction and social contagion. That is, infant girls are more attentive than boys to the emotional states of their mothers and those of other children. This heightened sensitivity to the emotional environment seems to be genetically based. Throughout life, women interact more, talk more and listen more than boys and men. Women are generally more tuned into the emotional environment than men. This seems to be true at all ages and in all cultures.

This general tendency for women to be sensitive to the emotional environment means they imbibe emotional messages and cultural ideas more rapidly and easily than men. Religion takes advantage of this tendency by creating guilt messages that are uniquely targeted at women.

All major religions put most of the responsibility for sexual morality on women. Religions teach that women should remain chaste and should control and hide their sexuality so men will not be tempted. Once a woman is infected with ideas of chastity, modesty and sexual morality, she is more susceptible to guilt when these are violated or she imagines that they have been violated. If the woman "gives in" to the man, it is her fault. If she tempts a man, it is her fault. Some religions even blame the woman if she is raped.

Sarah Hargreaves, a rape counselor and group facilitator, writes:

> Women agonize over Matthew 6:14-16, "For if you forgive men when they sin against you, your heavenly Father will also forgive you. But if you do not forgive men their sins, your Father will not

forgive your sins." They torture themselves trying to forgive the person who humiliated and terrorized them. Or worse, yet, they stifle their genuine emotions because they believe forgiveness is the magic cure for fixing their anger and resentment. If they cannot forgive their attacker something is wrong with them and they will not be able to heal. These are frankly crazy ideas because it assumes the rapist is worthy of forgiveness.[43]

With this intense programming, women experience religious sexual guilt more often and more strongly than men. They are encouraged to get relief by going to their religion. They are told, it is their duty to forgive or they are not worthy of Jesus.

These religious ideas are the ultimate distortion. Women can pray, attend services, go to mass, do Bible study, go to women's religious meetings, but the fact remains, they are guilty of being a woman. Just as Eve was guilty of the "fall of man," all women are guilty in the context of Christianity and Islam, as well as many other religions.

Further, religions often teach that women are responsible for children's moral development. Not taking their children to church is a sign of moral neglect. The guilt messages are so strong that even non-religious mothers have been known to take their children to church or send them. In the church, children are exposed to abstinence-only messages, purity rings, and most of all, messages about female responsibility in most sexual matters.

Alan Miller and John Hoffman looked at gender differences in religiosity as a function of risk aversion. The more risk averse a person is, the higher his or her religiosity and church attendance. In other words, risk-averse people don't want to take a chance on getting on the wrong side of god.[44] This would fit well with our guilt hypothesis. Women who are most afraid of divine consequences (as taught in shame and guilt training) are more likely than men to engage in fear- and guilt-reducing activities, like attending church. Men who are less fearful of divine retribution or less risk-averse see less need to be involved in religion.

---

43   From a speech titled "Rape and Religion," delivered at SlutWalk KC in Kansas City, Sept. 2011.

44   Miller, A.S. and Hoffman, J.P. (March 1995). "Risk and Religion: An Explanation of Gender Differences in Religiosity," *Journal for the Scientific Study of Religion*, 34(1).

Christopher Hitchens articulated a similar argument in a recent speech:[45]

> The loss of a child is incredibly traumatic to a woman. No doubt men are traumatized as well, but it is the woman who carries the baby to term and spends much of her waking hours with the child. She has the strongest bond. ... If a woman thinks that there is even a tiny advantage in preserving her child through prayer or giving to a priest, she will do so, and I cannot blame her. I can blame the priest for taking advantage of such a deeply held love and devotion for his own gain.

This is a powerful psychological argument that explains why mothers are often much more concerned with taking children to church and teaching them religious ideas than fathers.

### How Guilt Disrupts Sexual Communication

The guilt cycle also works well to inhibit sexual communication between religious married people and keeps them feeling both guilty and sexually frustrated. Here is how it works. Sexual preferences develop, evolve and change over a lifetime. Some marry before they recognize they are homosexual. Others find their spouse has a frustratingly high or low sex drive. Or they discover that they have a fetish. Without opportunities for sexual exploration and discovery, how is a 19 to 20-year-old to learn what he or she likes and how his or her body reacts?

The younger a religious person is when she gets married, the less she understands and knows about her sexuality. Add to this the incredible fear of talking about sexual fantasies, masturbation, experimentation and pornography, and a young adult enters marriage with a serious handicap that can inhibit sexual development for life.

Such people have no template for communication except through their guilt-based training. Interacting and working with hundreds of people, I have found a huge difference in the sexual skill level of religious newly-weds and newly-weds raised in a secular environment. The former are often groping in the dark, sometimes literally. Even if they do have some experience or skill with regard to sex and sexuality, they are often reluctant to display it for fear of giving away previous sexual experience. The abstinence-only programs

---

45  Delivered at the Texas Freethought Convention, 2011. Available on DVD.

and reclaimed-virginity movement make men and women ashamed of being sexual creatures before or outside of marriage.

For a woman, the result is denial even as she is having sex with her husband. If she was successfully abstinent before marriage, she enters into sex with great ignorance. Her husband dares not speak of any partners he has had, since it would quickly betray a double standard. Since it is highly likely that one or both had partners before marriage, they start the relationship on a lie.

A woman who "reclaims her virginity" is buying into the same guilt.[46] Aside from the ludicrous idea that one can reclaim virginity or innocence, it is simply religion's attempt to inject guilt and control sexuality. Should the woman remarry, how does she communicate about her previous sexual experiences except in derogatory ways? All she learned and experienced from previous partners is by definition bad and wrong. Her new husband is her only sexual partner since she has renewed her virginity. It is an amazing mental gymnastic that only a religion or a schizophrenic could contrive.

Of course, this insanity is not unique to women. I have known many Christian men who experience the male equivalent. Their sexual ideas and inhibitions are deeply rooted in religious doctrine and teachings. Catholic priests and nuns are among the best at teaching this. Those with the least experience in sex are also the ones perpetuating highly destructive ideas. The 1998 documentary *Sex in a Cold Climate* on the Irish Magdalene homes is instructive by documenting the incredibly cruel sexual messages and training of the Magdelene nuns.

Here is what one woman wrote me several years ago:

> *At 22, I married a good Catholic man and converted. I had been raised in a fairly non-religious home, but his religiosity seemed a part of the attraction at the time. It was something I had not seen or experienced before, and it held a certain attraction. We seemed to click in most areas. I liked his integrity and honesty. He had an air of confidence about him that just seemed to melt me. It was clear from the start that he was sexually inexperienced. While I was never promiscuous, I had been around the block a few times with a couple of other boyfriends. I wasn't as uptight about sex*

---

46  For example, "Can you become a virgin again?" by Tim Stafford, available at http://www.christianitytoday.com/iyf/hottopics/sexabstinence/7c2041.html.

*as he was but figured he would loosen up after we got married. We did sleep together before we got married, but it was not that great. He seemed wracked with guilt about our premarital sex, so I stopped tempting him.*

*After we got married, it went south quickly. Our first night I decided to give him a treat and go down on him. Before we were married, he insisted on strictly missionary position and nothing else. I figured now that we are married, what we do in the bedroom is our business. Boy was I wrong! He nearly bit my head off when he figured out what I was getting ready to do. Little did I know I was committing a mortal sin. I had never heard any sermons that prohibited oral sex, and none of the premarital counseling we did with the Priest indicated it was wrong. Well, it was wrong as far as he was concerned. "Only prostitutes did that, my wife will never do that." He couldn't even say the word! That should have been my first clue. In three years of trying, I could never communicate with him about sex. He seemed totally uninterested in what I wanted and absolutely refused to relax and try something different once in a while. He responded to me like I was from outer space, if I suggested anything.*

*About three and a half years into the marriage, when I was totally sick of going to church and climbing the walls in sexual frustration, I discovered he was visiting prostitutes when he was out of town. I tried talking to him about it, but there was no talking as far as he was concerned. He was definitely embarrassed and contrite, but it didn't change anything. I look back and think how stupid I was. All the signs were there, I just didn't pay attention to them. We got divorced soon after.*

This is not uncommon for religious newly-weds. An otherwise compatible couple finds they are utterly unable to communicate about sex or adjust their sexual styles and preferences. They cannot even grow and experiment together. Jesus is always watching and sin is always lurking.

Among secularists, sex seems to be taken more in stride. In many cases, both have had several previous partners and communicating about what they like and want, while awkward at first, does not seem to be a major problem. The evidence for this comes from my own survey research and clinical experience. Those raised secular are much more comfortable with their bodies, easily admit to masturbating, openly discuss ways to negotiate safe sex and condom use and generally have no reluctance in talking about sexual ideas. Many of the discussions I have had with secular groups on campuses or in humanist or atheist community groups have been easy and natural. The same discussion and content would get me kicked out of a Campus Crusade for Christ meeting or a Baptist Sunday School.

## The Urge for Variety

In marriage, the urge for variety and change arises within a few years. She will want to do something more than missionary position; he will want to experiment with oral sex; she will want him to pull her hair occasionally; he will want to have her dress up like a slut sometimes. Unfortunately, none of this will happen if both think these are potentially sinful behaviors.

The guilt cycle works to keep both sides quiet, within narrow sexual boundaries. Unable to communicate and fearful of their spouse's judgment, sex slowly dies over a period of years, but the sex drive does not go away. He will start using pornography and masturbating more. She will avoid his physical advances. She will start reading more romance novels and engulf herself in children or church activities. He will go out with friends and spend huge amounts of time doing his hobbies in the garage.

Eventually, she may find his porn stash and feel extremely hurt and rejected. She may lash out at him, berating him for defiling their marriage. For his part, he may see her reading dozens of trashy novels and feel that she may be interested in romance but not in him. The hurt may come out as verbal abuse or constantly finding fault in one another.

If things get bad enough, they may go for marital counseling with their minister, who will pray with them. That is about all he can do, since advice on actual sexual behavior runs the risk of revealing unbiblical thinking. If he is a Catholic priest, it is even worse, since he's not supposed to have any first-hand experience with sex.

The double problem for the Protestant minister is that he is very likely having the same problems as his members, but he and his wife cannot discuss or reveal them to anyone or talk to each other. It is a religiously transmitted disease but no one will admit it.

## Thought Police

The cycle of behavior we have described has consequences far beyond the church. Religious training and indoctrination creates internal states that are in conflict with natural urges and drives. A person feels condemned by his own sex drive. God has created him as a sexual being and then condemns him for acting on that drive. Indoctrination tells him that the church's teaching cannot be wrong, so it must be his sinful nature and Satan tempting him.

Such misattribution means the root cause will not be found and no cure or treatment is possible. It is like a diabetic who refuses to believe that her diabetes is caused or exacerbated by the five cokes and pint of ice cream she eats each day. There may be medical treatments to reduce the symptoms, but sooner or later the disease will flare up with all its consequences.

Religion is a master at thought diversion. For example, if you have a normal sexual thought, religion can distort and divert that thought into something guilt-inducing.

Compare these thinking processes:

*A religious person:*
1. "God hates porn. I succumbed to temptation and feel guilty for looking at a porn site last night."
2. "I love my husband, but the new minister really turns me on. I am a loathsome person for even thinking about such things."

*A non-religious person:*
1. "It was fun looking at that porn site last night. Glad I found it. It gave me some ideas for my wife and me to explore, and I enjoyed masturbating to one of the scenes."
2. "That new man at work really turns me on. I think I'll tell my husband about him. He seems to enjoy knowing I get turned on by other men."

Which of these individuals will have a better time tonight? Who is more in tune with their sexuality? Which of these is likely to experience a flood of inappropriate behavior or uncontrolled emotions?

Here is a story that illustrates this thinking style. It was sent to me by an ex-Christian woman, Candace Gorham, of the Ebony Exodus project:[47]

> *Countless religious experiences in my childhood through early adulthood (Jehovah's Witnesses, United Methodists, Non-*

---

47   Listen to more of Candace's story at LivingAfterFaith.com, episode #26.

*denominational/evangelical, Baptists) taught me that sex was something to be feared. Despite the fact that everyone said that sex was good once married, the messages about sex outside of marriage were very different. Sex became this terrifying, disease-spreading monster that had the ability to ruin your life and tarnish your reputation forever. I cannot think of a single time when I was young that I got straightforward, non-religiously biased information about sexuality, safe sex, masturbation or even general education about male/female differences from religious institutions. They only taught abstinence. All that I learned about sex came from fifth grade D.A.R.E. classes, science classes about reproduction, one ninth grade health class, and obviously, friends and personal experience.*

*There was guilt and shame in "touching yourself" and kissing. Even what I call 'appreciating the beauty of the feminine' was wrong because, if I were a lesbian, it would mean that god would hate me more than if I were a heterosexual fornicator. Though not a lesbian, my strong appreciation for that particular form worried me, sometimes more intensely than heterosexual encounters.*

*During my first sexual relationship in high school, I was less worried about pregnancy and disease and more embarrassed that God was watching me every time I "did it." I was sure that he hated me for giving up my virtue and felt that I deserved eternal hell. Regardless, I kept doing it anyway. At times, the guilt and shame were so extreme that I would feel physically ill afterward. I would literally have to roll over in bed and lie still for a few minutes afraid I would vomit.*

*When I went off to college, I was resolute to abstain from sex before marriage. Shame ensued after my one and only one-night stand. Another one-time-only experience involved fairly innocent 'messing around' in a group. Both incidences were followed by periods of abstinent contrition.*

*Once in a solid relationship, I convinced myself that God would recognize the purity of my heart and love me anyway. Sadly to say, that optimism didn't last, and I entered a downward spiral into a deep depression sparked by my fear of God and love of man. How does one choose between the intense pleasure of carnal love and the God who loves you, yet hates you?*

*My college love and I married at 20 because we believed a prophecy that God had ordained it and we shouldn't delay His plans. But even in our marriage, I struggled with my sexuality. Pornography? It repulsed me. Anal sex? It led to the destruction of Sodom and Gomorrah. Talking dirty? Profane! Trips to the 'toy' shop only produced gels and lotions. Suffice it to say that my husband's and my exodus from religion was one of the best things that we could do, not only for our marriage but also for our sex life. I once believed that religious prohibitions plus messages to play the sexy vixen plus the guilty sickness from sex that persisted into my marriage made the orgasm more drama than it was worth.*

*Now, I haven't felt that sickness in years. I can do anything as adventurous or traditional as my husband and I agree to. Instead of telling people that only sex after marriage is good, we should be yelling from the mountain tops that sex after religion is better!*

Candace wrote her story in hopes that other people will find their way out of religion. Thus, her Ebony Exodus project is focused on helping black women get out of religion.

## Religious Dams

One of the myths that religionists perpetuate is that, without religion, people will go wild and do terrible sexual things. But the evidence doesn't support this. How many headlines read, "Atheist leader convicted of molesting dozens of boys." Or read, "Atheists have the highest divorce rate." Non-religious people often have better control over their sex lives and relationships because they don't have the constant interference of religious guilt. They don't try to dam up their desires; instead, they channel them in appropriate ways.

As we saw in Candace's story, religious guilt does not stop behavior. It may slow you down, but biology wins. Candace's behavior was not based on rational thinking and clear-headed decision-making. Religion put a dam across her sex drive. When it overflowed, she experienced horrible guilt, even physical revulsion. Guilt reduces the ability of a person to exercise rational control over sexual behavior. The result is something more unpredictable, even surprising to the religious person. Candace engaged in behavior at the most unexpected times and was horrified that she could not control it. It is a common pattern among people of all the major religions, including many of the leaders.

# CHAPTER 7:

# CONSPIRACY OF SILENCE:

# PROGRAMMING THE COLLECTIVE MIND

*Religion has the capacity to silence critical thinking and create blindness in entire groups of people. It can infect the minds of followers so completely as to allow the most egregious sexual acts against children and others to go unchallenged for centuries.*

*"When authorities warn you of the sinfulness of sex, there is an important lesson to be learned. Do not have sex with the authorities."*

*-Matt Groening*

### Where Is the Outrage?

In 2011 Brother Robert Best, principal of a Catholic school in Australia, was charged with raping dozens of boys over a period of years going back to 1969! The school chaplain, Gerald Ridsdale, was also charged as a serial rapist. Claims were made that 26 of the rape victims committed suicide in later years. How could these rapists go unnoticed and unreported for decades? And, where is the indignation and outrage?

Despite outrageously inappropriate or illegal actions by many ministers and priests, the Catholic Church's outcry and response are muted. When a pedophile priest is found, we often learn that he has harmed dozens of victims over many years. We also learn that church officials were notified, parents had complained, and even police reports had been filed, but to no avail. Protestants ministers who have affairs – whether straight or homosexual – can simply ask for forgiveness and keep their jobs. Some ministers caught raping children quietly pay off the family (from the church coffers) and keep preaching.

Compare this to a teacher or principal in a public school. A public school principal doing anything sexual with a student is instantly fired. There is a huge difference in accountability between the two systems – public accountability and private, religious accountability. In some church cases, parents complained, bishops were notified and letters were sent from lawyers, sometimes over a 20-year span. In the public school system of the United States, such complaints tend to get immediate attention. Secular school principals get into serious trouble for simply failing to report even suspected abuse, let alone doing it themselves. In the Catholic system, clergy are not reprimanded or held to public account by the church. It generally requires intervention by civil authorities or lawsuits to get action.

Some think this is changing, but it is hard to tell. New cases seem to crop up constantly. While the church is under legal pressure in the developed world, legal pressure is non-existent for Catholic and Evangelical churches in Africa, South and Central America. Undoubtedly, abuse is at least as prevalent in these areas as the United States and Europe. There is no evidence that the churches are proactively investigating abuse in these areas. They have covered it up for centuries in the West, why would they not be doing the same in countries where there is little legal pressure?

## Institutional Accountability

In order to maintain a healthy environment, an institution needs a mix of ingrown tradition and outside fresh air. All institutions have a tendency to isolate themselves. Whether the local utility company or the military, they don't like people snooping around and they don't like outsiders telling them what to do. In my 28 years as an organizational psychologist, I saw dozens of examples of high-level people making huge ethical mistakes in the name of corporate profit. They were usually mistakes rooted in narrow, institutional thinking.

Wise CEOs will make efforts to bring in "fresh air." They may mandate outside audits, even if not required by regulation, hire outsiders occasionally and reassign people to new and challenging areas. They may insist on continuing education and open discussion of the latest industry ideas to keep ideas flowing throughout the organization. This is the best prevention against insular thinking.

Does any of this describe the Catholic Church? Catholicism is the oldest and largest institution in the world. It has been around in some form for at least 1,800 years. It is the ultimate case study of an insular institution. Over the centuries many have attempted reform, but most of them were excommunicated, if they were lucky; executed if unlucky. Many point to Vatican II (1963) as an effective reform, but it was a desperate attempt to make the church more relevant. No key reforms were made, especially in matters of sex: nuns and priests still remained celibate, birth control forbidden, women still the lesser of the sexes, abstinence only before marriage, etc. Insular institutions don't reform themselves. Many Catholics have changed, but they are attending the church while ignoring its commandments. The church may update its techniques and methods, but it is always in service of the institutional organism. This is one of the reasons why the pedophile priest issue is and will remain an endemic disease in the Catholic Church.

While I have focused on the Catholic Church, Protestant organizations are just as loathe to be visited by outside inspectors. They quietly pass along ministers to other congregations or out the door when there is a sex scandal. Criminal charges are rarely brought, and sexual misconduct of a non-criminal nature (for example, an adulterous preacher) is often ignored the first time or two. As long as the wife keeps her mouth shut, no crime was committed.

As a helping professional, a psychologist, psychiatrist, medical doctor or social worker can be thrown out of his or her profession, even criminally prosecuted, for engaging in a sexual relationship with a client. The nature of the therapeutic relationship is seen as sacrosanct. Sexual contact with a client is among the most serious of ethical violations. Ministers and priests are also seen as helping professionals but there is no such ethical or legal oversight. Religion gives special protection to clergy, which gives cover for abuse.

The most protected of ministers are those who bring in the most members and the most money; hard to fire a million-dollar man. Once a mega-church has been built, the mortgage requires a charismatic leader to bring in the money. That same man often convinces the board of directors to take on the financial burden of building the large new facility. With $2-3 million a year coming in from a charismatic preacher and a huge mortgage, you can overlook a little adultery. The alternative: Object to a preacher's behavior and face being voted off the board or shamed out of the congregation – usually both.

Where is the outcry? The answer involves the brains of the followers and has at least two components – childhood infection and anesthetization of the mind.

### Childhood Infection

Silencing of the adult mind begins with infecting the mind of the child and creating an unquestioning blindness to religious authority. Childhood indoctrination is carried out in many ways but begins with things like apparently innocent children's songs in church like "Jesus Loves the Little Children," "Daniel in the Lion's Den," or "Jesus Loves Me," and stories that emphasize the benevolent Jesus. The early message of unconditional love lulls the young mind into a feeling of safety and security. The message fits the developmental stage of the young child, who craves security in a frightening world of large and potentially dangerous adults. The songs and stories convey a subtle message of a wonderfully kind and loving god who is always good and protective. No stories of children being eaten by she bears or executed for disobedience.[48]

In the child's mind, the priest or minister takes on the same good qualities as the god. It is simple association. The person who tells the child about the

---

48    Such as the stories related in 2 Kings, 2:23-24 and Deuteronomy, 21:18-2.

wonderful, loving and protective god must also have those qualities. This idea and association is carried into adulthood. Add to this the messages about respect for authority, and most children easily defer to any religious figure and continue that behavior as adults.

Once the safety and security message has been implanted, the message changes at or around preadolescence. The new message is, "You can't have the unconditional love unless you follow the rules of the god." Here is where the message of sin and shame is seriously introduced. The preadolescent and adolescent learns that it is their own evil nature that is responsible for their problems.

This powerful combination of messages puts the mind in an inferior state. God is all good, the child-adolescent-adult is fundamentally flawed and sinful, especially females. Such a confusing and false idea is accepted because the young human mind is open to anything that has perceived survival value.[49] If all the adults in your life, including priests and ministers, say, "God is important for your safety or salvation," a child will probably find that compelling. It often takes a lot of Sunday School, catechism or temple to deeply infect a child with these concepts.

We acquire both the language and religious concepts from our immediate culture – at the same time. A child cannot discriminate between useful survival information and the emotional and psychological manipulations of religion. Once infected, these ideas are deeply embedded and almost impossible to change. Just as you would be hard pressed to unlearn your language, it's hard to unlearn your religion. Then add the mystique that most religions put on the leaders. Since they are leaders, they must be closer to the good god than you are. What they say must have more power and authority than your little opinion.

All of this has the power to create a mythology about religious leaders. They are more knowing, more powerful, more important and closer to god than you. That, in turn, labels anyone daring to challenge as disloyal and, worse, disobeying god.

Ministers and priests automatically get unusual respect, even from people not of that faith. This is the power of the chief, shaman or headman in a clan or tribe. Most human groups obey some kind of hierarchy. Respect for the hierarchy has great survival value and offers protection from outside

---

49  We will further discuss the importance of imprinting in child development in Chapter 10..

groups and dangers. The child has strong survival motivation to identify powerful people, treat them with deference and fit into the group under the authority.[50]

Religion has hijacked the tendency to defer to authority. The priest is not the best hunter, best soldier, or the top salesman, but as a "man of god," he automatically gets higher status. Some would argue that going to the seminary for four years or earning a doctor of divinity or Ph.D. in Theology means he or she has earned something and deserves respect. Theology has not advanced an inch in the last 1,000 years. How much respect does a profession deserve if it cannot add to the knowledge and understanding of man? How much respect does a helping professional deserve who has little or no training in anything but superstition and is not required to adhere to a set of professional ethics?

The net result of this system is that Catholic clergy, charismatic preachers and imams can do no wrong; their word is god's word. Childhood infection creates an invisible, protective shield around and unquestioning blindness to the leaders of a religion. The shield does not necessarily extend to other religions. Protestants can see the immoral behavior of Catholic bishops protecting pedophile priests but be blind to the immoral or illegal behavior of their own minister.

## Anesthetization of the Mind

Now let's add a second component of the collective mind – anesthetization. If the majority of adherents in a religious community are trained in this fashion, they are positioned to ignore the aberrant behavior in the leader. Karl Marx famously said that religion is the opiate of the masses. His analysis was not far off. Religious people can ignore massive amounts of information in support of their religion's view of the world.

For example, most Protestants understand that the Catholic church has a major, institutional, endemic problem with sex abuse by clergy. They can even identify reasonable causes, like celibacy or protection coming from the hierarchy. Many cannot believe that Catholics are not more outraged at the continual, non-stop scandals. They are surprised that people continue to

---

50   See essay by Richard Dawkins, "The Emptiness of Theology," available online at http:// richarddawkins.net/ articles/88-the-emptiness-of-theology.

attend and give money to the Catholic Church. In other words, a rational observer can often see the problem with clarity.

At the same time, ask Catholics as they are leaving mass about these same issues. The answers range from "One bad apple spoils the lot" argument to "It's is a big problem but the Church is 2,000 years old and has seen worse," to "The Church is under attack by the secular world," to "My priest would never do anything like that." That refrain was heard for years even from people whose own children were being molested by priests.[51] Even as the scandals become public and well documented, nothing could stop these people from attending mass, giving money and praying for the priest. Their minds are anesthetized so effectively that no rational process will influence them.

The mechanisms of such anesthetization can be traced back to the childhood indoctrination. Most children don't question their religion. It would not occur to a child to ask, "Why aren't you teaching me Islam rather than Catholicism?"

That same childlike acceptance resides in the minds of most adults of the faith. Once installed, the religious map prevents critical thinking about itself, though critical thinking about other religions works fine. With sufficient people infected, there is little chance of a clergy being accused, let alone caught. Reading Irish reports on 80 years of Catholic sexual abuse in schools and orphanages, it is clear the mostly Catholic police were as good at ignoring complaints as the bishops, often discounting victims reports and even threatening the victims.[52] While a Protestant police officer in the United States does not have the same religion, he does have the same clergy blindness. Whether a Baptist minister or a Catholic priest, the victim often has less standing than the clergy and, therefore, less credibility in the eyes of the authorities.

## Changing Times

Fortunately, times are a-changing for the better. The more secular a society becomes, the more difficult it is to maintain a collective religious mind. As a result, decades of abuse are finally beginning to be exposed.

51   See the documentary *Deliver Us From Evil* (Lionsgate, 2006), about the decades-long abuse by Father O'Grady in California.

52   The Irish Government Commission to Inquire into Child Abuse Orphanages and School for the Deaf, available online at http://www.childabusecommission.com/rpt/ExecSummary.php.

Police are better trained and have a healthy skepticism as they document cases. The Internet allows people far more information about the church and the predators within and more opportunities to communicate across distances.

Catholic church attendance rates have fallen since 1990 and 10% of U.S. parishes have closed, along with a 24% decrease in active priests. Growth in U.S. Catholicism is almost entirely fueled by immigration, and many new priests are immigrants themselves.[53] According to a 2009 Pew Research study, among American-born Catholics, four have left the Catholic church for every new convert.[54] Some of this decline may well be attributable to the sex scandals. Others may reflect the Internet generation coming of age. Even highly anesthetized minds may awaken as a result of the avalanche of evidence revealing church complicity.

Unfortunately, people who were abused often stay deeply loyal to the institution that allowed and hid the abuse. On the face of it, it is irrational to stay loyal to an organization that has ruined your sex life, caused untold emotional anguish and abuse and knowingly protected predators for years. *The Unbreakable Child* (2010) by Kim Michele Richardson is the story of a woman who was sexually abused for years in a Catholic orphanage. She and 40 other women were the first to gain a settlement from Roman Catholic nuns. It is a horrendous story, yet she remains a loyal Catholic and even sends her children to Catholic schools. Such is the power of childhood infection and abuse. One reviewer says, "Hers is a beautifully told story about strength and an enduring faith that can lead but one place: to forgiveness."[55] Why would forgiveness even be considered except in the context of religious infection? The primary purpose of forgiveness, in these kinds of cases, is to allow the victim to continue in the religion. The church perpetuates the notion that failure to forgive means something is wrong with you. Forgiveness is an attempt to resolve the cognitive dissonance for the victim. It doesn't work and takes the focus off of the perpetrator. Only by forgiving can she justify

---

53    "The Disturbing Trends behind Parish Closings" by Joseph Claude Harris, May 2005. Available online at http://www.americamagazine.org/content/article.cfm?article_id=4164.

54    "Faith in Flux: Changes in Religious Affiliation," 2009, revised 2011, available online at http://pewforum.org/Faith-in-Flux(3).aspx.

55    Amazon.com review by Mary Francis Wilkens, http://www.amazon.com/Unbreakable-Child-Kim-Michele-Richardson/dp/1933016914/ref=sr_1_1?s=books&ie=UTF8&qid=1321375789&sr=1-1.

her continued membership, giving her money and putting her own children back in the system!

This chapter focused mostly on Catholicism, but the same analysis could be done on Islam, Buddhism, Mormonism and Protestantism. The problems are not unique to Catholicism, just more obvious at this point in time. Visit StopBaptistPredators.org or read the Freedom From Religion Foundation's Black Collar Crime Blotter to see thousands of cases from other denominations.

While the religious are certainly anesthetized, we might help stop this pattern by asking, "Where is the outrage?" We can make it difficult for the religious to hide or ignore the sexual abuses and escapades of clergy in any religion. How to do this? By highlighting news stories in social media, letting friends know about local abuses and keeping the issue in front of people. The statistics show that there is not one bad apple but thousands in every religion. Don't let religionists downplay the devastating harm that religious leaders perpetuate on their followers.

# SECTION II:
# FOLLOW THE BIOLOGY

## CHAPTER 8:
## HOLY BIOLOGY

*It is impossible to understand sex and sexuality without a minimal understanding of biology. To ensure that we are fair and balanced in our approach, we will first look at religious biology, then examine scientific biology.*

## The Bible

Bible biology begins with all creatures coming from nowhere. The first man, Adam, was created out of dust. Adam was given the responsibility for creating a classification system for all the animals by naming them. Adam was a bit lonely so he was put to sleep and a rib was extracted to create a "help mate."[56]

In Genesis we find that at least one snake can talk and two trees have supernatural powers – the Tree of Knowledge of Good and Evil and the Tree of Life. Humans could live for hundreds of years (Adam lived 930 years with Methuselah taking the prize at 969).

We also know that animals were sexual creatures, hence Noah's task of bringing all the animals on board the Ark in twos. (There is no mention of asexually reproducing salamanders or lizards.)[57]

We are also told:

- Bats are birds (Leviticus 11:13-19).
- Rabbits are among the ruminants that chew their cud (Deuteronomy 14:7).
- Insects are four-legged creatures (Leviticus 11:2-23).
- Locusts, crickets and grasshoppers are acceptable to eat because they have legs above their feet (Leviticus 11:21).
- In Genesis Adam and Eve had two sons, one of whom murdered the other. The survivor, Cain, somehow acquired a wife and fathered Enoch. (Where the wife came from no one seems to know.)
- Only women are barren (men are never infertile). Fortunately, biblical biology trumps infertility. Sara, wife of Abraham, was over 80 years old when she conceived and "bore a son to Abraham" (Genesis 21:1-2).
- In the New Testament Paul was bitten by a poisonous snake while stranded on Malta (Acts 28:8-9). Never mind that there

---

56   As an interesting side note, many animals have a bone in their penis called a baculum. We will discuss this later, but the ancients may have noticed that while many animals have a baculum, humans do not. Some have theorized that god did not take a rib from Adam, since men and women have the same number of ribs, but instead took his baculum. And thus, men have no baculum.

57   Asexual reproduction is a mode of reproduction by which offspring arise from a single parent and inherit the genes of that parent only.

are no poisonous snakes on Malta and no evidence they ever existed on that island.

- In First Corinthians, Paul tells us that only a dead seed can germinate (15:36).
- People rose from the dead, including Lazarus. After Jesus was crucified, many holy people's tombs opened and they walked around Jerusalem (Matt. 27:52).
- A fig tree withered instantly when Jesus cursed it (Mark 11:12-14).
- Jesus multiplied fish to feed five thousand people (Mark 8:19).
- An epileptic boy was instantly cured with a single command from Jesus (Matt. 17:18).

## The Koran

From the Hadith, we learn a good deal about embryology. The process of gestation begins with male and female sperm for 40 days, the embryo becomes a clot for 40 days, then puts on flesh for 40 days. No mention of bones. In 86:6-7, the Koran says, "He [man] is made from a gushing fluid which issues from between the loins and ribs." No mention of ova.

In the area of botany, the Koran says (20:53) "... with it We have produced diverse pairs of plants each separate from others," failing to mention that many plants don't come in pairs but have both sex organs on one plant.

## Other Holy Books

We could have looked at the Book of Mormon and found that horses existed in America before Columbus arrived (although the Indians didn't seem to discover them until after Columbus came). Or we could read the Zoroastrian Avesta to find that all creatures were created from seeds.[58]

There simply isn't much biology in these religious texts and what there is is remarkably inaccurate. In the next chapter we will examine a wealth of information, not only about human sex but also of many other species, none of which shows up in any holy text.

---

58  Fargard II 27 (70): "Thither thou shalt bring the seeds of men and women, of the greatest, best, and finest kinds on this earth; thither thou shalt bring the seeds of every kind of cattle, of the greatest, best, and finest kinds on this earth."

# CHAPTER 9:

# UNHOLY BIOLOGY: BUSTING THE MONOGAMY MYTH

*Homosexuality is found in over 1,500 species. Homophobia is found in only one. Which seems more unnatural?*

**-Effox comment on HuffPosts**

## Follow the Biology

We have all heard the saying "Follow the money." In sexuality, it is important to follow the biology. To understand what religion is doing to us sexually, we need to understand what our natural biological tendencies are.

To understand human sexuality, we can study how the sex organs of other animals have evolved. Why are they so different from ours? Why are some large, others small? Why do some species have female sex organs that look like male organs?

Sex organs are among the most dynamic and adaptive organs in any species and give us a framework for understanding how evolution has shaped us and how we compare to other species. This study will help us understand the impact of religion on sexuality and provide some ideas for non-religious sexuality.

Carolus Linnaeus (1707-1778), the "father of modern biological classification," noticed that flowers were most easily classified by their sex organs: the pistil, stamen, petal.[59] For this reason, some said he was obsessed with sex. Modern evolutionary biology has confirmed that sex organs are important for classification, largely because they evolve and change more rapidly than most other organs. This rapid change allows us to make fine distinctions and shows how almost identical animals may be entirely different species, based on sex organ differences. Sex organs tell us a lot about what is going on in the world of sex and sexual selection with a particular species.

## Super Duck's Inflatable Penis

Ducks have a lot of sex. A female takes a liking to a certain male and waddles around in a seductive way to get his attention. Her behavior shows that she wants to mate with a specific male, but every male wants in on the act. She mates with her beau, then the others try to gang on. Though she struggles to escape, she is no match for three or four males at once. It is rape, pure and simple, and she doesn't like it.

For years this behavior was a mystery to scientists. Questions like, "Why is there so much rape among ducks?" "Does the female have any real control over who she mates with?" and "Why do ducks have large penises?"

---

59  One critic, botanist Johann Siegesbeck, called Linnaeus's plant classification system a "loathsome harlotry." See http://www.ucmp.berkeley.edu/history/linnaeus.html.

Dr. Patricia Brennan at the University of Sheffield, England, is an expert on duck sex. Thank goodness we have duck-sex workers. She unveiled the mystery of duck mating as summarized below.

The duck penis is amazingly large for such a small animal, often as long as the duck, and male ducks grow a new penis every mating season. Why carry that big thing around if you don't need it.[60] The male penis resides inside the bird and "everts" out in one third of a second. Eversion is like an erection, only inside out. When the duck is ready to mate, he pushes it out, like blowing a balloon out of his body.

When males are in large groups with other males, they grow their penises 15-25% longer.[61] If the competition is too tough, the less dominant males grow more moderate penises and start to absorb them back into their body weeks earlier than the males with huge members. Their chances for reproduction are slim in the face of competition, so they reabsorb their penises and hope for better luck next year.

According to Dr. Maydianne Andrade of the University of Toronto-Scarborough, "Ducks are essentially engineering their own phallus in response to social challenges."[62]

### Ms. Wonder Duck Fights Back

For decades, biologists marveled at the huge penises on such small animals. No one could come up with a good explanation for the duck penis that fit all the facts, until Dr. Brennan decided to do something radical; she dissected the female reproductive tract. Seems the male scientists had never bothered to look at the female. To her surprise, Dr. Brennan found that the female tract was extremely deep and shaped like a corkscrew, only in the opposite direction from the male (which would make it hard for the male to mate). There were dead-end pockets, where semen could get caught and not make it up to the eggs. Brennan's experiments showed that the female can relax her reproductive tract and make it easy for a male to get in or she can "corkscrew" it to make it difficult. In the evolutionary battle over who gets to fertilize the egg, the males had the brute force, but the females had an effective resistance strategy.

---

60   See a brief listing of articles by Brennan, et al, at http://www.yale.edu/eeb/prum/evolution.htm.

61   Also see a review of Brennan's studies by Susan Milius in *Wired* magazine, August 2010. Available online at http://www.wired.com/wiredscience/2010/08/duck-penises/.

62   Ibid.

On the male side, experiments showed that the male can get his penis up and put it in and ejaculate amazingly fast. Now it all makes sense. This is not just a war of the sexes; it is a war between the sex organs. Dr. Brennan hypothesized that this system has co-evolved to help the male penetrate and mate fast and help the female resist such rapid mating without her permission. To determine if the female has control over who actually fertilizes her eggs, Dr. Brennan did DNA testing on ducklings and found that 97% of all fertilized eggs were by the guy Ms. Duck liked.

Looking at a wide variety of duck species, researchers have shown that this is not a finished fight. Different species seem to be in different stages of this co-evolution. Depending on the mating strategy, male and female sex organs may have different shapes and sizes. This is called sexually antagonistic co-evolution, and it is found in many terrestrial species.

We can find many examples of sexually antagonistic co-evolution among spiders, insects, rabbits and hyenas. A study of 15 species of water striders showed that each had evolved strategies for male mating and female mate prevention. Each species has its own unique solution to the problem of how to mate, who to mate with and how to control the mating process.

Looking closely at all aspects of the reproductive organs and reproductive cycle in a species tells a lot about the current state of sexual competition, where it was in the past and, perhaps, how it got to the place it is now. Armed with the concept of sexual competition and antagonistic co-evolution, we can turn our attention to species more closely related to us and ask, "What does their sexual physiology and reproductive cycle tell us? Where are they now and how did they come to the current state?" We are going to explore a series of facts and then see where they point us.

## Size Matters: The Gorilla

Among most mammals, size difference between male and female is a good predictor of polygyny[63] in that species. The larger the size difference, the more females a male will mate with and try to control. Size difference between the sexes is known as sexual dimorphism.

---

63  Polygyny: many wives. It is often called polygamy in modern culture. The opposite, many husbands, is termed polyandry. Although these terms are related to the idea of marriage, we will use the term polygyny in relation to this discussion even though animals don't marry and most are not even monogamous, as we will see later.

Among all primates, gorillas have the greatest degree of sexual dimorphism. For gorillas, it is body size that counts. An adult male mountain gorilla may weigh 220 kg (484 lb) and a female, 97.7 kg (215 lb). Thus, the male is twice the size of the female. But the male's penis is only 4 cm (1.5 in) long.

Gorillas also have a baculum or penis bone. The baculum is a bone in the penis that assists in mating. Most mammals have a baculum including all primates, except humans. A few other species have also lost their baculum: elephants, horses, whales and dolphins, to name a few.

A silverback male gorilla generally has a harem of two to five females with whom he has exclusive mating rights even if other "black back" (immature) males are present. While the male guards his females from other silverbacks, a female is free to leave and join another group whenever she wants. The average female changes groups two or three times in her lifetime. She may even go off and mate with a single male. Actual sex among gorillas only lasts about a minute, so a quick dalliance can be pulled off easily if the conditions are right.

The largest male usually dominates the local group, which can be as big as 20-30 individuals. While silverbacks rarely fight to the death, they do put on an impressive show of force to convince any potential usurpers to back off.

Females generally leave their home troop when they are about 7 or 8 years old in search of a silverback that they might move in with. While they may be sexually mature at that age, they often don't begin mating until they are 12–14 years old. By comparison, males leave their troop when they reach 10 or 11. Males often lead a solitary life until they can attract their own females and begin mating at 15 to 18 years old. There is a lot of competition in the gorilla world for females. Not every male will establish a harem. Those who cannot may join a group as a submissive male with no mating privileges, or they may continue to live alone.

Gorillas are at the opposite end of the penis spectrum than ducks. As long as they have imposing physical size, gorillas do not need to have a large penis. Gorillas also have sex far less frequently than the three other great apes (chimps, bonobos and humans). As a result, a male doesn't need to produce as much sperm, and his testes are less than half the size of humans' and a quarter the size of chimps'.

## May the Best Sperm Win: The Chimpanzee

Compared to gorillas, chimps are extremely sexual. Females may mate several times a day. When the female is ovulating, her sex organs swell and become pink, advertising the fact. A female in estrus (commonly called "heat") attracts the attention of every male in the troop, but while chimp females are very sexual, they don't mate randomly. The top males get most access and they only mate when in estrus. Males of lower rank may or may not get to mate.

Alpha males may attain their position through intelligence and social skill. For example, a male that can put together an alliance of males may dominate the group through sheer force of will and intelligence. Jane Goodall, in her book *In the Shadow of Man* (1971), tells the story of Mike, a low-ranking male who spent years on the outer edge of the group. One day he discovered the power of empty gasoline cans. Picking them up, making a display, then running with the cans in hand or pushing them, he found that he could intimidate all the other males. It took Mike about four months to ascend to his throne as the alpha male of the group.

Chimp sexual anatomy contrasts sharply with that of gorillas. First of all, the chimp penis is much larger and longer, 8 cm (3 in.). Chimps also have very large testes, twice as large as humans'. With all that sex, they need to produce a lot of semen. Males can mate many times a day but are only interested in females who are in estrus, as the naturalist Carly Wilson has noted:

> Chimps have giant balls, the biggest of any primate and twice the size of the average man ... They use these giant balls to produce in excess enough semen to flush out the lingering semen of any males to which their partners may have recently mated. In essence, male chimps have big balls because female chimps are whores. Ouch. To be fair, the males are whores, too though.[64]

To go a step farther into semenology, within the semen of chimps is a substance that forms a plug.[65] This plug, formed by a protein that coagulates,

---

64 From Wilson's blog, available at http://carlywilson.com/2010/08/free-love-in-the-animal-kingdom/.

65 Kingan, et al, (2003). "Reduced Polymorphism in the Chimpanzee Semen Coagulating Protein, Semenogelin I." *Journal of Molecular Evolution*, 57:159–169. Available online at http://www.oeb.harvard.edu/faculty/edwards/people/postdocs/papers/Kingan2003.pdf.

prevents subsequent males' sperm from fertilizing the egg. Many species use this strategy.[66] With all the sex going on among chimps, a male has to have a way to stop other males from getting to the egg.

This is called sperm competition. There are two kinds of sperm competition. The first is simply producing more sperm than the other guy. The second is having a method for preventing the other guy from getting to the egg. The plug is one part of the prevention strategy.

But there is another layer to sperm competition. While the sperm may be fighting and plugging away, the semen from the second guy contains a liquefying agent known as PSA that can dissolve a plug from the first donor and allow the second donor's sperm to get on with the race. How is that for a fight? It's an entire war going on inside the female chimp and an entire level of evolutionary pressure independent of the size of the animal, shape of the penis or reproductive details of the female.

Following the biology of chimps and discovering the highly developed sperm competition system probably means there has been a lot of mating going on between females and multiple males for thousands of generations. "Follow the biology" tells the story of what is really going on in a species' mating strategies.

## The Feminine Mystique: The Bonobo

Mating strategies are often very different even between closely related species, and the bonobo are very different from the gorilla and the chimp. The bonobo is the smallest and rarest of the four great apes. It was once thought to be a chimp and was commonly called the pygmy chimp because it was about 10% smaller, but DNA evidence shows that bonobos are actually a different species.

Bonobos seem more human than chimps. For example, while chimps prefer sex doggy-style, bonobos greatly prefer face-to-face, missionary style. Bonobos even like to kiss, and they are not too concerned about what gender they are having sex with. Frans de Waal, the great Dutch primatologist,

---

66   In many polyandrous species (mates with many males), the males tend to carry a couple of genes that allow the semen to create a plug. Only in a species where there are multiple male partners would such a gene be useful. Bonobos and chimps have these genes (SEMG1 and SEMG2), and so do humans.

notes his student's astonishment when he shows them a video of two male bonobos giving each other a long French kiss.[67]

Imagine a fundamentalist church taking a field trip to the zoo to give a lesson in creationism and coming across a couple of bonobos gazing into one another's eyes while having sex and kissing. It might throw a monkey wrench into the lesson plans.

Sex is far more important as a bonding, tension reliever and conflict management tool than for procreation. When two bonobos get into conflict, they often end up rubbing genitals or having sex to dissipate the tension or conflict. When a bonobo finds a particularly good fruit tree or food source, he or she gets very excited and often has sex with another bonobo before settling down to eat. When nervous tension is present in the group, many engage in tension-releasing sex.

Bonobos have sex frequently and with many partners. In bonobo culture, females rule. A committee of closely allied females makes sure the male testosterone doesn't get out of control. When a male tries to over-assert himself, the top two or three females gang up on him to let him know where he stands. When food is found, the top females get the prime picks while the sons and daughters of high-status females are next in line.

In the bonobo world, the female leaves her natal group to wander out to find another. She joins a new group by finding one of the senior females and approaching her sexually. This takes the form of rubbing clitorises and grooming the senior female. If the younger female is accepted, the two will bond. All females in the group are bonded to each other more than to any male, and the bonding activity continues throughout life. Females may have as much or more sex with each other as with males.

Males, on the other hand, stay with their birth group and maintain a strong bond with their mothers. Sons of high-status mothers will have high status, but the female always is in the alpha position.

The female clitoris is enormous, the size of a little finger. Bonobos seem to get a great deal of enjoyment out of clitoral stimulation, including orgasm. According to Frans de Waal, the expression on female bonobos looks very similar to human females when they are having an orgasm, including clenched teeth and an expression of intense concentration.[68] They also engage

---

67   Noted in de Waal's *Our Inner Ape*, (2005), p. 90.

68   Ibid., p. 95.

in a wide variety of hand-to-genital stimulation with themselves and others. Every combination of masturbation and sex has been observed and all are frequent enough to be a normal part of sexual expression.

Unique among mammals, bonobos have semi-hidden estrus. Only humans have a similar strategy. Most mammals mate only when they are in heat or fertile, but bonobos seem to mate any time. When females are in estrus, they display more pink genitals, but this sign of fertility is not an invitation to have lots of sex (like chimps) since they are already having lots of sex.

When a female bonobo becomes pregnant and gives birth, she generally cares for her baby for four to five years and does not conceive again until the baby is weaned. But the sex goes on. It is the same in humans. As long as a woman is nursing, her fertility cycle usually will be suppressed. It's nature's way of saying, "Don't have another baby until this one is able to take care of itself." Because modern women do not nurse as long or as much, they become fertile much sooner after a pregnancy than our hunter-gatherer ancestors and bonobos.

Bonobo anatomy is interesting for its differences and similarities to other primates. Like chimps, the penis is large relative to body size and has a baculum (penis bone). Like humans, the females have breasts. They are small, but clearly present compared to the flat-chested chimps. Male testes are very large and produce copious amounts of semen, presumably to flush out and compete with the semen of other males who went before. And, as in the chimp, bonobo semen has the same methods for blocking and fighting other sperm. Bonobos are also the masters of the "quickie." A typical sexual encounter lasts as little as 7-15 seconds.[69]

Comparing gorilla, chimp and bonobo sex, we can see a spectrum of sexual strategies from the gorilla's highly male-dominated polygynous system, to the chimp's male-dominated multimate system, to the highly female-oriented multimate bonobo system. These three species are genetically tied to a particular sexual strategy for their species.

## Humans: The Penis Puzzle

What were humans doing 20,000 years ago when all of humanity were hunters and gatherers? There are hints at our previous sex lives in our genes,

---

69  See Jared Diamond's *The Third Chimpanzee: The Evolution and Future of the Human Animal*, (2006), p. 75.

physiology and anatomy. For example, human males have testes that are far larger than those of the polygynous gorilla but half the size of the highly sexual chimp and bonobo. Humans produce a large amount of semen compared to the gorilla but not nearly as much as the bonobo or chimp. What might that say about our sexual tendencies in the past and now?

Just like the bonobo, humans have a hidden estrus and can mate at any time, indicating that sex serves more of a social bonding than a reproduction role. The sexual dimorphism and larger testes point to a polygynous tendency, or multimate strategy, and counter any idea that humans are monogamous. The female breasts are totally puzzling in terms of evolutionary causes, but we can be sure they are important and sexually selected in our history because they attract so much attention from both men and women.

Human females are strongly affected by their biology in the type of male they prefer. For years, researchers got conflicting results on the types of bodies and faces that women found attractive. Johnston and colleagues cracked the puzzle when they took into account where a woman was in her menstrual cycle.[70] During fertility, women preferred very masculine faces. When they were not fertile, women preferred more feminine faces. In other research, Hughes and Gallup found that male shoulder-to-hip ratio was predictive of sexual activity at a younger age, with more partners and extra pair couplings.[71] Apparently, women find this male body type very attractive. All of this gives a strong indication that women and men are unconsciously driven by their biology.

The human penis does not have a baculum (penis bone) and is totally dependent upon a pressurizing system to get an erection. With a baculum bone, a male can easily get an erection. Without it, a human male has to be in good health in order to get an erection. As with many traits in nature, females often select the male who shows the best "health traits."

The human penis is far larger than in other primates, both in absolute size and relative to body size. What would cause this larger size in humans? Geoffrey Miller in his book, *The Mating Mind* (2001), writes:

> Given two otherwise identical hominid males, if female hom-
> inids consistently preferred the one with the longer, thicker, more

70  Johnston, V. S., Hagel, R., et al. (2001). "Male facial attractiveness: Evidence for Hormone-Mediated Adaptive Design." *Evolution and Human Behavior*, 22(4).

71  Hughes. S. M., Dispenza, F., and Gallup, J. G. G. (2004). "Ratings of Voice Attractiveness Predict Sexual Behavior and Body Configuration." *Evolution and Human Behavior*, 25.

flexible penis to the one with the shorter, thinner, less flexible one, then the genes for large penises would have spread. Given the relatively large size of modern human penis, it is clear that size mattered. If it had not, modern males would have chimp-sized sexual organs. ... The male human penis does not appear to be especially well adapted for producing auditory, olfactory, or gustatory stimulation. That leaves the sense of touch as the medium for female choice.

Another theory is that the penis evolved along with the vagina. As the human head got larger, the birth canal also had to enlarge, hence the penis enlarged as well.

Besides size, the human penis is shaped differently from those of the other great apes. The glans or penis head is enlarged, giving it a mushroom-type shape at the top. This shape is so distinct and different from other primates as to suggest some important evolutionary function. The differences between human and other primate penises indicate that some level of competitive pressure drove the change since we split from the chimp/bonobo line around 4.1 million years ago. But why this particular shape? What benefit might it confer to the owner?

Robin Baker, biology professor at the University of Manchester, England, found that the penis shape serves perfectly as a pump – to pump semen out of the vagina![72] The penis can pump up to 80% of semen out of the vagina, removing semen from any previous mate. This simple fact of penis shape as a pump explains several other things. Why does human copulation last so much longer compared to that of other primates? A chimp or bonobo is finished in 7-15 seconds and gorillas in one minute, whereas humans go for four minutes or longer.[73] While pleasurable for both parties, it allows the man enough time to pump out the previous fellow's semen before depositing his own. Once ejaculation happens, the human male goes flaccid rapidly so as not to pump his own semen out.

Following up on Baker's research, Gallup and Burch of the State University of New York found:

> The displacement of simulated semen was robust across different prosthetic phalluses, different artificial vaginas, different semen

---

72   For a explanation by Robin Baker on this phenomenon, see the video available online at http://www.robin-baker. com/videos/v2/

73   Noted in Diamond's *The Third Chimpanzee*, p. 75.

recipes, and different semen viscosities. The magnitude of semen displacement was directly proportional to the depth of thrusting and inversely proportional to semen viscosity. By manipulating different characteristics of artificial phalluses, the coronal ridge and frenulum were identified as key morphological features involved in mediating the semen displacement effect.[74]

Going beyond penis anatomy, the ejaculate of human males shares with chimps (and other animals) the ability to coagulate. Some researchers have noted that semen coagulates within seconds after ejaculation.[75] This may serve to keep semen in place while sperm make their way to the egg and/or it may serve to prevent other sperm from getting to the egg. While humans do not make as strong a semen plug as chimps and bonobos, human semen does create an obstruction.

Why would evolution reshape the penis, enlarge the testes, eliminate the baculum bone and create semen plugs? Because humans are a polygynous species and may be a multimale, multifemale species. This may sound radical, but genetic evidence shows that about 80% of women have reproduced throughout our history but only 40% of men.[76] This stunning fact means that over time, women have been more successful at reproducing than men and that successful men have reproduced with two or more women. While this may seem to go against common sense, we must remember that over history, men have consistently had the most dangerous positions in society. Even today, 93% of the people killed on the job are men. It was undoubtedly worse with our hunter-gathering ancestors as well as the warrior cultures of later civilization. In the course of our species, many young men died before they could reproduce. In addition, the men at the top of almost any society have access to more women than the men at the bottom (the Hugh Hefner effect). Human females are also more attracted to high-status men.

74   Gallup, G.G. and Burch, R.L., (2004). "Semen displacement as a sperm competition strategy in humans." *Evolutionary Psychology*, 2.

75   As noted previously, in Kingan, et al, 2003 article "Reduced polymorphism in the chimpanzee semen coagulating protein," as well as studies by Dixson and Anderson, (2002),"Sexual selection, seminal coagulation and copulatory plug formation in primates." (*Folia Primatologica; International Journal of Primatology*, 73(2-3)) and by Dorus, Wyckoff, et al., (2004), "Rate of molecular evolution of the seminal protein gene SEMG2 correlates with levels of female promiscuity." (*Nature Genetics*, 36).

76   Roy Baumeister, "Is There Anything Good About Men?" American Psychological Association, Invited Address, 2007. Transcript available online at http://www.psy.fsu.edu/~baumeistertice/goodaboutmen.htm.

All of these facts, penis shape and size, loss of baculum bone, larger testes, longer coitus, point to adaptations in response to intense reproductive pressure on men. Human male sex organs evolved in a highly competitive environment that involved a multimate system. Women evolved attraction to certain types of males, men evolved strategies to displace other male's sperm and ensure their sperm gets to the egg first – to name just a few of the evolved characteristics. It is a dance between males and females, between male sex organs and female sex organs, between male semen chemistry and female vaginal chemistry. The result is a mating strategy that resembles other primates in some ways, but is unique to our species.

## The Sex Partner Mystery

For decades, researchers could not understand how men could report far more sexual partners than women. Some suspected that men exaggerated; others suspected women underreported. The mystery was solved when Alexander and Fisher[77] found that women reported far fewer sexual partners when they thought their answers might be seen by a researcher. They reported more partners when they thought their answers were anonymous and even more when they thought they were hooked up to a lie detector machine. Under the "lie detector" condition, women's answers were equal to those of men. Men's answers did not vary. The researchers attributed underreporting to the social expectation of purity placed upon women in our culture.

Over the last 60 years, vast amounts of research have been conducted on human sexuality and behavior. Depending on the study, 90-95% of all people have had sex before marriage and most of those with partners they do not ultimately marry. In addition, Kinsey found that 50% of men and 26% of women had extramarital affairs.[78] Then we must consider that 50% of couples get divorced and most go on to have sex with one or more people before they marry again. While it is difficult to determine exact numbers, there is no doubt that a high proportion of people have multiple sex partners in a lifetime.

Humans are not now – and never have been – monogamous. According to the research, humans have been a multimate species for millions of

---

77  Alexander, M.G. and Fisher, T.D. (2003). "Truth and Consequences: Using the bogus pipeline to examine sex differences in self-reported sexuality." *The Journal of Sex Research*, Vol. 40.

78  Data from Kinsey's studies available online at http://www.kinseyinstitute.org/research/ak-data.html#extramaritalcoitus.

years. At best we are serial polygamists (one mate with two or more mates, without regard to sex of the partner), bonding with someone for a time and then moving on to other mates.[79]

"Follow the biology" tells us much more about who we are than any religion. If you want more information, take a look at some of the books or studies in the bibliography.[80] Next, we will look at how biology, among other things, affects our development into unique sexual human beings.

---

79  I use the term serial polygamist intentionally since the idea of "serial monogamy" makes little sense. Monogamy is simply defined as one sexual partner for life. That is certainly the definition used by Jesus and the one followed by most Christian sects. If you have more than one partner in your life, you do not fit that definition of monogamy. You are multimate.

80  See these books in the bibliography: *The Myth of Monogamy* by Barash and Lipton, *Sex at Dawn: The Prehistoric Origins of Modern Sexuality*, by Ryan and Jetha, and *Sperm Wars: Infidelity, Sexual Conflict and other Bedroom Battles*, by Robin Baker.

# CHAPTER 10:

# MAPPING YOUR SEXUALITY

Our sexual behavior and preferences are the product of many influences. We often have no awareness or control over these influences.

*"Disgust is intuitive microbiology."*
**- Steven Pinker,** *The Blank Slate: The Modern Denial of Human Nature*

## Your Invisible Map

The sexual biology discussed in the previous chapters lays a foundation for understanding the many forces that make us unique sexual beings. To frame this discussion, I will use the idea of a map: a map that resides in our genes, our neurological wiring and our cultural training. It helps us navigate the sexual world, often without conscious thought. The processes that create an erection or female lubrication need no thinking, just proper stimulation. In fact, thinking can interfere. This is but one example of the unconsciousness of sex. Our sexual map determines why one person turns you on but another turns you off. Let's examine the origin of our sexual maps and answer these questions.

- How is the brain programmed to seek a mate and have sex?
- Where does the program come from? How much of it is genetic and how much is culturally specific?

Our sexual map is the way we understand and negotiate our sexual world, which includes our own minds and bodies as well as those of everyone else. The map motivates you to give your phone number to one person and recoil at the thought of giving it to another.

Let's begin with how the brain is programmed – which parts are "hard wired" and which ones are more flexible and responsive to training and the environment. The brain is put together in unique developmental stages. For example, at birth the infant brain has to recognize and respond to its parents. Research shows that infants tackle this task within a few weeks. How does the baby know the difference between a mother and, say, a cat or dog? A template is genetically programmed into the human brain that allows the baby to recognize a human face as opposed to the dog or cat.

The baby's next task is to fill in the details of his or her particular parent's face. Recognizing mom or dad allows the baby to relax and feel secure. If the baby is not allowed to form a secure attachment, he or she may demonstrate poorer coping skills in later life, including intolerance to change and stress.[81]

A similar process seems to be involved in mate selection. One large study of adopted daughters found that women tended to chose husbands who resembled their adoptive father. The researchers found that the more

81   Schore, A. (2001). "Effects Of A Secure Attachment Relationship On Right Brain Development, Affect Regulation, And Infant Mental Health" *Infant Mental Health Journal*, 22(1–2).

supportive the adoptive father was of the daughter, the more often she chose a husband who resembled him.

Why study adopted daughters? Because they are genetically unrelated to the man who raised them. Any tendency to choose a similar-looking husband, therefore, would be the product of conditioning or imprinting, not from genes she received from her father.

While these results did not account for all the variance in mate choice, it is evidence that some kind of imprinting is going on in the female mind. Women may have some unconscious programming to look for faces similar to their father or the man who nurtures them as they are growing up, as long as they had a positive attachment to him. Using the same methodology, the researchers found no evidence of this type of programming in boys.[82]

How does the brain know who an appropriate mate is? A study of 3,000 marriages from the Israeli kibbutz system found that unrelated children raised together until at least six years of age never married one another. This is called the Westermarck effect[83] and theorizes that the brain of a child is programmed to lose sexual interest in anyone raised too close to him or her – presumably to minimize the risk of incest.

These are two examples of innate programming. They demonstrate that sexual preferences and choices are often formed outside of our awareness, an invisible map that guides us whether we know it or not.

While evolution has shaped the penis, breasts, hips and other outward signs of gender, as we can see from mate-selection research, it has also shaped the human brain. The following discussion is an oversimplification of the complex topic of the neuroscience of sex. Our purpose is to examine the complexities of sexual development with a particular focus on how religion impacts us at the most basic levels.

### The Three-Tiered Map

Human brains have three layers of programming. Each layer adds a twist or turn to sexual preferences and tendencies. The first layer is genetic

---

82  Bereczkei, T., Gyuris, P. and Weisfeld, G. (2004). "Sexual imprinting in human mate choice." *The Royal Society*, 271.

83  After Edvard Alexander Westermarck (1862–1939). He was a Swedish-speaking Finnish philosopher and sociologist who studied marriage, exogamy and the incest taboo. He was the first to propose that there is a biological reason people are not attracted to close relatives and there is little evidence that an incest taboo is necessary as Freud proposed.

programming from the inherited genes. The second involves environmental influences that impact genes and their expression. The third level deals with the way we "fill in the blanks" as social and cultural beings. This level can then become a feedback loop that influences the inherited genes by influencing with whom we choose to have sex.

### Tier One – Sex in Your Genes

An XX or an XY set of chromosomes and the genes on them largely determines gender.[84] Within these genes is the programming to shape a male or female brain with some of the behaviors needed for reproduction.

Many people believe that these chromosomes are the only influence on sexuality. However, many studies show that sex and sexual behavior are influenced by a number of things beyond which chromosomes and genes we inherit. As a fetus develops, genes perform a specific task, such as forming an organ or type of cell. Once the task is done, the gene may turn off. In the womb, the fetus develops as a result of a series of on-and-off events triggered by many conditions, both inside and outside the fetus. The process is governed by a hierarchical sequence unique to our species, but similar to that of many other species. This is the first level of sexual programming.

Several twin studies have shown a significant genetic role in the type of partner a person chooses. One of the largest included 7,200 twins born in Sweden.[85] The study concluded that 18-39% of sexual preference was genetic. In another study, J. Michael Bailey and Richard C. Pillard found that 52% of the identical twins of male homosexuals were also homosexual, compared to only 22% of non-identical twins.[86] Likewise, they found that if one identical twin is lesbian, in almost 50% of the cases studied, the other twin is lesbian as well, in comparison to 16% of the non-identical twins. This tells us that a large part of sexual preference is determined by genetics.

---

84    I recognize that this ignores other possibilities that can influence sex. These are far less common, even rare. In the interest of simplicity, we will stick to the basics but will explore some other influences when we discuss tier-two epigenetics.

85    Långström N, Rahman Q, Carlström E, Lichtenstein P. (2010). "Genetic and environmental effects on same-sex sexual behavior: a population study of twins in Sweden." *Archives of Sexual Behavior*, 39(1).

86    Bailey, J.M., Pillard, R.C. (1991). "A Genetic Study of Male Sexual Orientation." *Archives of General Psychiatry*, 48(12).

This "tier one" – or genetic – component of our sexual map is hard-wired and unlikely to change. But the two other levels of programming have their say as well.

### Tier Two: Epigenetics – Your Genes on Drugs

The second level also takes place in the womb. The fetus is surrounded by a chemical mix in the amniotic fluid and receives nourishment from the mother through the umbilical cord. If all goes well, the genes switch on and off in a proper sequence and form a nice healthy baby. The process of fetal development is an extremely complex chain of chemical reactions.

From the perspective of the mother's body, the fetus is an invasive foreign object. For this reason, it is largely protected from direct contact with the mother's blood because it might provoke the mother's immune system to attack.

This protection also keeps many of the pollutants and dangerous chemicals in the mother's system from entering the fetus. Unfortunately, some chemicals and pollutants can cross the barrier between mother and fetus. Some medications and supplements can also interfere with the development of the fetus. Other things can also influence development such as what the mother eats, smokes or drinks, or her amount of stress. There is also a delicate balancing act between the mother and fetus. The fetus wants to grow as large as possible but the mother needs to limit growth so she can live to have more babies. The result of this "battle" can influence the development of the fetus and its sexual development, especially for males.

In the last decade or so, research has shown that genes are impacted by external effects or "epigenetics." For example, high stress causes major changes in the behavior of adult male rats, making them less masculine. Exposure to nicotine can change the testes of male rats. The plasticizer diethylhexyl phthalate causes malformations in rat testes. Their testes weigh less and testosterone levels go down to female levels in male rats.[87] These effects have been seen in many animals, and evidence is accumulating that it is no different for humans.

Occasionally, extreme changes can even alter the sex of the fetus. Estrogen is the default hormone in the uterus. If a male fetus with a full

---

87   Parks, L., Ostby, J, et al. (2000). "The Plasticizer Diethylhexyl Phthalate Induces Malformations by Decreasing Fetal Testosterone Synthesis during Sexual Differentiation in the Male Rat." *Toxicological Sciences*, 58(2).

XY complement is somehow deprived of testosterone, he will develop into a female. Similarly, if a female with XX chromosome is exposed to high levels of testosterone in utero, she will develop a penis and testes.

## Your Inner Female

All human embryos start as female. A male is the product of thousands of chemical sequences beginning at conception that slowly masculinize the body. A disruption in any number of these sequences can make a man more macsuline or less masculine.

During the intrauterine period of development, the male brain is programmed by a surge of testosterone acting on the nervous system. If something interferes with or reduces this surge, the male brain will program differently. This is one reason for the variety of sexual orientations – homosexual, heterosexual, bisexual or transsexual. The genes, hormones and environment create a unique human being. In some cases that human being's body and mind do not conform to religious notions of male or female.

One example of how hormones and genetics work to create a sexual person is seen in Androgen Insensitivity Syndrome (AIS). AIS is a rare condition that creates sexual characteristics that are somewhere in between male and female or a complete reversal of sexual characteristics. There are two types of AIS: Complete AIS and Incomplete AIS. In Complete AIS a male fetus becomes a girl because he inherits a lack of sensitivity to androgens – insensitivity to the hormones that tell his body to become a man. As a result, development follows the natural route to a female body even though he has the male Y chromosome.[88]

Incomplete AIS comes from partial insensitivity to androgen hormones. When this happens, the baby may develop gender ambiguity such as growing breasts, testes not descending or the urethra developing below the penis rather from the tip. The partial insensitivity gives the developing fetus mixed signals. As a result, male and female characteristics develop in a male fetus.

AIS demonstrates that gender is not as simple as religionists might claim. There are at least 7,000 people in the United States with Complete AIS – they look and act like women but their genes are male.

---

88   Hanan, Mary, "Women With Male DNA All Female." Avaiable online at http://abcnews. go.com/Health/MedicalMysteries/story?id=5465752&page=1.

Genetics and epigenetics are far more important in sexuality than any idea of choice. No evidence has been found that anyone chooses their sexuality. Choice is a theological concept, not a biological one.

## Tier Three – Sex in Your Jeans

The third tier of programming happens from birth through early adulthood. Our genes don't tell us how to get a date or what sexual position we most enjoy. We develop our sexuality through a multilayered process.

The child and adolescent move through developmental stages that are genetically programmed but are also susceptible to epigenetic impact and cultural influence. For example, children absorb any language in their environment until about age 12, at which time the brain seems to slow down or switch off language acquisition.

In addition, children learn only the language or languages in their immediate environment. They easily learn the grammar and syntax, vocabulary and many subtle inflections and accents, effortlessly absorbing a critical aspect of human culture. Two children raised in the same house may even learn very different versions of the same language. For example, in pre-Civil War United States, slave children were raised right next to the plantation owner's children, yet they spoke very different versions of the same language. In England, servants and aristocrats spoke different dialects. Cultural pressures can have strong influences on language acquisition.

The same is true of sex. While some aspects of sex are determined at tier one and two, others are susceptible to tier three – cultural learning. At the onset of puberty, with hormones rushing, adolescents are primed to absorb everything they can about sex. During this time, humans develop a good deal of their likes and dislikes, including primary and secondary sexual preferences.[89] Primary sexual preference is a person's main orientation: homosexual, heterosexual, bisexual, transsexual. But primary sexual preference is only the scaffolding for sexuality; much needs to be filled in to make a complete sexual being. This is where secondary sexual preferences come in – sexual fetishes to body type preferences actually drive behavior. They are what turn people on.

A woman may be attracted to men with hair on their chest. A man may like women with a certain breast size. A woman may enjoy a man with a

---

89   I owe a debt of gratitude to my friend Dr. Dan Dana for his development of this idea.

sensuous mouth who can kiss well. A man may want a woman who acts seductively and dresses to achieve that effect. A woman may enjoy a man who is extremely intelligent. The list of secondary preferences is virtually infinite but limited within any given person. For example, a woman may prefer men with broad shoulders and a deep voice. That would probably preclude tall lanky tenors, which another woman may prefer.

Adolescents seek clues about sex and sexuality within their environment. The same experience may impact two teenagers entirely differently. One girl may find that she is strongly attracted to risk-taking "bad boys," whereas her sister is turned off by that type. While these attractions manifest themselves in adolescence, they are a product of all three levels of the sexual map – genetic, epigenetic and cultural.

The drive to identify sexual cues in the environment is incredibly intense and susceptible to influence from events and experiences. Here are two stories, the first from a 28-year-old man named Charlie:

> *I was raised Catholic and, therefore, went through that whole shame cycle of being Catholic and gay. However, there was a third ingredient – I also had a fetish for seeing men burst balloons. Seriously!*
>
> *It began as a phobia of balloons popping, but somehow during my adolescence it became something of a fetish. Much like a kid who was spanked over the knee of his father and later goes on to sexualize the act, I took that fear and turned it into something erotic – those guys who popped balloons for fun were so scary to me, but somehow incredibly sexy.*

Here's a story from a 46-year-old man:

> *My brother and I liked to go through the trash of a local army surplus store. We often found all sorts of fun and interesting stuff. One day we hit the jackpot with a half dozen porn magazines. It wasn't the first time we had found porn but definitely the best. We brought it home and secretly went through it. One magazine featured several bondage scenes. Those images just burned in my mind. I was so turned on by the idea of tying someone up I didn't even think about having sex. Just the thought of tying a woman up turned me on. Years later, my brother and I were talking about "the good old days." He and I can talk about anything. He has always been more adventurous about sex than I. To my surprise*

*he mentioned that magazine and how much it turned him on. And here is the mind-blowing thing, he was turned on by the idea of being tied up! He told me it had been a fantasy of his for decades. He liked the idea of a woman being in total control of him. Neither of us had ever thought about bondage before we saw that magazine. We discovered both of us had engaged in different bondage things over the intervening years.*

Secondary preferences often dictate what kind of sex is most stimulating and satisfying. Both sexes have secondary preferences that influence mate selection. An acquaintance of mine seemed to have a new girlfriend every six months or so. Over the course of five years, I noticed many of his girlfriends were amazingly similar in body type. When I met his mother, it all made sense: she was an older version of every woman he had dated.

Adolescents seek out sexual cues in their environment, learning what is and what is not attractive in their culture. If the culture tells boys that small feet or large breasts are attractive, that is what they will most likely focus on as adults. If the culture tells girls that the best bear hunter or the best singer on *American Idol* is the most desirable, that may impact them.

Secondary sexual preferences can come to dominate entire cultures *and* determine what genes get passed on. We see the evidence in female body types. Women in some cultures have large bottoms. Over thousands of years, these characteristics have been sexually selected. The genes do not tell a man to choose a woman with a large butt, but genes program the brain to look for cues in the environment and in certain areas of the body. Just as the human brain is programmed to recognize the human facial configuration but not any specific face, we are programmed to recognize parts of the body that have sexual significance. The culture then tells you what that significance is.

The ebb and flow of sex hormones impacts the brain at all ages, but especially before age 20. If something happens while the brain is being inundated with sex hormones, it may have a permanent impact on sexual behavior and preference. If it happens consistently within a culture, it can literally shape the body type of an entire people.

## Learning Social Cues for the Map

The social environment tells our sexual map when to increase or decrease hormones. This part of our sexual map runs automatically. Much of it was learned early in life. The male duck learns to recognize his dominance level and where he fits into the duck hierarchy. Humans do much the same. When we walk into a party, we unconsciously evaluate the people and cues and adjust our behavior to fit the social structure of the group. We unconsciously look at how many men or women are in the room, how they are dressed, where they are standing and the posture and nonverbal gestures they use. With these signals, we often determine who the most important people are and act accordingly.

Were we to look at hormone levels, we would find that high-status men and women in the room have higher testosterone than lower-status individuals. Research has also shown that testosterone and other hormones can increase or decrease when perceived status changes.[90]

Research on male aggression and competition shows that men engaged in sports or in watching sports evidence a testosterone surge when their team wins. Further, many men experience a strong need to have sex after the victory. If they lose, testosterone declines. Winning primes men to compete and losing primes them to be less aggressive in the face of a superior foe.[91]

In this regard, humans are like many other species. Males experience changes in hormonal levels in the presence of competition and aggression, and want sex when they win. Women also show changes in testosterone levels in response to watching or participating in sporting events and in risk-taking behavior.

Is it possible that religion impacts hormones? Could testosterone increase or decrease in response to religious activities? No one has researched this, but most religious services are based on the idea of submission and evoke submissive behavior such as the following:[92]

- Bowing the head during prayer
- Kneeling
- Prostrating on a mat during prayer
- Singing songs about submission

90   Josephs, R. A., Sellers, J. G., Newman, M. L., Mehta, P. H. (2006). "The mismatch effect: When testosterone and status are at odds." *Journal of Personality and Social Psychology*, 90(6).

91   Bernhardt P.C., Dabbs, J.M. Jr., Fielden, J.A, Lutter, C.D. (1998). "Testosterone changes during vicarious experiences of winning and losing among fans at sporting events." *Physiology & Behavior*, 65(1).

92   The word "Islam" means "submit" in Arabic, but Christianity, Buddhism, Hinduism, Bahai'a and any number of other religions might as well use it as their slogan as well.

- Women covering their head or men taking hats off
- Listening silently, without question to the priest or minister
- Using submissive language when speaking to the deity
- Engaging in rituals of supplication

*– all of these acts are acts of social submission, particularly for women.*

Going to church may reduce testosterone levels through constant submission. Not everyone's testosterone levels will be lowered, however. At least one person's hormones in the group will likely go up – the priest or minister's. Standing on a podium, telling hundreds, even thousands of people to submit is not much different than a gorilla or chimp doing a dominance display. I have interviewed many former ministers in my research. All tell of the emotional high they got from standing in front of the congregation and preaching. Clearly, there is a strong hormonal response from telling others to submit.

Hormones are important for our motivational systems. Testosterone is not the only hormone involved in motivation, dominance or submission, but it is an important one. Many other variables are involved, but one fact stands out – the more educated and financially successful, the less religious a person is likely to be. The opposite is also generally true; the more religious, the less educated and financially stable.

Could religion's constant message of submission have an impact on other areas of life and achievement? For example, given that the most religious people are often of lower educational and socioeconomic status, does religion's message of submission have a negative impact on educational achievement and economic development? In the United States, the most religious states generally have the lowest levels of economic development and educational status – Utah being the exception. Is this related to high levels of religiosity? Where submission to religious authority is valued, creationism and opposition to teaching evolution seem to thrive. It is a controversial topic for which there is little or no research. I would suggest it is an area ripe for exploration. How much does religion impact motivation and educational achievement?

### Your Brain on Metaphors

In a wonderful essay "This Is Your Brain on Metaphors," the renowned professor of neurology, Robert Sapolsky, writes about how our brains use the same regions to process physical experiences and metaphors.[93] Human brains are not so much designed as duct-taped. Evolution did not give us a metaphor processing center, so our brains use a center that already processes similar information. When you smell or taste something rotten, a region in the brain called the insula responds with gustatory disgust. The same area of your brain responds to the thought of something disgusting. Tasting is not the same as thinking about tasting, yet the brain processes the two in the same area. To some degree, the brain cannot distinguish between a bad taste and the thought of a bad taste.

How is this relevant for religion and sexuality? Religious training is full of messages about sex and sexuality that map to the parts of the brain that process disgust and other negative responses. How many times do you have to hear, "Homosexuality is disgusting," before you map homosexuality to the disgust part of your brain? Even someone who is homosexual maps disgust about his or her sexuality based on this kind of religious training. This does not stop them from being homosexual, but it does make them feel disgusted with their behavior.[94]

An elder in the church I attended as a young adult was fond of talking about all the disgusting things shown on TV. A friend and I were at his house one day. A talk show was on the TV, and when someone on the show mentioned oral sex, the elder stomped to the TV set and turned it off. "That is the most disgusting thing I have ever heard on TV," he said. He looked like he had just bitten into a rotten apple with a big worm in it. The expression of metaphorical disgust processed through the insula as if it were a physical experience.

Religious programming has the power to distort normal, natural and intensely pleasurable behavior into something inconceivably disgusting. Decades later, this same elder was accused of molesting two of his children. Could the conflict between his religious map and his biological map have contributed to his abusive behavior?

---

93    Robert Sapolsky, "This is Your Brain on Metaphors." *The New York Times*, 14 Nov 2010.

94    For further discussion of religion and disgust see *The Better Angels of Our Nature: Why Violence Has Declined*, by Steven Pinker (2011).

## Religious Mapping – The Two-Party Brain

Adolescents may integrate cultural messages intoning that sex is wrong, that masturbation is a violation of your body and that nothing sexual is permitted until marriage. While these messages often don't stop them from having sex, they can make adolescents feel disgusted with themselves as well as guilty.

The sexual behavior is driven from one part of the brain while the disgust and guilt are contained in a different area. The two are not necessarily connected, yet we have the illusion that we are one unified person with one unified brain and that we are in control of our behavior. When we do something that is not consistent with our ideas of control, we have elaborate ways of justifying and rationalizing the behavior.

Mark Regnerus explores the impact of religion in adolescents in his book *Forbidden Fruit* (2007). Based on extensive study, he shows how little impact religion has on most teenagers, even those who are most religious. He concludes:

> It is popularly held that evangelical Protestants are the most conservative American religious tradition with respect to sexual attitudes and behaviors .... Evangelicals do in fact maintain more conservative attitudes about sex than do mainline Protestants, black Protestants and Jewish youth. They are the second most likely (after Mormons) to think that having sex will make them feel guilty, least likely to think that sex is pleasurable, and most likely to think that having sex will cause their partner to disrespect them. But evangelical Protestant youth are not the religious group least likely to have sex. Indeed, in both data sets, they are largely indistinguishable from the rest of American adolescents.

These results are consistent with many studies, including my own research. For example, in an on-line survey of 10,000 people, I found almost no difference in sexual behavior between people raised to be very religious and those raised least religiously.[95] The only difference was in the level of guilt. Religious teenagers feel far more guilty, but they still have sex. This is strong evidence that teenagers are of two minds. One part of their brain

---

95  Ray, D.W. and Brown, A. (2011). "Sex and Secularism: What Happens When You Leave Religion." See IPCPress.com for the full report. We will discuss this research in Chapter 16.

holds certain religious beliefs and the other drives their natural sexuality. The two areas don't talk to each other very much. The religious part of the brain certainly doesn't stop them from having sex:

This story from a formerly religious young woman shows this disconnect:

*My boyfriend and I were really hot for each other, but being students in a fundamentalist college, we had it beaten into our heads that sex before marriage was absolutely forbidden. If we were caught, we would be expelled. As a result, we did about everything short of intercourse until one night my boyfriend suggested that we get married in "God's eyes." We knelt down and prayed fervently that God bless us and our marriage, and consider us married on that very night. Then we hopped into bed and fucked like rabbits. It was an amazing night, one that I will never forget. I had never felt so close to another person, never experienced such intense pleasure, never felt so safe, never enjoyed such warmth. There was no doubt in my mind that it was a night blessed by God.*

*Over the next few days, I was totally cool with what we had done, but my boyfriend acted strange and distant. I tried to talk to him but got nothing. I asked him when we could go out again, and he just mumbled. It began to drive me crazy. What had happened to us being married? What happened to that amazing man who kissed me and made me feel so loved, warm and safe?*

*Weeks went by, and we hardly saw each other. Then one night, he called and said, "We have to talk." I met him at a private corner of the library and found that he was wracked with guilt and felt we had to go confess to the dean of the school and promise not to have sex again. I tried to tell him that I was perfectly O.K. with what we did, even if he didn't want to be married, but nothing would change his mind. I refused to go confess anything to the dean because what we had done was beautiful and certainly God-given. I knew that if he talked to the dean without me, I would get kicked out. The semester was almost over, so I asked him to wait until after finals. I got out of there as soon as finals were finished and transferred to a secular university. I never spoke to him again. That was the beginning of the end for my religion. How can anything so beautiful be wrong? It just did not make sense to me.*

*I am happy to say that after several wonderful lovers, I found a man who makes me happy. He is a little religious, but it doesn't get in the way of great sex and a great relationship.*

The boyfriend's sexual map went through Jesus, a circuitous route based on the erroneous idea that the mind is one entity. As a result, he could not integrate the two areas of his brain. The only way he could deal with the disgust he experienced in one part of his brain was to confess from another part, keeping these two areas separate and unable to communicate or integrate. Chances are he will engage in future sexual behavior that will puzzle him and create huge guilt and remorse.

## Adult Maps

Once adolescents are imprinted, those cultural sexual patterns remain an important part of their sexual preferences.[96] Let's look at some religious maps and how they might impact adult sexuality. Throughout adolescence, Muslim men receive strong messages about male dominance in marriage. The Koran is highly male-focused, with women being of little importance. Mohammed married as many women as he wanted, even a nine-year-old girl. Polygamy was acceptable and women were given in marriage with little consideration. Rules and punishments for women are far harsher than for men. The sexes are separated from childhood and male privilege is obvious in their disparate treatment of the sexes. In many Muslim countries, boys get an education, especially a religious one, whereas girls get minimal schooling outside of the home. Women are told that their purpose is to please the man and have children. Men are taught that sex with an infidel woman, especially in another country, is not a sin against Allah. For a Muslim woman, sex with any man except her husband is a crime.

With these messages imprinted in adolescence, Muslim men have ideas about women that are misogynistic by Western standards. Here is a story I received from an American woman who met a wealthy Arab man on-line and started dating him long distance:

*The first few times we met in person, he flew here. We would spend a week or two together and have the greatest time. I really fell for this guy. He was educated in a very prestigious United*

---

96  For more information see Ogi Ogas and Sai Gaddam, *A Billion Wicked Thoughts: What the world's largest experiment reveals about human desire,* (2011).

*States university and was a thriving professional in Lebanon. He was very secular and seemed to have no use for Islam though his family was still religious. He knew how to treat a woman and was amazing in bed. I am pretty poor most of the time with a kid in college so I wasn't in a position to fly to the Middle East. After almost a year and several visits to the United States, he offered to fly me over for a visit. It was an exciting opportunity. When I arrived, his father met me at the airport – not him! We went directly to his father's house where I waited for almost a day until my friend arrived. His father and mother treated me O.K., but it was very uncomfortable. They spoke very little English and I spoke no Arabic. When he arrived, he acted glad to see me, but he didn't even touch me or give me one of those passionate kisses I loved. I soon learned that I would be staying with his parents for the entire two weeks I was there. I had little or no time alone with him. Everywhere we went, his father was with us.*

*The most disturbing thing was how much his personality had changed. He was not affectionate at all and often talked to his parents as if I was not there. In public, he seemed nervous, and definitely did not want me getting close to him. Not once did he take me to his house. I tried to talk to him about it, but there was little privacy, and he never seemed in the mood to talk about serious things.*

*We did manage to have sex a couple of times, but it was hardly what we had in the States. I could go on and on about this bizarre trip. I enjoyed seeing a new country, but didn't have any interest in him or that culture after that.*

One might chalk this up to "cultural differences," but this guy's sexual map came from Islam. While he was able to act like an American man when in the United States, his sexual map was strongly influenced by the religious culture when he was in his home country. His personality seemed to change when he was home. More likely, his sexual map changed. In the United States, he could effectively ignore his Muslim sexual map for a few weeks, but he could not do so in his home country.

## The Effect of Submission

What might the hormonal response be if a person is subjected to a steady barrage of submission messages from birth? Whether Islam, Christianity or others, religious messages have an impact as sex hormones battle stress hormones within the religious person. The body says, "take action on your sexual urges," while religion says, "you will go to hell for doing so." Such constant conflict will eventually distort sexuality.

Religious restrictions and fear messages combined with normal biological urges inevitably lead to stress. In his work with baboons, Robert Sapolsky has used direct measurements of testosterone, steroids and stress hormones to show the impact of social connection to health and well-being. His research is important because humans under stress show similar hormonal patterns to baboons. For decades social isolation has been noted as one of the most stressful events a person can experience, but only recently have measurements actually shown how extremely stressful this can be for both humans and baboons.[97] Social isolation can lead to major depression, illness, gastrointestinal disease and suppressed immune response, among many other mental and physical problems.

Religions use the threat and practice of social isolation to maintain control and loyalty in followers. Leaving religion means risking social isolation and all the physical and mental consequences that may follow. Submission messages, combined with threat of social ostracism, deter people from leaving the church. For many churches, social isolation is a key tool for maintaining conformity. Those escaping often report strong sanctions and isolation from their former communities and families. Those who stay in religion can be stressed by pressure to suppress and ignore their biological map, are given powerful guilt messages and condemned for thinking about sex. This often leads to depression, emotional problems and stress-related illness.

## Maps in Conflict

We have multiple sexual maps – from genetic and epigenetic influences that are largely out of our consciousness to social and cultural influences that may or may not be within our awareness. We are a social and biological species with sexual patterns and tendencies that exist independent of any

---

97  Discussed in Robert Sapolsky's *A Primate's Memoir: A Neuroscientist's Unconventional Life Among the Baboons*, (2002).

religion. Religions attempt to force sex into a one-size-fits-all box, placing a layer of complexity on sexuality that is neither realistic nor related to the biological roots of our species. In the next section we will take a look at what other cultures can tell us about human sexuality.

# SECTION III:
# FOLLOW THE CULTURE

## CHAPTER 11:
## SEX BEFORE GOD

Western ideas of sex and sexuality reflect a tiny slice of human experience. The varieties of sexual experience, belief and practice are vast. In understanding sexual variety, we will see how the major religions limit sexuality to an arbitrarily narrow area of acceptable practice.

*"Whatever the main biological function of human copulation, it isn't conception, which is just an occasional by-product."*

**-Jared Diamond**

## Sex Before Buddha, Jesus or Mohammed

Before agriculture, virtually every society engaged in hunting and gathering. While "modern" societies have marginalized or eliminated hunter-gatherer societies, there are still sufficient numbers in places like the Amazon and Africa to study and make an educated guess about life before agriculture and what sexual practices may have looked like before the major religions came along.

For tens of thousands of years, hunter-gatherers maintained a steady population with very slow growth. It was a successful lifestyle, with less disease and greater overall health and lifespan than those of agriculturalists. To put it another way, we lived successfully as hunter-gatherers for 99.5% of human history.[98]

The hunter-gatherer lifestyle had characteristics very different from those of the agriculturalists that supplanted many of them. For example, unlike agriculturalists, hunter-gatherers could not afford too many children. No woman can efficiently gather roots, nuts and berries, and carry more than one child. Infanticide was a form of population control but may not have been practiced often because nursing women are less fertile. Women among hunter-gatherers often nurse far longer than those in agricultural societies, up to four years. Children were not weaned in many cultures until they were capable of learning how to help with gathering. As a result, children were spaced about four years apart.

Women also provided 60-70% of the calories to the family through gathering. This can be seen in the archeology of preagricultural societies and in today's hunter-gatherers. In many ways, the evidence is still present in Africa, Australia and South America, as well as North America, until the very recent past.

Compared to agricultural communities, hunter-gatherers exploit their environment more evenly and completely. The food and medical knowledge of these societies is astounding and their diet often consists of 10-12 times more food items than that of most agriculturalists.

To understand the importance of farming on religious and sexual ideas, we first need to understand what religion and sex were like before agricul-

---

98  For an excellent summary of the negative impact of agriculture on human health, see http://www.scribd.com/doc/2100251/Jared-Diamond-*The-Worst-Mistake-in-the-History-of-the-Human-Race* or read Jared Diamond's book, *Guns, Germs and Steel* (2005).

ture. Then we will examine the evolution of sex and religion through early agricultural societies up through the advent of the major religions of today.

## Preagricultural or Semiagricultural

How did sex and religion interact before agriculture? Cultures in Africa, Polynesia, the Amazon and China can show us a variety of religious and sexual practices that probably existed before agriculture. By examining these, we can see how today's religions impact and determine sexuality in modern culture.

### The Hadza of Tanzania and the Rift Valley

The Hadza people live in the Rift Valley close to the cradle of human evolution and near where the original fossils of Australopithecus were found by Mary Leaky in 1959.[99] A hunter-gatherer tribe, they have resisted the movement to agriculture for centuries. As a result, they have been pushed onto marginal land and have lost 90% of their traditional area. They live a mobile life and use the resources of the land. They have little concept of time. Their genetic stock may be 100,000 years old or much closer to the root of humanity than almost any other group.

They live in such low-density populations that diseases do not cause significant problems. Violence and murder are rare. They have lived in the same area for thousands of years but have left hardly a trace. Since they move frequently, the Hadza do not need or want possessions. Besides, they do not recognize official leadership. The community is very fluid, with people coming and going, joining and leaving local groups regularly.

Women provide a majority of the calories and men provide protein from hunting meat. Unlike their agricultural neighbors, they store no food and experience no droughts. They can always find something to eat. Their diet is varied and rich in nutrients. In addition, they spend a relatively small amount of time gathering food and a great deal of time socializing. While they have remained small in number, compared to the agriculturalists, the Hadza people maintain strong health.

Their religion has been described by Frank Marlowe, Harvard anthropologist, as minimalist. Until a generation ago, they didn't even bury their dead. Today they bury the dead but make no ceremony and show little or no

---

99  For an excellent article on the Hadza, see *National Geographic*, Dec. 2009.

emotion. They have no concept of an afterlife. Death seems to be just another part of life. The focus is on living today and enjoying social connections. According to Marlowe, one of the few rituals they have:

> ... is the Mai-toh-ko, or female puberty initiation, which happens when the berries are ripening. Pubertal girls gather in a camp where they are covered with animal fat and adorned with beads, then chase boys and try to hit them with their fertility sticks.[100]

Quite different from any Christian or Muslim religious ritual, the ritual is sexual and shows that women hold a powerful place in the society.

Over the last century, there has been constant pressure to get the Hadza to settle down and farm. Most efforts were a combination of government and missionary work. Many included force or coercion. In every case, most Hadza soon returned to foraging. As Frank Marlowe observes:

> Missionaries sometimes come to Mongo wa Mono and try to make converts. Usually, they do not last longer than a few months. Hadza children and teen-agers often sing Christian songs, and the Hadza welcome the food provided by missionaries, but there has been little conversion to Christianity. Many observers felt the settlements would mean the end of Hadza foraging, but surprisingly, they did not. Even today, few Hadza practice any kind of agriculture. Although most adult Hadza have lived in a settlement at some point in time, such experiences have been short-term and have not prevented them from continuing their foraging lifestyle and maintaining much of their traditional culture.[101]

With respect to sex and relationships, the woman is in charge. A man and a woman stay together for a few years, then they split up and find other mates. Most Hadza go through several partners in a lifetime. There is no marriage or divorce. If a woman doesn't like the way a man treats her, she simply leaves him. Occasionally, a man has more than one wife. While rare, this isn't forbidden by the culture. Children are well cared for within the groups, and men seem to be very interested in the welfare of all children. The Hadza are not particularly concerned with paternity:

100   Frank Marlowe, "Why the Hadza are Still Hunter-Gatherers," in *Ethnicity, Hunter-Gatherers, and the "Other,"* edited by Susan Kent (2002), p. 252.

101   Ibid., p.255

Up to 5% of Hadza women marry men from neighboring cultures.
Often after a Hadza woman does marry an outsider and
has a child, she leaves him and returns to raise the child in a
Hadza camp. This may well be because Hadza women are too
independent to put up with the sort of treatment they get from
non-Hadza men. When they do return, they do not experience
any noticeable stigmatism.[102]
The children of such outside marriages are treated no differently.

One recurring theme among the Hadza people as well as other hunter-
gathering peoples is the independence of women. How does a husband
control a woman when she provides as much or more of the calories as the
man and she can roam anywhere she likes? She is not seen as property and
has as much support and freedom within the community as any man. She
is seen as an independent sexual person from adolescence, with full rights
to choose whom she likes.

## Mangaians of Polynesia

In Polynesia, sex-positive,[103] egalitarian cultures thrived for thousands of
years. The Mangaians are good examples. They are a fishing and gardening
society on an isolated island in the South Pacific. Sex within the culture is
seen as positive in most respects, with a focus on sexual pleasure, particularly
female satisfaction and multiple orgasms. Romantic love is not necessarily
linked to sex. There are few restrictions, and most of those are on the kings
and queens or elites.

Mangaian youths do not date. There is no gradual increase of intimacy
beginning with kissing, necking and petting. For the youth, coitus is the
expected outcome of the intimate encounter.

According to Donald Marshall, a cultural anthropologist, fewer than
one out of one hundred girls or boys have not had "substantial sexual
experience."[104] Young people are encouraged to have as many partners as

102   Ibid., p. 256

103   Sex positivity is an attitude towards human sexuality that regards all consensual sexual activities
as fundamentally healthy and pleasurable, and encourages sexual pleasure and experimentation.

104   Marshall, D.S. in *Human Sexual Behavior: Variations in the Ethnographic Spectrum*, (1971),
edited by Robert C. Suggs , p. 103.

possible prior to marriage. Masturbation is seen as normal and encouraged.[105] After a boy goes through supercision,[106] he is taught sexual techniques in great detail by a male mentor. Also, as he becomes sexually active, he is expected to know a great deal about female anatomy. Young Mangaian males (early teens to early twenties) average three orgasms per night, seven nights a week. At 28 years of age, they average two orgasms per night, five to six times a week. The expectation is that the male will strive to have his partner have two to three orgasms to his one.[107]

Before Western contact, Mangaian women were seen as sexually equal, even superior to men. Women could expect their lovers to please her, and they might also wish to play with other women from time to time. Mangaian religion was not heavily involved in sex and sexuality. Little or no evidence exists of sexual prohibitions based on religion. What the initial English missionaries found looked nothing like their Victorian sexuality so they worked hard to infect the culture with the restrictive practices and ideas of Christianity.

In present-day Mangaian culture, Christianity has taken over, but missionaries have largely failed in their attempts to impose religious sexual values. Christian sexual guilt and shame do not infect the Mangaians. Premarital sex is still widely practiced. The purpose of sex is still seen as largely recreational.

### The Na of China

Hunter-gatherers gave way to societies that farmed or gardened while hunting or herding. When the soil was depleted, they moved on with their herds. The Na is such a culture.

The Na, also called the Mosuo, are a tribe of about 40,000 who live on the border of the Yunnan and Sichuan provinces in China. They are particularly interesting in this context because they seem to break many of our religious notions about marriage and childrearing.

---

105    Worell, J. in *Encyclopedia of Women and Gender: sex similarities and differences, Vol.1* (2002), p. 295..

106    A partial cutting of the foreskin of the penis but not like circumcision. It is mainly practiced in Polynesian cultures.

107    Noted by Donald Symons in *The Evolution of Human Sexuality*, (1981), p. 263.

The Na do not practice marriage – their language does not even have a word for husband or wife. In the Na culture, boys and girls pass directly from childhood to adulthood at puberty. Upon achieving adulthood, they are sexually free. The Na are matriarchal, as kinship is traced through the mother, and most people develop close relationships with maternal aunts and uncles. In matriarchal societies, women lead in different ways than men in a patriarchy. Women are more consultative and cooperative in decision-making; control of others is not the objective, but rather harmony and a prosperous family for all. It bears some similarities to the bonobo chimp matriarchal system discussed in Chapter 9.

The girl's residence is the primary place for sex. A man always visits a woman, but he must be out of the house by morning. Men and women do not live together. Fatherhood is unimportant. A child is raised by his mother in the home of her mother. The uncles are the male figures in the child's life. The mother may not know or care who the father is. Women guard their sexual freedom as do the men. The number of lovers a person has can be a point of pride, though not something that is openly discussed.

Within the family, women can talk to other women about their sexual experiences as do men to men, but it is considered improper to discuss sex in mixed company. The Na women are famous for their openness to sex, even with people outside their tribe. Marco Polo visited them in 1265 and wrote, "They do not consider it objectionable for a foreigner, or any other man, to have his way with their wives, daughters, sisters, or any other women in their home."[108] Being a macho Italian, Polo failed to realize that it was the women who chose to enjoy the foreigners.

The Na show us that humans are not programmed for any particular sexual arrangement. Women can be as independent as men in matters of sex, and healthy successful childrearing does not require a Western-style family. Finally, the Na cannot be easily classified into any of our preconceived relationship types. Men and women are equal in almost every way.

The Na people are very religious and follow a form of Buddhism as well as their own ancient religion, Dabaism. It has many gods, including the rain, mountain and cave gods. Many deities are genderless, but some of the most important gods are gendered. As with many cultures, their gods

---

108    As noted in Ryan and Jetha's *Sex at Dawn: How We Mate, Why We Stray, and What it Means for Modern Relationships*, (2007), p. 127.

reflect the sexual power dynamics of the culture. The sun is female and the moon male.[109] The primary deity of the Na is a goddess, Gemu.[110]

In the 1950s, the Chinese government attempted to force the Na to marry. The government put pressure on the tribe in many cruel ways. Chinese communism is notoriously conservative with respect to sex, even prudish, just as the major religions, so the ways of the Na were seen as being out of line with the dogma. In recent years, the government has relaxed control and pressure, and, as a result, the Na reverted back to their original sexual practices.[111]

### Religious Dogma and Sex

The major religions have many dogmatic ideas about marriage, childrearing and sexuality. They also make claims about human nature and sexuality. They proclaim that a child must be raised by two opposite-sex parents, that sexual activity before marriage will harm the marriage, that marriage is essential for the greatest human happiness, that masturbation is unnatural, that women must be subordinate to men, etc. They say that without religious sexual control, humans will run amok, behaving immorally and without regard to families and children.

Among these three cultures we can see that none of these dogmas hold water. People have lived happily and productively for thousands of years without the sexual, marital and childrearing practices of Jesus, Mohammed, Joseph Smith or Buddha. Comparing these cultures with our own, we can see that modern religions make claims about human nature and sex that are not supported by the data. Even if we cannot say exactly what human sexuality is, it definitively is not what Western religions claim.

109   *Encyclopedia of Sex and Gender: Men and Women in the World's Cultures*, edited by Carol R. Ember and Melvin Ember, (2003), p. 702.

110   Ibid., p. 608.

111   Ibid., p. 704.

# CHAPTER 12:

# SEX AND EARLY RELIGION

*How did the religion of early agricultural societies impact sex?*

## Elimination of Hunter-Gatherer Religion

The transition from hunter-gatherer to agriculturalist took place rapidly in the fertile crescent in Iran and Iraq, and other places like China and India, more than 9,000 years ago. Since farming can increase food availability by 100 times and can support 100 times more people, the farmers quickly outpaced the birth rate of foragers, resulting in steady encroachment of agriculture upon hunter-gathering groups.

The conflict between foragers and farmers and herders has played out over the world for 10,000 years. Throughout the 20th century, scholars debated, "What happened to the Europeans who inhabited Europe before agriculture?" Some thought they learned farming from the neighboring groups and eventually became farmers themselves, but a 2009 study of ancient European DNA from graves over 7,500 years old concluded:

> … there is little evidence of a direct genetic link between the hunter-gatherers and the early farmers. Today's Europeans share few if any of the genes found in the early Europeans.[112]

It is a recurring theme: farmers don't integrate with hunter-gatherers; they eliminate them.

Invading farmers rarely adopt the cultural practices of those they replace. The result is a totally new set of sexual and religious practices. Even if a fraction of the people survive the farmer invasion, the religions don't. The religion of the Great Plains Indians in the United States did not survive; Christianity took over. Tribal religions of Afganistan in the 800s CE did not survive; Islam took over. This change is especially true of sexual practices and gender relationships with invading religions.

Among hunter-gathering societies, social and political equality between the sexes is more common. In 74.3% of foraging societies, a married couple can live with either side of the family.[113] Foraging groups tend to trace lineage through both parents.

This all makes sense if marriage is fluid, even unofficial, but this pattern changes decisively with agriculture. Property ownership made a huge impact on human societies. The focus of human activity changed to support the massive population load that came with more food. Equality between the

---

112   Bramanti B, et al. (2009). "Genetic discontinuity between local hunter-gatherers and Central Europe's first farmers." *Science*, 326(137).

113   Marlowe, F. (2004). "Marital Residence among Foragers," *Current Anthropology*, 45(2).

sexes became far less common. Women began having children every two years rather than every four, and children became important for labor. Farmers had to acquire and defend their land, plant and harvest crops, and build storage areas for produce and animals. All of this requires a concentration of labor and resources very different from hunter-gatherers.

Marriage was much more structured among landowners and not as structured among those who were not owners. Control of the land depended on control of the children, who would inherit it. This, in turn, meant sexual control of the wife. While the Hadza woman may decide to have a new husband or have a dalliance with another man, such thinking was taboo in agricultural societies. The landowner's children must inherit the land, not some interloper.

## Religion and Sex in Early Agricultural Civilizations

All cultures seem to have some kind of taboos and restrictions on sex and sexuality, varying from extreme to almost non-existent. We will look at three ancient agricultural cultures that predated modern religion to see what sexual practices they had and how religion influenced them.

### Sacred Prostitutes and Gay Soldiers: Greek Sex

Ancient Greece was an agricultural and class-based society. The upper classes had large land holdings, the lower classes worked small plots and the slave class served both the land owners and the government.

Upper-class men tended not to marry until their 30s, and women were kept sequestered until marriage. As a result, prostitution was an important, even honorable, institution. Prostitutes were both male and female, and men might visit both. Not only was prostitution legal, Greek cities often owned and regulated houses of prostitution. For example, the great Athenian states-man Solon used tax money from brothels to finance a temple to Aphrodite. At some times and places in the Greek world, sacred prostitutes were part of some religious rituals and requirements.

The view of women was summarized by Demosthenes, "We have courtesans for pleasure, concubines to provide for our daily needs, and our spouses to give us legitimate children and to be the faithful guardians of our homes."[114] At the same time, the law dealt severely with women who had sex outside of marriage.

Older Greek men often had sexual relationships with boys and younger men. In military life, soldiers generally mentored boys. During his training, the boy might perform sexual services for his mentor. Once a man came of age, he was expected to marry, have children and perhaps take on a boy himself. Same-sex relations among equals was discouraged.

The gods of Greece were overtly sexual. They had sex, marriage, illicit lovers, illegitimate children and much more. They raped other gods, had sex with humans and murdered or harmed one another over sex and sexual partners. The whole drama of human sex was played out in Greek religion, a mirror of Greek sexual practices, mores and taboos.

As with many contemporary agricultural societies, Greek religion and sex were closely connected to the requirements of agriculture. Women were seen as inferior and under the control and ownership of their husbands or fathers. Upper-class women were expected to stay in the house and out of sight, whereas lower-class women might be seen going about their daily chores and duties in the streets. Women had little political power, and arranged marriages were the norm.

Greek religious practices were quite different from those of Christianity and Islam with respect to sex and sexuality. Unlike modern religions, Greek religion had less impact on sex and sexuality. Sexual rules were more governed by the partriarchal need for control of property and progeny than by a god or gods. While one might strongly disagree with the treatment of both women and children, there was little in the way of religious guilt around sex, especially for men.

### Don't Love Your Wife Too Much: Roman Sex

Similar to the Greeks, Roman religion had little to say about sex. The ruling classes were concerned with paternity and modest and upright behavior. Married women were sexually restricted to their husbands, but husbands could have sex outside the marriage as long as it was not with a married woman. Not surprisingly, prostitution was a common part of Roman society. Homosexual behavior between peers was strongly sanctioned, but a master could have sex with a slave or male prostitute.

114		Pseudo-Demosthenes, *Against Neaera*, 122.

Too much love for one's wife was seen as a lack of masculinity. In fact, Pompey the Great was ridiculed by many in the Roman Senate for being too much in love with his wife.

With the discovery and excavation of the buried city of Pompeii in 1748, much was learned about Roman sex, especially pornography. Elaborate sexual scenes were found on the walls of homes and houses of prostitution, indicating the Romans enjoyed visual stimulation as much as Internet porn viewers today.

Roman religion was a conglomerate of religious ideas and gods from Greek, Etruscan and other cultures. The head of the family was responsible for deciding which gods to worship and ensuring the gods were satisfied. There was still great superstition, as in the wide practice of astrology, but no monolithic religious structure dominated Rome until the ascendance of Christianity in the 300s CE.

Nevertheless, there were brief periods of sexual repression, such as when Augustus (63 BCE to 14 CE) attempted to reign in the adulterous upper and middle classes. He used religious justifications, in part, but it did not last long, and he had trouble following his own laws.

With the rise of Christianity, sexual repression began in earnest. Christian writers in the late imperial period had a fixation on sex and sexuality. They railed against pagan sexual behavior and championed such concepts as the virgin birth and celibacy.

From the Greeks and Romans, we can see a well-formed agricultural pattern of sexuality. Religion is not a major influence over sexual practices, though religion does support concepts like male superiority and sacred prostitution.

### Yin and Yang But Only for Men: Chinese Culture

Any number of sexual ideas and theories were developed and practiced in ancient China. But around 1000 CE, the culture became more conservative, and Confucianism almost took on the role that early Catholicism and later Puritanism played in the West. Sexual texts were suppressed and destroyed, and public discussion and display of sexual ideas and art was discouraged. As a result, Chinese culture lost sexual art and ideas for 1,000 years. Scholars are only now discovering some of the lost texts and artwork of the pre-Confucian era. In 1999, a Chinese sex museum was established in Hong Kong.[115] It was very controversial and was almost closed down several times. Its exhibits contain sexual toys, sexual art, sex texts and much more. It represents an entire cultural heritage that was otherwise unknown to modern Chinese.

The idea of an exchange of energy between the man and the woman was prevalent in Chinese sexual beliefs, especially in Taoism. A certain kind of sex with a specific kind of woman was thought to revitalize the man. Further, specific sexual positions and practices, if properly done, were thought to prevent or cure illness and extend the man's life and health. The woman's pleasure and excitement was important for the proper exchange of Yin and Yang. Unfortunately, this slowly came to focus less on the woman and more on the man. Ultimately, the practices treated women as objects through which men could achieve greater life and health.

The religious beliefs were related to the notion of heaven and earth. These were represented in men and women as separate aspects of heaven and earth and reunified in the sex act. It was also believed that in order to send life force, called Qi, to the brain, men must not ejaculate inside the woman. These ideas changed and evolved for two thousand years and were not universally accepted or practiced at all times and places.

Pre-Confucian Chinese culture integrated religion and sex to a larger degree than either Greece or Rome, but the pattern was still agricultural with male dominance and ownership and inheritance issues being tantamount.

### Where Are the Women?

In almost all agricultural societies, women are relegated to the back room. Greece and Rome were not friendly places for women and by today's standards would be characterized as misogynistic. Chinese sexual ideas, while interesting and somewhat in line with actual human biology, were not particularly friendly to women either and gradually became more male focused.

### The Scope of Human Sexuality

Preagricultural societies engaged in sexual practices spanning the full spectrum of sexuality. With the advent of agriculture, sexual options narrowed

---

115  For more information about the Ancient China Sex Culture Museum, see http://www.regenttour.com/chinaplanner/sha/sha-sights-sex.htm.

the role of women and became more constricted and restricted. Our analysis could go on across many more agricultural societies, including Maya, Inca, Egyptian, Indian, etc., but the results are all the same.

This brief survey of cultures shows the breadth of human sexual ideas and practices compared to the current religious environment. It also shows the roots of male dominance in agriculture that influences today's religions.

Humans are capable of a wide range of sexual behaviors. We may tend to practice certain sexual styles, but those tendencies can and are shaped by the culture we live in. For example, we may have a genetic tendency toward polygyny as a species, but not as strongly as gorillas – besides, our religious map tries to push us closer to or farther away from our biological map.

As we have seen in our discussion of other species and of different cultures, humans do not seem to have a strongly predetermined sexual style. We are not gibbons that live in comparative isolation and have one mate for life, although some people do that. We are not gorillas with many wives where the male shows grand displays of aggression to keep competing males away, although some people and cultures have that configuration. We are not chimps with their male displays of dominance and multiple mating systems, although we have individuals and cultures that value aggression and dominance over other males and females. Finally, we are not bonobos with females that rule the roost and keep male aggressive tendencies in line, but there have been many cultures with that approach. We are all and none of these. Humans are the most sexually flexible mammals on the planet.

Within this wide range of sexuality, tribal religions existed for tens of thousands of years. Each tribe had its unique set of sexual practices. Two cultures with very different sexual practices could exist almost side-by-side, each justifying its norms with religious stories that were centuries old. For example, the matriarchal/matrilineal Hopi and Navaho lived in the geographic vicinity of the patriarchal/patrilineal Apache. The practices of each were thought to be a product of their godlike ancestors. Before modern religion, sexual practices throughout the world showed no evidence of a biologically predetermined pattern.

Next, we will look at how development of the major religions changed all of this, creating a set of practices and beliefs that prohibit and preclude the full range of sexuality.

# CHAPTER 13:

## MODERN RELIGIONS AND THE MISOGYNY OF GOD

Religions have systematized violence against women for thousands of years. What is the cost of this repression?

*"Let your women keep silence in the churches: for it is not permitted unto them to speak; but they are commanded to be under obedience, as also saith the law."*

**1 Corinthians 14:34 KJV**

## Double Standards

The most sexually restrictive cultures have strong double standards for male and female behavior. Women and men are supposed to act in prescribed ways, with men allowed more leeway and freedom in many cases. For example, a woman is often blamed when she is raped. The laws often make it difficult, if not impossible, to prove rape, and the man is assumed to have been lured and tempted by the woman. In sexually repressive cultures, women are always more oppressed than men.

Islam, Judaism, Buddhism and Christianity all claim that their laws and rules around sexuality are necessary to control the evils of sexual sin – humans simply cannot be trusted to control themselves without religious restrictions. But what is really going on? We know from examples of other cultures like the Na and Hadza that people do quite well in their sex lives without religious restrictions.

Most sex-positive cultures don't seem to have problems with rape or sexual abuse, for example. Why are rape and sexual exploitation such terrible problems in many religious cultures and not in the less religious ones? In the sexually uptight Hindu, Muslim and Christian cultures, sexual exploitation is a major problem. Is religion actually encouraging and supporting abuse toward women and children? Does the assumed moral superiority of men give cover for abusive behavior?

## Western Religious Distortions

We look in horror at the murderous sexual laws of Saudi Arabia today: women and men are publicly executed for adultery; women are publicly whipped for violating the strict dress codes of the kingdom; religious police have the power to condemn and punish even the smallest sexual indiscretion. These laws and practices are barbaric, but they are remarkably similar to those of Israel in 500 BCE. They are the laws of a monotheistic, patriarchal religion that has eliminated the female role from the pantheon forever. Whether the male Jewish Yahweh, Allah or Christian Jesus, there is no room for female gods, and the feminine is to be suspected, devalued and feared. This is very different from almost every agricultural religion that came before. Greek, Roman, Parthian, Indian, Egyptian, Persian and most other agricultural religions had female gods, often related to human, animal or crop fertility. We will discuss this transition in the next chapter, but for now, let's look at the effects this new monotheistic approach had on sexuality.

## The Jewish Distortion

Early Jewish law, as among Muslims in Saudi Arabia today, had a constant message of female uncleanliness. How did that impact young Jewish women and girls? How much did the message of male dominance in the home and total control over the children impact male and female sexual expression and development? A Jewish father had complete discretion over who and when his children could marry. How did that affect sexual development? How many women or daughters were beaten, ostracized, sold into slavery or executed for having sex before marriage? How many boys were berated and beaten for masturbating? How many homosexual men were put to death under Jewish law for expressing their sexuality?

Of all the possible avenues for sexual expression, Jewish children could choose from a very narrow set. To step outside of them meant punishment or banishment from the community, shame for the person and the family and guilt over the transgression against "god's laws."

When Judaism became monotheistic, it also eliminated sexuality from its deity. A single god has no sex partner – it is essentially asexual. Just as the Greek gods reflected the sexual mores and taboos of that society, the Jewish god reflected the sexual ideas of Jewish society.

For Judaism, a single god meant the ultimate domination of the masculine over the feminine in the culture. With this came stringent restrictions on sexual behavior, especially for women. Polygyny, which was widely practiced throughout Judaism among the upper classes, gradually changed to monogamy. Divorce became more difficult, especially for women, and sexual rules were abundant, as can be seen in Leviticus. From birth, women were seen as inferior. Menstruating and bearing children were seen as unclean. Even touching a woman during menstruation made another unclean. Here are examples of some of the Jewish laws:

> **Leviticus 15:19,** And if a woman have an issue, and her issue in her flesh be blood, she shall be put apart seven days: and whosoever toucheth her shall be unclean until the even.
>
> **12:5,** But if she bear a maid child, then she shall be unclean two weeks (one week for boys), as in her separation: and she shall continue in the blood of her purifying threescore and six days.

Prohibitions on sex during menstruation are common in many cultures, but the Jews take it to an extreme in this verse:

20:18, And if a man shall lie with a woman having her sickness, and shall uncover her nakedness; he hath discovered her fountain, and she hath uncovered the fountain of her blood: and both of them shall be cut off from among their people.

While males have fewer rules and restrictions, there are still plenty. For example, regarding masturbation:

15:16, And if any man's seed of copulation go out from him, then he shall wash all his flesh in water, and be unclean until the even.

So if he has a wet dream, he is unclean the rest of the day.

In all of these rules, we can see clear distortions of sexuality based on the idea of ritual cleanliness. These restrictions have no basis in biology, ethics or psychology, they are simply responses to ancient superstitions, based in patriarchal, agricultural society, and give religion control of sex and sexuality.

Non-agricultural tribes may have had similar taboos, but the menstruating woman was not necessarily treated like a pariah. Most hunter-gatherer societies also showed little concern about masturbation.

Many modern apologists claim that these religious rules were primitive ways to control the spread of disease, but ritual cleanliness was based in supernaturalism and had nothing to do with disease or germs. In many instances, ritual cleanliness actually promoted disease. For example, male circumcision using unsterilized instruments was dangerous. Even today, the risks are substantial. In 2005, Orthodox mohels using an ancient practice infected a number of babies with herpes, which is very dangerous to infants and some babies died.

Further, ritual washing was anything but clean. Ancient rituals used fonts, bowls or instruments that were never washed. While the water may have been replaced, the hands and instruments of ritual cleansing were never sterilized. What better way to spread water-borne diseases than to use the same bowl for days or even years without sterilization?

When Jews, Catholics, Muslims or any other group claim that ancient rituals prevented disease, they are speaking from a modern perspective. Ritual cleansing and cleanliness were totally unrelated to actual sanitary cleanliness. Ritual cleanliness is designed to protect the individual and community from contamination from deities and invisible powers and forces. When a woman brings two doves for a burnt offering, as in Leviticus 12:8, she is trying to rid herself of spiritual filth that comes from having a child and just being a woman.

In Judaism the notion of ritual purity is critical. Jewish culture, while having many food restrictions and taboos, placed much more emphasis on sexual purity than many other cultures. Looking at modern Judaism, it may be hard to believe that the harsh and specific penalties of Leviticus and other books were actually practiced, but we have only to look at the laws and practices of Saudi Arabia today to see what life was probably like in Israel in 500 BCE. Today a couple caught in adultery, for example, can be stoned to death or beheaded. Sounds exactly like Leviticus. There is no reason to believe Israel of that day was not like it is described in the Bible.

Judaism brought intense sexual control in the service of the patriarchal Yahweh god in order to propagate the religion. Jewish culture continued with this straitjacket until only a few hundred years ago when it slowly began to change. Still today, the more conservative forms of Judaism contain a good deal of sexual guilt and repression.

You may think that these old scriptures mean little today, that nobody stones people for adultery or sells errant daughters into slavery, but millions of Jews and Christians actually read these Old Testament books and believe that their god dictated the words. How can those words not have some impact?

## The Christian Distortion

By the first century CE, both Greek and Roman sexual views and practices had been circulating in and around Palestine for several centuries. The Jewish response was to tighten up the system to keep pagan practices from seeping into Judaism. The advent of Christianity came within this context. The apostle Paul led the new cult with a hyper-controlling sexuality.

Here is a list of verses from Paul. It is hard to see any positive sexuality in these:

> 1 Corinthians 6:9, Do you not know that the wicked will not inherit the kingdom of God? Do not be deceived: Neither the sexually immoral nor idolaters nor adulterers nor male prostitutes nor homosexual offenders.
>
> 1 Corinthians 6:15, Do you not know that your bodies are members of Christ himself? Shall I then take the members of Christ and unite them with a prostitute? Never!

**2 Corinthians 12:21**, I am afraid that when I come again my God will humble me before you, and I will be grieved over many who have sinned earlier and have not repented of the impurity, sexual sin and debauchery in which they have indulged.

**1 Thessalonians 4:5**, not in passionate lust like the pagans, who do not know God;

**2 Corinthians 6:14**, Do not be yoked together with unbelievers. For what do righteousness and wickedness have in common? Or what fellowship can light have with darkness?

**1 Timothy 2:11-15**, A woman should learn in quietness and full submission. I do not permit a woman to teach or to assume authority over a man; she must be quiet. For Adam was formed first, then Eve. And Adam was not the one deceived; it was the woman who was deceived and became a sinner. But women will be saved through childbearing – if they continue in faith, love and holiness with propriety.

While the statements of Jesus on sex and marriage were restrictive, Paul's became explicit. Women should keep their mouths shut and heads covered and defer to men in all things.

From the earliest Christian writings of the Ante-Nicene fathers, sexual repression was a recurring theme. Tertullian (150-230 CE), the great Christian apologist from Carthage, makes hundreds of sex-negative references about women. Here is his central idea:

Do you not know that you are each an Eve? The sentence of God on this sex of yours lives in this age: the guilt must of necessity live too. You are the Devil's gateway: You are the unsealer of the forbidden tree: You are the first deserter of the divine law: You are she who persuaded him whom the devil was not valiant enough to attack. You destroyed so easily God's image, man. On account of your desert even the Son of God had to die.

Tertullian, often called the father of Latin Christianity, is a revered saint of the Catholic church. He was also married. Imagine being this guy's wife! He is still studied and quoted by the highest church scholars and officials. Tertullian set the pace for sexual distortion with many others to follow, but he was also reflecting the already misogynistic environment of Christianity.

### Celibacy

One of the most incredible distortions of Christianity is celibacy of the clergy and others. Given that the Christian god is asexual, celibacy is seen as a way to achieve a kind of communion with the god. Paul writes:

> 1 Corinthians 7:8-9, Now to the unmarried and the widows I say: It is good for them to stay unmarried, as I do. But if they cannot control themselves, they should marry, for it is better to marry than to burn with passion.

On this and other passages, the Catholic church has built a justification for celibacy of the clergy. The result has been two thousand years of pedophilia, priests with mistresses, illegitimate children of priests and nuns, and Popes with illegitimate children and several "nieces" living in the Vatican.

When sex is suppressed, it tends to come out in strange places. Over the centuries, thousands have been executed throughout Europe by both Catholic and Protestant authorities for sodomy, witchcraft, homosexuality, adultery and bestiality. A total of 150,000 to 250,000 people, the majority of whom were women, were executed throughout Europe in the 16th century for crimes that frequently seemed to be related to sex or sexuality. How many of these people were executed because of the sexual paranoia of some celibate priest or sexually repressed Calvinist minister?

### The Muslim Distortion

Ayaan Hirsi Ali tells a number of heart-rending stories in her books, *Infidel* (2006) and *Nomad* (2010), about her journey from Somalia and Ethiopia to Europe and the United States. The themes are consistent: a woman's body belongs to men – father first, brothers and cousins second and, finally, her husband when she marries. She has little or no choice in the matter.

Islam is consumed with sex and sexuality; consumed with the suppression and control of female sexuality. To be Muslim is to be sexually pure, especially if you are a woman. Everything from masturbation to sex before or outside of marriage is forbidden for women. While there are also behaviors forbidden for men, the sex police tend to look the other way when men transgress. Mohammed himself allowed men to engage in sex while in foreign countries or serving in the armies of Allah. No such permission was given to women. On the contrary, for women to travel in a foreign country without a male escort was almost unheard of until very recently.

Having sexual relations with a non-Muslim woman does not taint a man. Infidel women are seen as less than human, and Allah gives Muslim men the right to use them. A Muslim man traveling from Saudi Arabia to Amsterdam may have no compunction about visiting the red-light district and engaging a prostitute or dating a Dutch woman. Should a Muslim woman have sex with an infidel, on the other hand, she is rendered impure, and in some Muslim countries, may pay with her life. If the legal system does not execute her, her family probably will.

In her memoir, *Nomad*, Ayaan Hirsi Ali tells this revealing story of her cousin, who came to America as a refugee. She fled her native country and at some point acquired AIDS. Unable to admit that she had ever had sex, she became involved with a European man but never told him she had AIDS. As a result, he too became infected. She was deeply shamed and felt that she should be stoned or beaten for sinning against Allah. When he confronted her about it, she accused him of giving it to her. Even then, she could not admit to him, or anyone, that she had engaged in sex and became infected before she met him.

In other stories, Ayaan Hirsi Ali tells of Muslim men who, when informed that they had AIDS, responded by saying, "I don't have that! I'm a Muslim! And Somali! We don't get Aydis (AIDS)!" The delusion and self-deception rooted in religious dogma facilitate the spread of both biological and religious viruses.

### An Invasive Species

When Islam swept out of the Arabian Peninsula, it became an invasive species to both the pagan and Christian areas it conquered. With it came the sexual practices of a very patriarchal, polygamist culture. While the religions it displaced were not particularly sex positive, Islamic sexual practices, on the whole, were uniformly sex negative.

The invasion of Islam into India led to the decline of some sex-positive religious practices, but to be fair, Hindu, Jain, Buddhist and other religions in the region were already very patriarchal and sex negative. Much of what the upper classes practiced in India was less restrictive than for the masses. For example, the early highly sexualized art of the period after 500 BCE was the result of royal patronage and polygyny among the ruling classes. In southern India, it was customary for most people – both men and women – to wear nothing above the waist in that hot climate, as is customary in many other hot climates. This changed with the conquests of the Muslim Moguls. Islamic sexualization of the female body required women to cover themselves, regardless of their religion. The result was a dramatic change in sexual attitudes and practices across India. Where local cultures had different dress and sexual practices, new pressures forced the population to dress "modestly" and restrict women's rights. Thus, Islam ensured that the culture was more uniformly sex negative.

With the coming of the British Empire and the collapse of the Mogul empire, Christianity infected India. While it did a poor job of converting people, it did a good job of reinforcing Christian sexual mores throughout India, especially on the aristocracy. What Islam started, Christianity finished. Today India is a bastion of sexual conservatism. All media are highly censored for sexual content, even kissing in public is forbidden as Richard Gere learned in 2007 when he kissed the Indian actress Shilpa Shetty on stage. An arrest warrant was issued for this infraction of public decency.[116] Does that sound like a culture that produced the Kama Sutra?

Wherever sexually restrictive religions invade, they bring the tools of repression with them – fear of punishment, shame if caught, guilt that the deity watches and terror of punishment. Islam, Christianity and Judaism, with their patriarchal, asexual god, have systematically overcome local sexual ideas throughout the world and infected cultures with sex-negative practices. Women and children are most affected, but it impacts men in many ways as well.

In this section we explored many different cultures and practices from hunter-gatherers to Greeks and Romans to the current major religions. Hunter-gatherer women were generally not seen as property and had much more freedom. Agriculture had a decided impact on sexual practices as a result of property ownership and labor needs. Today's religious sexual maps are deeply rooted in the property and inheritance ideas of ancient people.

In the next section we will look at the psychological tools these religions use to ensure sexual conformity. How does religion distort sexuality in our culture today? Why are religions so opposed to sex education? What happens to your sex life when you leave religion?

---

116  See "Arrest Warrant Issued for Richard Gere Over Kiss," *People Magazine*, 26 April 2007. Available online at http://www.people.com/people/article/0,,20036905,00.html.

# SECTION IV:
# THE PSYCHOLOGY OF RELIGION AND SEX

## CHAPTER 14:
## THE TOOLS OF DISTORTION

*Religion uses natural emotional, psychological and biological processes to distort and shape our sexuality.*

### The Rise of Universal Religions

Christianity was founded on sexual ideas and practices that were designed to create guilt and shame around what is a perfectly normal drive. As a result, when the Christian religion infects a culture, it immediately creates a sex-negative environment.

Tribal religions generally say nothing about other religions, except "my gods are better than your gods." They are specific to a given tribe and make no claim to universality. Religion and the culture are indistinguishable. One must be born into the culture to practice the religion.

The notion that there are universal religious principles that supersede any individual culture emerged around 600 BCE. Zoroastrianism may have been the first universal religion in the West. It grew, developed and declined in Persia from about 600 BCE to 100 BCE, but it continued to be a significant influence for another five hundred years. About the same time, Buddhism began in the East and spread rapidly, its universal message often replacing tribal religions wherever it went.

With Christianity in the first century and Islam in the seventh, universal religion became a permanent part of Western culture. Local custom and practice was superseded by the idea that a single god created humans with one sexual style. Obedience to that god meant following one narrow set of sexual practices; all others were sinful.

You may be thinking, "That fits Islam and Christianity, but not Buddhism." But in a practical sense, Buddhism functions much like any other religion. Mosr Buddhist monks and nuns are celibate. The current Dalai Lama follows the traditional Tibetan Buddhist assertion that inappropriate sexual behavior includes lesbian and gay sex, and any sex other than penis-vagina intercourse with one's own monogamous partner, including oral sex, anal sex, and masturbation.

The universal religions proposed a revolutionary idea, that religion supersedes culture. Behaving like an invasive species, universal religions decimated tribal religions and infected the minds of tribal cultures, often with the help of armies and diseases. The conquistadors of Spain not only brought armament and missionaries but also devastating diseases. The combination can be very convincing to a people.

One of the most important propagation methods was sex. We find examples of sexual practices similar to those of Christianty or Islam in many tribal cultures, but the idea of a Supreme Being capable of knowing your every thought and watching you at every moment was a huge step beyond what tribal religions claimed. Tribal religion looked more like a partnership between the tribe and its gods, although they could be as sex negative and oppressive as the universal religions. Universal religions enforced one sex-negative patriarchal standard on anyone infected with the religion, regardless of past tribal traditions and practices. As a result, as soon as a tribe adopted Christianity, for example, there was strong pressure for the tribe to adopt male dominance patterns even if the tribe was once matriarchal.

Whether the tribal religion was more sex positive or sex negative, it became much more sex negative when infected with the universal religion. To most tribal cultures, notions of sin, obedience, spiritual kingdoms, eternal life and heaven made little or no sense when people had lived thousands of years with local gods that brought them rain, crops, game and fertility. The Spanish missionaries worked for 150 years to convert the Hopi with little success. The Hopi eventually revolted, burning churches and killing priests. The Animists of the Sahel desert have successfully resisted conversion for centuries. The Celts of Northern Europe resisted infection for centuries and often secretly kept their rituals and beliefs long after their official conversion. The universal religions have little to offer these cultures. So how do they get converted?

## How Religion Uses Disease

Political and military power and disease led to conversion. Islam swept out of Saudi Arabia and imposed its will on the great, but weak and failing, Persian empire. In the process, it largely supplanted Zoroastrianism. The Persian empire was famously tolerant of all religions, but with Islam's conquest, local populations were coerced into conversion because non-Muslim tribes were taxed and their influence limited.

Disease was the best ally of Western religions as they sought to infect new cultures. When explorers and missionaries arrived in North and South America, they brought foreign viruses and germs. Conservative estimates are that 80% of the population was killed over just a few decades.[117] Measles, influenza and small pox combined to devastate entire nations. One well-

---

117   Jared Diamond provides this estimate in *Guns, Germs, and Steel: the Fates of Human Societies*, (1997), p 357.

documented example was the Wyandotte (Huron) tribe. In the 1630s, smallpox killed over half of its people.[118]

Many tribes interpreted this devastation as abandonment by their gods, and the missionaries encouraged such thinking. Just as the small pox or measles attacked the immune system of individuals, Christianity attacked the cultural immune system of these tribes. In this way, the population of much of the Western hemisphere was converted or eliminated.

In the cultures that were not eliminated, the survivors quickly learned that following the god of the conquerors was the best way to avoid future disaster. Much of the message sent by both Islam and Christianity was about abandoning old sexual practices and adopting those of the new religion. Missionaries to Hawaii preached that the devastating epidemics of cholera, measles and gonorrhea were part of divine judgment. From 1779 to 1848, up to 80% of the population died of Western diseases, inadvertently brought by the missionaries and traders.

Once converted, people's enthusiasm for their new religion could be remarkable. Hence, the Maori of New Zealand are much more fervently Presbyterian or Mormon than the island's European descendants. Central American Indians practice Catholicism more devoutly than the Spanish who initially gave them the religious disease. Blacks in the United States are more devoutly Christian than the whites who held them in slavery.

The religious conversion process continues today, and it is tied closely to sex. In Africa, Catholics and Evangelicals preach that condoms do not work. Those who distribute condoms or teach their use are vilified as instruments of the devil, encouraging people to have sex. The message is, "You will die of AIDS if you do not conform to Christian notions of monogamy." When people get AIDS, it is seen as evidence of sinful behavior and divine retribution for not following Jesus.

Throughout history, religion and illness have worked together. Through prayer, religion promises healing from disease and heaven if the disease wins. In every way, religion wins. All too often doctors don't get credit because missionaries say god guided the doctor's hand. Missionary doctors are among the worst at spreading this idea.

---

118   See, for example, Ronald Robertson's discussion in *Rotting face: smallpox and the American Indian*, (2001), pp.107-108.

## Death Neurosis and Sex

Many hunter-gatherer tribes have no afterlife concept. The idea of an "afterlife" probably caught on with agriculture and took on many different forms. It may mean reincarnation as a lower or higher being, eternal torture or bliss, promise of heaven and many virgins, or your own planet. There are many afterlife ideas and little agreement on what it may be.

Why do the major religions focus on the afterlife? What benefit do they derive? How is it tied into sex?

With the concept of an afterlife, religion creates a portal to infect people by means of terror and fear of death. Recall our discussion of the Toxic Trio in Chapter 1. If one has no concept of an afterlife, then fear of eternal punishment means nothing. But once one is thoroughly indoctrinated with the idea of living forever, then the fear of torture and punishment becomes an effective way to convince people of the need to perform specific rituals and live a certain way.

It is a brilliant psychological tool that leads to death neurosis, an excessive or irrational fear of death. As conscious beings, we are capable of understanding that we will die some day. We also have the ability to imagine a world after we die. Religion hijacks this ability and injects fear of eternal torture and abandonment as well as the promise of eternal bliss. A perfect carrot and stick approach. The ability to imagine what is beyond the horizon of death is what allows religion to take control and make us do unnatural things.

People who have a death neurosis will spend fortunes building monuments to their god. They will pray and ask invisible beings to help them escape punishment. They may pay priests, auditors, ministers or imams huge sums to ensure they get into the next level or go to heaven, etc.

A neurotic person behaves in unnatural ways. Once one is convinced of the idea of eternal life or death, the person may do almost anything to achieve the reward or avoid the punishment. He may fly an airplane into a building or become a missionary to another country. She may become a celibate nun or vow to raise a quiver full of children and homeschool them according to her religion. At the very least, the person will attend church regularly, give money, pray and do other things to ensure good standing with the deity. The root of this action is the hope for a reward and avoidance of punishment.

The entire edifice of the major religions rests on the concept of an afterlife. To make the idea stick in the minds of the followers, there must be an omniscient being who audits your thoughts and behavior to determine if you conformed sufficiently to the rituals and proscriptions to be given the reward or if you failed to do so and, therefore, are sent to punishment or oblivion. This creates the notion of a god watching all the time. It is simple to convince a small child that Jesus is watching her, that angels are present or that some god audits her thoughts. Children already believe that adults have huge powers; it's not hard to believe that a god does as well.

Using the death neurosis, religion ties your sexual thoughts and behavior to possible reward or punishment. In essence, it says, "You will die eternal death if you have the wrong kind of sex," extending our natural fear of death into our sex life. What is the psychological effect on a person when he is taught all his life that sex is not only bad but leads to death? How much does death programming lead to sexual dysfunction, fear of sex, sexual impotence and the fear of having too much fun in bed?

As we have seen in earlier chapters, the primary purpose of the human sex drive is to connect people to one another and to the culture. Death neurosis disrupts the joy of sex and reduces the connection that sex brings to people. Loss of positive sexual connection has consequences, including depression and inappropriate sexual expression.

### Scandalous Breasts: How Religion Sexualizes the Normal

Humans love sex. Both men and women are wired to be sexually responsive. Sex is the social glue of the human species. It takes heavy-handed training or trauma to kill a human's sex drive.

Religion has that power. Sexual training in guilt, shame and fear begins virtually at birth by sexualizing nudity. The religious signal is that nudity is always sexual and the body must be covered for modesty. The Adam and Eve story is taught to young children even though they have no way to know what it means.

Next comes the sexualization of breastfeeding. Most tribal religions pay little or no attention to a mother nursing a child. With the religious fear of nudity, however, breastfeeding is carefully hidden. Thus, one of the most natural things a human can do is turned into something shameful. A simple Web search of "breastfeeding scandals" yields a trove of controversy over this simple and natural act. Read the anti-breastfeeding comments, and it is quickly apparent that many people see it as a sexual act or a provocation, partly because it is associated with bodily pleasure.

Breastfeeding was not seen as sexual in earlier Christian culture. Medieval and Renaissance religious art is replete with pictures of Mary breastfeeding Jesus. If we are to take that as an indication of the attitude to breastfeeding in that day, it appears that breastfeeding was not sexualized.

Hundreds of statues in U.S. courthouses and capitols contain the "blind lady of justice" with one breast showing. It is often a classical Greek or Roman likeness that was virtually unnoticed for decades until in 2002, when then U.S. attorney general, John Ashcroft, ordered a statue in the U.S. Justice Department covered. Perhaps, he felt it was pornographic. The art deco statue has stood since the 1930s in the Justice Department and one day the extremely religious Protestant attorney general decides it is pornographic. This is the same mentality as the Taliban in Afghanistan or Muslims in India or Pakistan destroying ancient Hindu or Buddhist art because it shows nudity.

Such is the mindset of large puritanical segments of all the major religions. Whether Hindu, or Muslim, Protestant or Catholic, these groups thrive on demonizing sex. These, among many other signals, infect children and sexualize things that are not necessarily sexual.

## Religion and Physical Marking

For thousands of years, cultures have used physical marking and circumcision to denote membership in the group. Many religions have adopted this practice to signal religious membership and mark the child from birth or early adolescence. It is no coincidence that the primary marking method of Judaism, Islam and Christianity deals with male sex organs primarily and female sex organs less often. Many cultures use tattoos, scarification or other markings, but these religions have reduced the ritual marking of children to the genitals. It is a strong indication that sex and sexuality belong to the religion and supersede local cultural ideas.

## Male Circumcision

Many religions attempt to mark children from an early age. While the psychological indoctrination is insidious, the physical marking can be horrendous. Male circumcision is seen as "normal" among Christians and is mandatory in Judaism and much of Islam. For Islam and Judaism, it marks one as a member. The uncircumcised may be considered unclean and may not be allowed to marry members of the religion.

An atheist couple who are cultural Jews refused to circumcise their boy. While both sets of grandparents are not religious, they were extremely upset, leading to disruption of communication between the parents and grandparents for many months. The message from the grandparents was, "Be an atheist if you want, but get your child circumcised so he can remain a member of the tribe."

In male circumcision, Jewish parents are making the choice that their child will be Jewish. While some Jewish groups, including humanistic and reformed Jews, have declared that circumcision is not necessary for Jewish identity, that is not the stance of orthodox and other conservative Jewish groups. In one television interview about circumcision, one rabbi stated, "It's painful, it's abusive, it's traumatic, and if anybody does it who isn't in a covenant, they ought to be put in prison … I do abusive things because I'm in covenant with god."[119]

It is an amazing admission that belief in an invisible, voyeuristic god gives license for criminal abuse of an infant.

In many Muslim communities, male circumcision is considered a sunnah, or practice instituted by Mohammed himself. Parents who refuse to circumcise their boy would be seen as unfaithful Muslims and could be ostracized or in danger. It is a permanent mark forced on the child by a religion he did not voluntarily join.

In addition, Muslim male circumcision is most generally done when the boy is around 12 years old. The pain and trauma of infant circumcision may not be remembered later in life, but it is for a 12-year-old. How is that not mutilation? How much does that affect the boy? In my family I have seen the damage this practice does. My grandmother forced my father to become circumcised when he was 12. It traumatized him at the time and left an emotional scar for the rest of his life. Even discussing it later in life, it brought back painful memories that he associated with his sexuality.

Circumcision was not common among Christians in North America until around 1900 when several threads of thought came together to increase and encourage its practice. Religious concern over adolescent masturbation

---

119   From the film *Cut: Slicing Through the Myths of Circumcision.* For additional information, see http://www.cutthefilm.com/Cut_Website/ Home.html.

led John Harvey Kellogg[120] to start a campaign for circumcision. He believed that circumcision decreased male adolescent response and inhibited male masturbation.

Other religious groups started preaching that an uncircumcised penis is dirty and unclean. While they often used fallacious medical arguments to convince parents to circumcise their children, the roots of the idea were religious. The fact that women bought into this idea and were often the persons making the decision to circumcise their sons meant that they began to see the uncircumcised penis as unclean. They passed the idea along to their daughters. Today, many women will not date an uncircumcised man. Some on-line dating sites even ask if the man is circumcised.

## Female Circumcision, Genital Mutilation

Female circumcision was practiced by tribes in the Arabian peninsula at the time of Mohammed. According to the Hadith, Mohammed apparently approved of the practice, though he cautioned against severe mutilation. The practice was adopted as a way to mark a woman as a Muslim, subject to Allah, her male family members and eventually her husband.

Some Islamic authorities believe that Mohammed was very clear in his instruction for both men and women to be circumcised.[121] Others argue that the practice is not a commandment or Sunnah from the Prophet. In any case, those who practice it today do it as a religious requirement based on dogma. While it may not have originated with Islam, it has become an integral part of the religious practice in many regions tied to notions of male dominance and control of female sexuality.

An estimated three million girls worldwide are subjected to genital mutilation and 500,000 in the immigrant communities of Europe.[122] Various

---

120   Of Kellogg cereal fame.

121   The following is often quoted as justification for female circumcision: "Um Atiyyat al-Ansariyyah said: A woman used to perform circumcision in Medina. The Prophet (pbuh) said to her: 'Do not cut too severely as that is better for a woman and more desirable for a husband'" (see http://www.religioustolerance.org/fem_cirm.htm). A recent example is referenced in the article "Cleric Says Female Circumcision Recommended by Islam" available online at http://www.rudaw.net/english/culture_art/3347.html.

122   World Health Organization, UNICEF, UNFPA, et al. "Eliminating Female genital mutilation: An interagency statement," Geneva, 1997, updated 2008. Available online at http://web.unfpa.org/upload/lib_pub_file/756_filename_fgm.pdf. In addition, see *Onze verborgen tranen* (Our Hidden Tears), (2005), by Waris Dirie.

forms of female circumcision are practiced by different communities; nevertheless, the practice always involves cutting a woman's genitalia in ways thought to reduce or eliminate sexual desire. The procedure is most generally done without anesthesia to girls age 10-12. They are kept in the dark about the procedure and may be deceived into thinking it is harmless and painless until the day it is done. It is difficult to describe such a process in words, but others have written about it in great detail. For example, Ayaan Hirsi Ali in her book *Nomad* gives an excellent, though horrifying, description based on her own experience.

The practice of female circumcision has grown in recent decades. Communities in Africa that never practiced it have been infected with more fundamentalist Islamic ideas that include stronger control of women. Further, the rapid increase of the practice in European Muslim communities is seen as a product of fundamentalist immigrants spreading conservative religious ideas. It is also seen as an attempt to control Muslim girls who may be tempted to become secular.

The practice has no value except in the context of religious control of women. In many African countries, it is illegal but often tolerated by authorities that look the other way. In Europe, entire Islamic communities conspire to hide the practice from the authorities, making it hard to find and prosecute.

### Distorting the Sexual Map

From fear of death to sexualizing the normal and marking children, religion is hell bent on creating an environment that is sexually negative – an environment that systematically and arbitrarily restricts options for people. Regardless of the biological map of an individual, religion will do its best to impose its map. The map is almost always focused on what *not* to do. Since humans can rarely, if ever, live up to such a restrictive standard, it gives religion a huge opportunity to develop guilt and shame, leading the person back to the religion for relief. **The map bears no resemblance to human sexuality.** It is an artificial and arbitrary set of rules imposed by the religion on its adherents. The result is oppression of women, sexual misinformation, fear of death, repression of homosexuals and much more.

# CHAPTER 15:

# DON'T TAMPER WITH THE FACTORY!

*Each religion has its own unique distortion pattern. The pattern combines with the historical and ethnic roots of the adherents to create their sexual map. Such a map is filled with conflicts that lead to guilt, shame and anxiety, all of which influence behavior and sexual satisfaction.*

### Sex Education, the Biggest Threat to Religion

When should a person start having sex? Religious groups are pretty clear about this one. You should have sex only after you are married and only with the person you are married to. But what they profess and what they do are two different things. Religion does not stop adolescents from having sex; it only makes them feel bad about the sex they do have. If they feel guilty, they will keep coming back to their church to get relief from the guilt the religion taught them.

A decade of research shows that religiosity has little or no impact on the onset of sexual activity. From masturbation to petting to oral sex and intercourse, religious kids start about the same time as secular children. U.S. government research on abstinence-only programs comes to the same conclusion.[123] Religious training delays sexual activity by months at best.

Why do religions preach against sex before marriage? They say it is to prevent disease and pregnancy. Some try to convince teens that sex before marriage damages the marriage later. Others say, "God says sex is sinful outside of marriage and you will burn in hell for violating god's law." Mormons and Muslims say sex is a sacred possession of woman that she gives only to her husband. These ideas inject guilt and shame into the young victim.

Open, fact-based sex education is among the biggest threats to religion. Knowing the facts about sex reveals the myths that religions preach. That is why most religions oppose secular sex education. Sex education also raises very uncomfortable questions for religious parents. Thus, good sex education will reveal that most people, including one's parents, masturbate, have sex before marriage, experiment with same sex partners, fantasize and use porn.

The vast majority of religious parents had sex before marriage, yet preach abstinence loudly to their children. It is rare that parents ever let their child know that they were sexually active before marriage. Instead, they tell their children of the hazards and horrors of having sex too early, never addressing the obvious question, "Mom or Dad, how did your premarital sex damage you, as you claim it will do to me?" If they ever answer that question, it is almost always in terms of religious guilt.

Humans have had premarital sex for most of the existence of the species. No credible evidence shows that premarital sex has any negative impact on sexuality, marriage or parenting ability. In Europe, the vast majority of

---

123   We will discuss this at length in Chapter 16.

teens have sex when they decide they are ready, and European civilization has not fallen apart.

European parents generally don't threaten, kill or beat their teenagers for engaging in sex. They educate their teens with some of the best sex education in the world. Teens are given the information to make their own rational decision about when to begin sex.[124] Adolescent sexual health outcomes are consistently better in France, Germany, the Netherlands and other European countries than in the United States.

## Life – A Balancing Act

Every life is a set of competing drives and goals. Achieving balance creates greater happiness and satisfaction. Sex requires balance as well. If one loses a sex partner, sexual feelings and behavior are disrupted. Eventually, sexual urges and desire will drive most people to do something about it. They may masturbate more, go out to places to meet possible partners, join an online dating service, etc. These behaviors are driven by natural sexual urges, so ignoring them is not an option for most people. Even those who say they can ignore or reduce their sex drive may not recognize it is being expressed in some other area of their lives.

Having a good sex life with a loving, caring partner or partners helps reduce stress and allows us to be more productive and creative in the other areas of our lives. It helps us create balance between our biological lives and our social and mental lives. Conversely, ignoring or distorting our biological map often leads to problems in our social and mental lives.

Using this naturalistic philosophy as a baseline, let's look at how different religions distort sexuality away from our natural tendencies.

## Distortion of the Catholic Priesthood

What did you know about sex before you started engaging in intercourse? That is the level of knowledge a priest has unless he is cheating with another man or woman, or both. People don't learn about their sexuality from books or discussions; they learn mostly from personal experience in bed with themselves or someone else – the opposite of what a priest is taught to do.

---

124   See "Adolescent Sexual Health in Europe and the US," available online at http://www. advocatesforyouth.org/publications/419?task=view.

Even if a priest is actively engaged in sex, it is illicit, by definition. What does secret, illicit sex teach you about sex and sexual relationships?

When I was in clinical practice, I worked with two priests who came to me for counseling. In both cases, their stories were those of perfectly normal 13-year-old boys. They masturbated a lot and loved to use pornography. They did not mention any pedophile tendencies, but years later one of them was arrested for just such behavior. In my few sessions with each of them, I could see nothing particularly wrong with their urges. What they were dealing with was an unnatural demand by their religion to forego a powerful drive and, as a result, they were suffering from guilt, angst and depression.

This experience helped me better understand the pedophile-priest phenomenon. If most priests are like the ones I worked with (as I have later come to learn is generally true), they are boys in men's bodies. Many are attracted to boys because that is the age at which their own development was arrested. It is the time at which their sexual map was formed. This is no excuse for the horrendous abuse that has been perpetrated by priests, but it does explain why the problem is so common and pervasive. It also points to a solution – stop asking humans to act like eunuchs when they are not.

Priestly misconduct is an example of religion distorting sexuality. It is like tying a young tree with a strong cord that pulls it hard in one direction and keeps tightening as the tree grows. The result will be a tree with a crooked trunk. As the cord bends the tree, the tree struggles to grow toward the sun. In the end, the trunk is bent at a very odd angle and cannot possibly support the weight it might have otherwise.

Most priests (and nuns) are drawn into the ministry before their hormones kick in. They cannot possibly know how powerful their biology is. Their religious sexual map teaches them sex is a crime against their god, but their biological map drives them to want sex intensely. All they know is that they are damned for having normal feelings and wanting to act on them.

Their education often starts when they are 12 or 13. Many who become priests or nuns attend same-sex "seminaries" or schools. They have little or no exposure to the opposite sex, and the celibate priests or nuns who instruct them are just as ignorant. Even if the boys are not abused by their instructor priests, they will probably engage in normal sexual behavior within their student group. The hormones are raging – what is a 15-year-old boy going to do if he is terrorized about masturbation and knows that sex with girls is a mortal sin? He will do what any normal boy does, experiment with the boys around him and then be torn with tremendous guilt. While other boys' brains are imprinting on normal sexual targets – women's faces, breasts, butts, voices, etc., the future priest's brain is being bombarded with messages that create fear of sex. Any sex he has will generate huge amounts of guilt that then feeds back into the religious sexual map. It is a formula for a very twisted and immature understanding of one's sexuality.

Combine this with the many other messages priests receive about being leaders of the church and moral models who give advice to those who are not as spiritually accomplished or advanced. The role they are given and the sexual feelings and drive they experience will almost inevitably lead to enormous internal conflict. Whether or not a given priest ever commits a crime against a child, the sexual map of such a person will be distorted simply because he is being forced into an unnatural sexuality. Celibacy is nothing if not abnormal. The human body and brain are not made for such programming. Whatever normal is, it does not include celibacy.

This same pattern can be seen in nuns as well. In my career, I had the opportunity to work in two institutions with nuns. I interacted with dozens of nuns and observed that their level of understanding about human sexuality was little better than that of a young girl. A few nuns were academically trained in sexual issues and were excellent listeners, but their adherence to Catholic sexual doctrine left them with few tools to understand or help people.

## Black Protestant Church Distortion

Black women are the most religious group in America. At the same time, they have among the highest number of unplanned pregnancies and receive 35% of all abortions, yet comprise only 13% of the population.[125] Polls show that Blacks oppose abortion more fervently than any other group in the United States.[126] Black Christianity is against homosexuality, masturbation, same-sex marriage, premarital sex, condom use, sex education and much more. It is among the most sexually conservative religions in America.

---

125   General Social Survey, NORC. 1977-2002. Available online at http://www3.norc.org/GSS+Website/.

126   From the Guttmacher Institute, "Characteristics of U.S. Abortion Patients, 2008," by Rachel K. Jones, Lawrence B. Finer and Susheela Sin. Available online at http://www.guttmacher.org/pubs/US-Abortion-Patients.pdf.

In an interview, the Black U.S. journalist and critic of religion, Jamila Bey, observed:

> Despite such strict mores about appropriate sexual behavior, 73% of African-American children in the United States are born to unmarried parents. So clearly, there is some disconnect that allows such strong adherents to fail so obviously, yet somehow maintain that they are indeed truly faithful.[127]

The Black Protestant church has avoided scrutiny for decades. Just like the Catholic church, it holds itself above reproach, making it taboo to criticize it. Outsiders who criticize are accused of racism, and members of the Black community who oppose the church suffer ostracism and worse.[128] Black atheists who call out the church are vilified.

In his excellent essay "The Invisibility of the Black Atheist," Wrath White observes,

> It can be argued that in most African American communities it is more acceptable to be a criminal who believes in God and goes to church on Sunday while selling drugs to kids all week than to be an atheist who has a good job, a good education, who contributes to society and supports his family. In these communities you find more tolerance towards gangbangers, drug addicts, and prostitutes, who pray to God for forgiveness than for honest productive citizens who deny the existence of God. This, for me, is one of the most embarrassing elements of Black culture, our zealous embracement of the God of our kidnappers, murderers, slavemasters and oppressors.[129]

The Black Protestant church holds itself out as the savior of the community and bastion of Black culture. However, the truth is something quite different. The Black church condemns all that is natural about sex and sexuality so effectively that it leaves church members with little or no useful information about their sexuality. The Black church creates an impossible sexual map, then condemns anyone who does not adhere to that map.

---

127    Interview with Jamila Bey on 31 October 2011.

128    For excellent analysis, see Sikivu Hutchinson's *Moral Combat: Black Atheists, Gender Politics, and the Values Wars,* (2011).

129    White's essay is available online at http://wordsofwrath.blogspot.com/2008/05/invisibility-of-black-atheist.html.

Black Christianity makes "women the sexual gatekeeper" even more strongly than white Christianity. It is women who are held responsible for remaining pure; it is women who are condemned and shamed when they fail. The shame and guilt effectively drive women back into the church so they can gain forgiveness. Seventy percent of Black church attendees are women. It is the guilt cycle writ large. According to Jamila Bey:

> This is actually advantageous, and serves to further the religious tradition. When a young woman has a child out of wedlock, and that child is a girl, the mother can show her willingness to repent by more stringently enforcing the rules of sexual behavior on her daughter. Thus, to not permit a young girl easy opportunity to play at normal dating and sexual behaviors, a mother may show her piety more strongly by keeping her girl in church and drilling her to protect her chastity, even though her mother did not. This serves the church by keeping more women inside. The younger ones are pressured to not displease their mothers by rebelling.

Black women and men are given a religious sexual map that requires sexual fidelity, monogamy, marriage, heterosexuality, no sex before marriage, no masturbation and no abortion, but their biological map takes them in an entirely different direction. The conflict between church teachings and natural desires results in guilt, shame and anger.

In a 2008 article from the Guttmacher Institute, Susan Cohen notes that Black women have three times the number of unintended pregnancies as white women and five times the number of abortions. This remains true even when education and income are accounted for.[130] She also notes that Black women are less likely to use birth control than white women, leaving them at risk for unintended pregnancies and needing abortion services. What Cohen does not say is that the likely reason for this difference is the sexual programming of the Black church.

The Black Protestant church's map is so distorted that it undermines healthy sexual and interpersonal relationships before they even get started. The result is low marriage rates, more abortions, persecution of gays, higher number of sexually transmitted infections (STIs), shame and ridicule over

---

130   Cohen, Susan A. "Abortion and Women of Color: The Bigger Picture," available online at http://www.guttmacher.org/pubs/gpr/11/3/gpr110302.html.

masturbation and more. The Black church's conservative message is similar to the white evangelical church's, and the results are similar. White evangelical churches are seeing a decrease in male attendance and an increase in out-of-wedlock births, STIs and abortions. The highest number of abortions in the United States is in the most religious areas. These problems have nothing to do with race and everything to do with the distorted sexual messages these churches preach.

Religious guilt causes people to deny their behavior even as they engage in it. Guilt short-circuits rational examination of behavior in favor of supernatural notions like "evil" and "the temptation of Satan." Replace the Black church's teachings on sex with factual knowledge about sex and sexuality and many problems would be solved. Unplanned births would plummet, STIs would be eliminated, abortions would be dramatically reduced, homosexuality would be accepted, even celebrated, and stable relationships could be established based on effective communication. The Black church is the problem, not the solution. You can take religion out of sex, but you cannot take sex out of the Black church. Sexual condemnation and guilt are the cornerstones upon which it thrives.

You may wonder, "Why isn't this the same for other churches, like the Catholics? Aren't they notorious for sexual restrictions and guilt?" It is true of some Catholics, especially Hispanics in the United States, but many American-born Catholics have learned to ignore the church and its teachings. The drop in attendance and dramatic decrease in large families tell us that American-born Catholics are not buying the map that the Catholic church is selling. Unfortunately, the Black church's sexual map is still selling well.

## The Fundamentalist Distortion

Baptist or Seventh Day Adventists, Pentecostals, Nazarenes, Evangelical and Jehovah's Witness are all shades of Christian fundamentalism. As such, their sexual views are universally restrictive. All are opposed to homosexuality, premarital sex, masturbation and many forms of sexual expression within marriage, such as anal and oral sex. While some of these churches are less vociferous than others, none is sex positive or offers a view of sexuality that resembles what human nature really is.

Austin Cline, in his Atheism newsletter, articulated the distorted logic that comes from many fundamental religions and the Catholic church:

Conservative evangelical objections to contraception, emergency contraception, and even abortion, can often be traced at least in part to their objections to 'irresponsible' sexual activity. Attempts to avoid pregnancy are thus attempts to avoid the consequences of one's 'irresponsible' choices. Since avoiding the consequences of irresponsible choices is itself irresponsible as well as something which makes such choices easier, it follows that people should be forced to bear those consequences. When it comes to sexual activity, this includes women accepting pregnancy.[131]

By this convoluted logic, pregnancy is a punishment resulting from having sex outside of marriage. The goal is to get women to just say no to any sex that is not approved by their church and to judge them as immoral if they say yes and use birth control.

Groups like Rick Warren's Saddleback Church use the same logic when they offer support to churches in Africa. They preach for abstinence-only and against condom use in areas with the highest number of AIDS victims. The result is a resurgence in AIDS in Central Africa, especially Uganda. Uganda had one of the most effective anti-AIDS programs in Africa and saw steady decline in the disease until Christian fundamentalists began preaching against condoms. It is a good example of the god virus and the AIDS virus working together to infect people.

The Evangelical anti-homosexuality message is incredibly destructive to people in Africa. Rick Warren and others encouraged anti-gay legislation in Uganda. The hatred and religious fervor the Evangelicals fostered may have been related to several attacks on homosexuals and the murder of David Kato, a gay rights leader.[132]

The sexual map of these churches leads to repression and subsequent acting out, not least among the clergy. Thus, all of these churches have problems controlling the clergy. Powerful, charismatic preachers can also be

---

131   Available online at http://atheism.about.com/od/religiousright/ig/Christian-Propaganda-Posters/Pregnancy-Punishment-Sex.htm.

132   The murder of David Kato is a prime example of religious hatred in Uganda. Legislation was even introduced by a prominent evangelical legislator to make homosexuality punishable by death and failing to report a homosexual as crime punishable by 5 years in prison. Only an international outcry stopped it from passing. See, for example, http://www.nytimes.com/2011/01/28/world/africa/28uganda.html.

very sexually attractive. This presents many opportunities for the successful preacher. To get a sample of this problem, visit the website **stopbaptist-predators.org**, an organization that has been documenting Baptist clergy sexual misconduct for years. Their investigations have shown cover-ups and behavior remarkably similar to those of the Catholic church. Other churches are equally culpable, but no one has yet publicly stepped up to investigate all of them.

The preachers who have been caught and those who helped cover up the crimes and misbehavior preach regularly about sexual sin. The guilt and shame they preach flow constantly from their literature, church services and Sunday Schools. Church-led sex education teaches only abstinence. Children are miseducated and deceived about their bodies and desires. At the same time, as mentioned earlier, the youth of these churches have the highest rate of teen pregnancies and STIs. Homosexual children in the churches are subjected to persecution by the church and terror by their own parents. It is not surprising that homosexual children raised in conservative communities also have the highest suicide rate.[133]

Fundamentalist sexual distortion that leads to suicide can only be characterized as the worst of all distortions. Were there better research on the subject, we would probably find that churches that program children to hate or fear sex push a significant number to behave in self-destructive ways, including suicide.

## The Mormon Distortion

Mormons are also against masturbation. They know it is going to happen, but they dare not say it is O.K. because Jesus said that to even have lustful thoughts is a sin. The leaders also know that they have done it many times in their life, yet they cannot admit it. Instead they talk around it, ignore it or just give inane advice to not do it.

One of the most humorous documents I have seen on the subject comes from Boyd K. Packer, who has held some of the highest positions in the Morman church, including president of the Quorum of the Twelve Apostles. In his six-page instruction, *To Young Men Only*, he never uses the

133  See, for example, Lindsay Tanner's "Gay Teen Suicides (And Straight) More Common In Politically Conservative Areas," at http://www.huffingtonpost.com/2011/04/18/gay-teen-suicides-and-str_n_850345.html.

term "masturbation" or "sex" once. This would be hilarious, if it weren't the actual view of the church. Here is an excerpt:[134]

> I wish to explain something that will help you understand your young manhood and help you develop self-control. When this power begins to form, it might be likened to having a little factory in your body, one designed to produce the product that can generate life.
>
> This little factory moves quietly into operation as a normal and expected pattern of growth and begins to produce the lifegiving substance. It will do so perhaps as long as you live. It works very slowly. That is the way it should be. For the most part, unless you tamper with it, you will hardly be aware that it is working at all.
>
> As you move closer to manhood, this little factory will sometimes produce an oversupply of this substance. The Lord has provided a way for that to be released. It will happen without any help or without any resistance from you. Perhaps, one night you will have a dream. In the course of it the release valve that controls the factory will open and release all that is excess.
>
> The factory and automatic release work on their own schedule. The Lord intended it to be that way. It is to regulate itself. This will not happen very often. You may go a longer period of time, and there will be no need for this to occur. When it does, you should not feel guilty. It is the nature of young manhood and is part of becoming a man.
>
> There is however, something you should not do. Sometimes a young man does not understand. Perhaps he is encouraged by unwise or unworthy companions to tamper with that factory. He might fondle himself and open that release valve. This you shouldn't do, for if you do that, the little factory will speed up. You will then be tempted again and again to release it. You can quickly be subjected to a habit, one that is not worthy, one that will leave you feeling depressed and feeling guilty. Resist that temptation. Do not be guilty of tampering or playing with this

134   This is a pamphlet that is given to every 12-year-old Mormon boy. For the full text, visit http://www.lds-mormon.com/only.shtml.

sacred power of creation. Keep it in reserve for the time when it can be righteously employed.

Many fundamentalist churches would probably agree with most of these ideas. This is an attempt to ensure that young Mormon boys feel shame and guilt about their normal sexual urges. DON'T TAMPER WITH THE FACTORY! – a simple but ineffective message.

This is a small sample of religions. A whole book could be devoted to the unique distortions of each cult and denomination, but this will suffice to illustrate the devastating impact of religion on the sex practices and sexuality of millions of people. Next we will take a look at what happens when people leave religion, and religion is no longer in the bedroom.

# CHAPTER 16:

# WHAT HAPPENS WHEN YOU LEAVE RELIGION

*What is the impact on sexuality when people leave religion? How do they benefit or suffer?*

### The Guilt Cycle and Various Denominations

In doing research for this book, I found few authors directly addressing religion's impact on sexuality and what happens to sex and sexuality when a person leaves religion. As a result, I determined to take a look myself. Amanda Brown, undergraduate at University of Kansas, and I conducted an Internet-based survey of 14,560 secular people in the United States. Most of our respondents were born and raised in a religious environment but have since left religion.[135]

We examined sex and religion from many different angles. We were most interested in the sexual guilt that people were taught or experienced in their religious training and how their sexual behavior changed once they left religion. We asked, "How would you rate what you were taught: How guilty you felt about sex and its implications on yourself?" We tabulated the results by the denomination in which respondents were raised. **Figure 1** shows that the fundamentalist religions use guilt more than liberal religions. It's not a surprise, but it is the first time that such data have been collected.

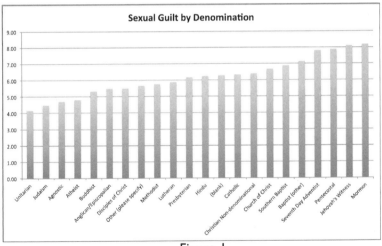

Figure 1

We went on to hypothesize that higher guilt led to poorer communication between parent and child about sex. To measure this, we asked respondents where they had received their sex education. A total of 38.2% of those from the least religious homes said that they got sex education from their parents,

135   The full report can be viewed at IPCPress.com, "Sex and Secularism: What Happens When You Leave Religion."

whereas only 13.5% respondents from more fundamentalist homes received parental sex education. In other words, those from the most guilt-based religions received the least amount of information from their parents.

Equally interesting were other sources of sexual information. For example, pornography was an important source of sexual information for 25.2% of the least religious, but the most religious cited it as important 33% of the time. This is part of a pattern that shows the most religious people often do the very thing their religion tells them not to, and they frequently do it at a higher rate than their more secular peers.

### Spanking the Monkey

Since masturbation is discouraged among many religions, we asked questions about how respondents' parents treated masturbation in the home. We asked, "Were you shamed or ridiculed by a parent or guardian for masturbatory activities?" A total of 5.5% of those from the most liberal homes said "yes," while 22.5% of those from the most religious homes said "yes."

For most questions, we also allowed respondents to make comments. Some of the responses from people raised in religious homes were heart-breaking:

- *… being caught masturbating caused me to be beaten until I couldn't stand up.*
- *I used to masturbate and then perform the Islamic ritual cleansing and beg Allah for forgiveness. I tried to stop, but my sexual desire was worse when I didn't than when I did. I worried not only about sin, but also about the fact that my mother told me that if I masturbated, I'd have problems with my future husband.*

Those raised in non-religious homes made comments that were very different, even funny:

- *My mom found my porn at one point. She informed me she didn't approve and kindly asked me to remove it from her hard drive (and put it on my own, portable, if I felt the need to).*
- *Not shamed exactly, but scolded for absconding with Dad's Playboy/ Penthouse magazines.*
- *My older sisters and their boyfriends would constantly ask, "Do you play with yourself?" Heck, yeah! Every chance I had.*

### Early Sexual Experience

We looked at the beginning of sexual behavior in adolescence and found remarkable similarities in four types of behavior, regardless of childhood religious training: masturbation, petting,[136] oral sex and intercourse.

As illustrated in **Figure 2**, there is very little difference in the beginning of these behaviors between those raised the most and least religious.

At about age 18, the largest difference appears, but it is only 9% for intercourse and that difference shrinks to 3.9% at age 21. All the sexual messages and guilt taught by religion have little or no effect on actual behavior. While this is just one study, we were careful to examine other studies that looked at similar behavior. For example, the national abstinence-only research funded by the federal government found that teaching children to abstain from sex has almost no effect on actual behavior.[137]

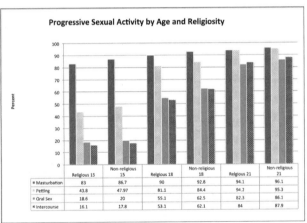

Figure 2

136   Petting: "making out" or foreplay without intercourse or other direct sexual contact.

137   The UCSF report found that "Not only is there no credible evidence that these millions of dollars have any positive effect, there is reason to be concerned that young people who receive the abstinence-only curricula in school will not have the tools to protect themselves in sexual situations." (Collins, C., Alagiri, P. and Summers, T. (2002). "Abstinence only vs. comprehensive sex education: What are the arguments? What is the evidence?" University of California, San Francisco: AIDS Research Institute).   Another research report stated, "Findings indicate that, despite the effects seen after the first year, programs had no statistically significant impact on eventual behavior. Based on data from the final follow-up survey, youth in the program group were no more likely to abstain from sex than their control group counterparts; among those who reported having had sex, program and control group youth had similar numbers of sexual partners and had initiated sex at the same mean age." (Christopher Trenholm, et. al.(2007). "Impacts of Four Title V, Section 510 Abstinence Education Programs: Final Report." Mathematica Policy Research, Inc.)

## Lust in Your Heart

Christian religions teach that even fantasizing is sinful, so we asked respondents if they felt it was wrong to fantasize sexually about others. A total of 46.1% of those raised most religious said it was wrong compared to 6.2% of the least religious. We also asked, "When you were religious, did you believe it was wrong to discuss or act out fantasies with your partner?" A total of 40% of the most religious said "yes," compared to 3.9% of the least religious.

## Talk Dirty to Me

Good sexual communication between partners includes the ability to share fantasies and other sexual ideas and desires. We can see from these data that respondents raised in more religious families were far more reluctant to communicate fantasies with their spouses or partners than the less religious. According to some religious leaders, sharing fantasies is sinful for both partners. Evangelicals take the "lust in your heart" idea very seriously.[138] This is evidence that religious people communicate far less about sex than the less religious.

## Sex After Religion

We also asked, "How has your sex life changed since leaving religion?"

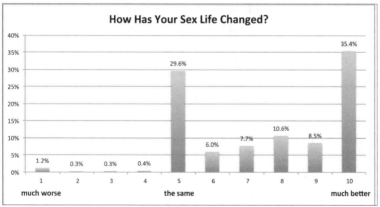

Figure 3

---

138  Matthew 5:27-28: "You have heard that it was said, 'You shall not commit adultery.' But I tell you that anyone who looks at a woman lustfully has already committed adultery with her in his heart."

As reflected in **Figure 3**, the difference was remarkable. On a scale of 1-10 with 10 as the most improved, 54.6% rated an 8, 9 or 10. The comments we received tell a story of great relief and satisfaction.

- *"I became comfortable with the idea of being a girl who actively wanted to have sex. I didn't know that was possible."*
- *"I have sex more frequently. I am less inhibited. I have felt more free to experiment and explore my sexuality."*
- *"Less embarrassment, more willing to act out fantasies, more comfortable and open about my own sexuality."*
- *"I find that my wife and I are less inhibited. We talk more openly about sex and regard it now, not as something merely for procreation, but for enjoyment and growing closer to each other."*
- *"I am more open to new things. I don't feel guilty about getting myself off, watching porn or needing to have sex. I enjoy sex, guilt free."*

We found that only 2.2% said their sex life worsened after leaving religion. Leaving religion disrupted some marital relationships; others found they had reduced access to possible partners.

- *"Since leaving religion, I have not had a physical or emotional relationship with my wife."*
- *"Since becoming an atheist, I have not met anyone who does not have some religious or 'spiritual' belief system. As a result, life is very lonely. I am proactively meeting new single members of the opposite sex in an effort to find someone who does not believe in the supernatural."*
- *"I used to be able to bed every girl in the Sunday School class; now they won't talk to me."*

Using the denominational information, we were able to see how much difference there was in sexual satisfaction depending on former religious affiliation. **Figure 4** shows how much sex life had changed. Sex improved for those leaving the most conservative and sexually repressive denominations, but every group showed some improvement.

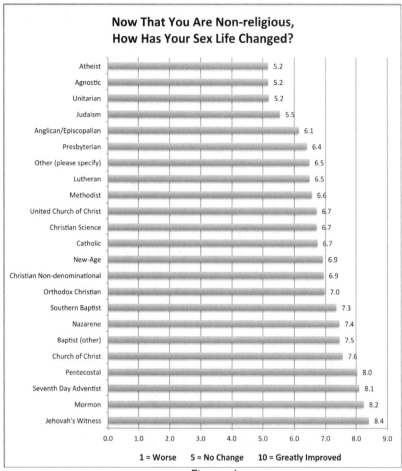

## Now That You Are Non-religious, How Has Your Sex Life Changed?

| Group | Value |
|---|---|
| Atheist | 5.2 |
| Agnostic | 5.2 |
| Unitarian | 5.2 |
| Judaism | 5.5 |
| Anglican/Episcopalian | 6.1 |
| Presbyterian | 6.4 |
| Other (please specify) | 6.5 |
| Lutheran | 6.5 |
| Methodist | 6.6 |
| United Church of Christ | 6.7 |
| Christian Science | 6.7 |
| Catholic | 6.7 |
| New-Age | 6.9 |
| Christian Non-denominational | 6.9 |
| Orthodox Christian | 7.0 |
| Southern Baptist | 7.3 |
| Nazarene | 7.4 |
| Baptist (other) | 7.5 |
| Church of Christ | 7.6 |
| Pentecostal | 8.0 |
| Seventh Day Adventist | 8.1 |
| Mormon | 8.2 |
| Jehovah's Witness | 8.4 |

1 = Worse    5 = No Change    10 = Greatly Improved

Figure 4

### Residual Effects

We hypothesized that guilt-based religious upbringing would have lasting or residual effects on people after leaving religion. Surprisingly, our data showed that sexual satisfaction was hardly impacted. In other words, those raised in the most restricted religious environments rapidly caught up with everyone else after leaving religion. It seems the guilt messages don't stick around very long.

At the same time, there was a difference felt between the most and the least religious groups in terms of anger they still feel about their religious training. In response to the question, "How much anger do you experience towards religion because of how it affected your sexuality?" the average rating among the most religious was 4.20 (10 being highest) while those from the least religious background scored 1.83. Among the most religious, 23% scored their anger at 8, 9 or 10 while only 4.3% among the least religious experienced high anger. As we can see from these results, some are still angry, but it does not seem to impact their current level of satisfaction.

### Lessons From the Research

While we were pleased that our results are consistent with major national studies in areas like first onset of adolescent sexual activities, none of those studies looked at what role religion may play in creating sexual behaviors. Religion has injected itself deeply into human sexuality; it is time to put it under the microscope and document the impact.

While much more needs to be done to understand how religion impacts sexuality, here are some conclusions to be drawn from this work.

1. Religions that use guilt the most also interfere and damage sexual satisfaction most. Less guilt-based religions do not impact sexual satisfaction as much.

2. If you wish to marry a religious person, make sure he or she belongs to a low-guilt religion like Unitarian, Episcopalian or some forms of Judaism. Your sex life will be less impacted.

3. The best thing you can do for your sex life is to leave religion, especially if you are in a high-guilt group like Mormon, Pentecostal, Jehovah's Witnesses, Seventh Day Adventist or Baptist.

4. Childhood and adolescent religious sexual training has little effect on sexual behavior. Adolescents begin sexual activity about the same time regardless of prior religious training. The danger is that religious children have not been given accurate information and may engage in more risky behavior leading to higher unwanted pregnancies, STIs and abortions among the most religious.

5. While secular parents are three times better at talking with their children about sex, it is still far too low, at 38%. There is much room for improvement.

In the next chapter we will explore some of the underlying psychological and biological reasons why sex is so compelling and why religion has so little impact on the behavior.

# CHAPTER 17:

# RELATIONSHIP CYCLES

Relationships have cycles that are related to our biology. Recognizing the biological basis of our cycles allows us to make rational choices and create greater happiness and commitment in our relationships.

*"Marriage requires a special talent, like acting. Monogamy requires genius."*

**-Warren Beatty**

*"When two people are under the influence of the most violent, most insane, most delusive, and most transient of passions, they are required to swear that they will remain in that excited, abnormal, and exhausting condition continuously until death do them part."*

**-George Bernard Shaw**

## New Relationship Energy (NRE)

If we were trying to understand the mating and bonding behavior of gibbons, we would take into account all aspects of behavior as well as brain chemical and neurological functioning. Our biology and chemistry is based on the same genetics and evolutionary history as the other great apes and other primates. Yet, religion paints us as non-animal, spiritual beings that are somehow disconnected from our biology. This fallacy prevents examination of what we really are and why we may behave in certain ways. Many religionists (and romantics) believe that understanding our biology and psychology detracts from sexual enjoyment. This myth allows religion to keep people ignorant and dependent upon Bronze Age ideas of sexuality.

When people begin a sexual relationship, they experience the rush of endorphins, opiate-like chemicals in the brain that make them feel euphoric. Some have called this "new relationship energy" or NRE.[139] Anyone who has been in love knows the feeling of new love. Art and literature are filled with stories of people like Romeo and Juliet in the throes of NRE. People want the sense of well-being and euphoria that comes from interaction with their lover.

NRE is an incredibly powerful part of our species' reproductive strategy. As an important first step in the bonding process, it lasts a limited time and then either dissolves or evolves into a second type of long-term bonding. Long-term bonding is dependent on another set of chemical and neurological processes that generate very different feelings from NRE. We will call this long-term security or LTS and will discuss it in detail in Chapter 23. Briefly, LTS is when people feel satisfied and secure in a relationship. Unlike the powerful emotions of NRE, LTS feels solid and reliable.

The fact that NRE can be almost uncontrollable is frightening to parents and religious leaders. Thus, all the major religions fear and condemn NRE. Some religions try to prevent it from happening. For example, arranged marriages effectively prevent NRE from undermining social, religious, political and familial order.

Most major religions have been involved in and supportive of arranged marriages at some time in their history. The practice allows for careful selection of socially or politically advantageous in-laws, thus ensuring that the

---

139  Probably first coined by Zhahai Stewart in the 1980s but more widely used in the 1990s. For a full discussion, see an article by Stewart in *Loving More* magazine, Issue 26, "What's All This NRE Stuff, Anyway?"

religion is propagated as well. While arranged marriages are less common today, taboos against marrying outside one's religion are still enforced in most cultures. Mormons and Jehovah's Witnesses, among others, work to ensure young people marry within the religion. This is designed to prevent people from falling in love and diluting religious control over the offspring.

In India, no Hindu father would select a Muslim husband for his daughter. An Orthodox Jew would never consider marrying a Christian. If a Christian married a Muslim in the United States, both families would likely disapprove.

In modern U.S. Christianity, all the conservative religions preach against "succumbing to the passions of youth." Abstinence-only courses focus on helping youth avoid the pitfalls of sex before marriage. None of this training works, and it sets the youth up for failure and guilt that will keep them tied to the church.[140] Educating children on the entire spectrum of sexuality, including realistic ideas about NRE, would prevent many unwanted pregnancies, diseases and divorces. Unfortunately, the church's motivation is not prevention through education, but guilt induction for religious propagation.

## Attachment

After NRE ends, humans may transition into attachment (LTS), the easy, comfortable feeling a person can achieve with a long-time partner. The brain uses the same pathways for adult attachment it used in childhood attachment to parents. The chemistry of attachment uses the brain chemical oxytocin to create the feeling of wellbeing. The same chemical is released during orgasm, breast feeding and other intimate encounters. It bonds married couples, best friends and pets. That is why some people can feel so strongly about their pets. All objects of attachment evoke similar neural pathways and chemistry in our brains. Oxytocin makes us feel safe, trusting and comfortable. It is an important part of the cycle of attachment.

If the sex is adequate for both parties, the relationship can settle at this level for decades, if not a lifetime. If the sex is not adequate for one party, the relationship may appear settled, but that party may seek outside stimulation.

---

140   From "Abstinence-Only Education Does Not Lead to Abstinent Behavior, Researchers Find" in *ScienceDaily*. Available online at http://www.sciencedaily.com/releases/2011/11/111129185925.htm.

The attachment may still be strong, but the need for stimulation and variety is not being satisfied.

## The Unwritten Rules of Marriage

A marriage contract is surrounded by cultural norms and expectations. Some are unwritten, others have been put into law like "Only one spouse per person" and "No sex outside of this legally sanctioned marriage." Religious marriages may be subject to additional rules such as:

- No birth control.
- The woman is under divine obligation to keep her husband satisfied, except when she is pregnant.
- The man is the head of the house.

There are also a host of other unwritten rules. For example,

- You cannot lust after another person.
- You may not masturbate while married.
- You may not think about other people while having sex with your spouse.
- You may not talk about sexual topics to a person you are not married to.

Another unwritten rule is that one partner has full control over the other partner's sexual expression. The ultimate expression of control is when one spouse decides he or she doesn't want sex any more. In other words, involuntary celibacy is imposed by one spouse on the other.

This kind of celibacy is quite common among religious couples or couples where one is religious and the other is not. If one partner decides he or she does not want to be sexually active, religious ideas about sex and marriage preclude a rational discussion of the issue.

I was once the guest co-host on *The Atheist Experience* TV show.[141] The subject was sex and religion. Rich Lyons from Seattle called in and told us he had been a Pentecostal minister for 20 years. He had been married for 21 years, and he and his wife had had sex only about 12 times during their marriage due to religious guilt and inhibition. He went on to say that during those 20 years, virtually every male member of his congregation came to him for counseling about their wives' lack of interest in sex. The only thing

---

141    *The Atheist Experience Television,* #688. Available at http://www.youtube.com/watch?v=YO8eubj23dQ.

he knew to suggest was to have them pray with him. In his words, "That did little good."

Women have a sex drive and capacity for sex that is equal to or greater than that of men. What could possibly have happened to a whole congregation of married Pentecostal women to tamp down that powerful drive and make them not want sex with their husbands?

Guilt around sex often preys upon one partner more than the other. Once child bearing is over, the justification for sex is gone. As a result, the most guilt-ridden partner often decides it is easier to go without sex than to deal with the guilt associated with it. The natural aging process may also mean that one partner has less of a sex drive than the other. Less drive combined with more guilt makes it easy to refuse sex. The other partner may still have a strong sex drive but no where and no way to express it.

The very religious state of Utah has consistently had the highest consumption of pornography.[142] In addition, porn use in the United States is generally higher in the most religious zip codes. This points towards the notion that sexual energy has to go somewhere, despite strong religious teachings and sanctions.

While religious guilt does not explain all sexual dysfunction within a marriage, it explains a large proportion. Issues often have roots in religious dogma taught in childhood and adolescence. For example, a man or woman may be turned off by oral sex. If asked, they may say, "I just don't feel comfortable with it." All too often a Sunday School teacher or minister told them that it was dirty and unnatural.

When children are starting puberty, they are extremely susceptible to religious messages. In my research, I encountered hundreds of stories about people being warned about eternal damnation for certain sexual activities. These messages often come from trusted adults, and the children carried them into adulthood and marriage. How does a woman relax and enjoy a good oral sex orgasm with her husband when she believes that it is an act only "Satan himself would teach."

142   "Red Light States: Who Buys Online Adult Entertainment?" by Benjamin Edelman, *Journal of Economic Perspectives*, 23 (1), Winter 2009.

### Satiation: "Not Tonight, Honey; I Have a Headache"

If you were forced to eat your favorite dessert every day for the rest of your life, you would probably be sick of it within weeks. Sex is similar. We need stimulation and variety. Children quickly tire of playing with the same toy and want new things. Most will go out of their way to invent new games. The same is true of adults and sex.

Sooner or later, NRE comes to an end. The novelty wears off; the excitement is less frequent or gone. At that point, the bond that holds a couple together must transition to something more settled, or they may break up. That is probably why the highest divorce rate is around four years of marriage, the maximum length of NRE.[143] If they make the transition, sex may continue, but at a lower level. It may taper off over the next decade or two as it becomes harder and harder for the partners to stimulate one another. It doesn't mean the sex drive goes away; they just have a harder time directing it toward each other.

What would that couple look and act like if they were members of the Hadza or Na cultures? In all probability, they wouldn't stress over a lifelong marriage. Each of the partners would have several long-term relationships over a lifetime. The children would still get great care and teaching from aunts and uncles and others in the village.

### Relationship Cycle

Religious notions of fidelity and marriage do not hold up to cultural and biological scrutiny. The basis for monogamy is rooted in the need for agriculturalists to control labor and inheritance. At the same time, religion takes advantage of this agricultural necessity to ensure that it is passed on to subsequent generations.[144] The farther our society gets from agriculture, the fewer economic restrictions on women. This, in turn, weakens religion's ability to propagate through sexual rules and guilt focused on the submission of women.

With more economic and educational options for women, we may be seeing the natural course of biology take place. Just as many hunter-gatherer

143   See Helen Fisher's discussion of the four-year itch in *Anatomy of Love: The Natural History of Monogamy, Adultery, and Divorce*, (1992).

144   Arranged marriages were still the norm in Europe as recently as the 1700s. "Love marriages" did not become common until the 1800s. Stephanie Coontz, *Marriage, a History: How Love Conquered Marriage*, (2005).

women have significant independence within their tribal structure, modern women have more power to decide who, when and whether to marry.

This does not mean that lifelong relationships are not possible, even desirable. It *does* mean that we should recognize the nature of love and attraction in humans. It is normal to get tired of your mate and desire someone else. The question is, what do you do about it?

The current religious model for marriage allows no path for discussing attraction issues. As a result, people may feel trapped, unloved, and angry. These unexpressed feelings often are acted out in destructive ways like becoming hypercritical of one another, undermining the financial security of the relationship, having an affair, etc.

Eliminate religious ideas of marriage and monogamy, and many options open up. A couple can talk openly about what they like and want. What would stimulate them and give them more satisfaction? They can also discuss and explore issues of insecurity, inadequacy and jealousy that are typically ignored or suppressed. Ignoring these slowly undermines the relationship. It is never easy to talk about these things, but the practice of doing it strengthens the relationship and keeps it alive.

Through these discussions profound love can develop – love that goes far beyond NRE and still has the power to evoke NRE chemistry. We will explore this further in Section V and develop some practical ways to manage the relationship cycle.

# CHAPTER 18:

# MOMMY, DID YOU HAVE SEX

# BEFORE YOU MARRIED DADDY?

*Why are religious parents poor at sex education? What inhibits and prevents them from being honest with their children? Sexual guilt in marriage and childrearing creates problems for everyone.*

Sex and God: The Psychology of Religion and Sex

## Children, Parents and Sex

Rarely can parents talk easily and intelligently to their children about sex; moreover, rarely do children want to talk about sex with their parents. As a result, even the most well-intentioned, best-educated parent has great difficulty with the conversation. The problem is often quite simple – deeply ingrained religious guilt.

In his research on adolescents and sexual communication with parents (*Forbidden Fruit*, 2007), Mark Regnerus reports:

> … parents for whom religion is important communicate less often about birth control than parents whose religious faith is not important. This suggests that when devoutly religious parents say they are talking regularly with their adolescents about sex and birth control, it means they are talking with them about morality rather than sharing information.

In our own research, discussed in Chapter 16, we also found that religious children got more of their information about sex from experience, peers and porn than from their parents. Thirteen percent of religious parents talked to their children about sex compared to 38% of secular parents. According to thousands of survey respondents, religious parents are much poorer than non-religious parents are at talking about sex. Something is interfering with the communication, and religious guilt is the probable cause.

Religious guilt around premarital sex may be one possible inhibitor. Ninety-five percent of the U.S. population has had premarital sex, even religious people.[145] The religious taboo against premarital sex is so strong that religious people cannot admit to this, especially to their children. This creates a barrier to communication between parent and child. As one religious parent told me, "What if my daughter asks if I had sex before marriage? Do I lie to her and tell her no, or do I tell her I did but she shouldn't do it? How do I justify my behavior to my daughter? It's just easier not to talk about it at all."

There is also the possibility that one or both of the parents have deceived the other partner about having premarital sex. This creates further guilt and conflict. If religious parents admit that they could not resist premarital sex,

---

145   National Survey of Family Growth, 2006. Available online at http://www.icpsr.umich.edu/icpsrweb/ICPSR/series/48.

how can they ask their children to resist it? The answer seems to be: better to lie or not talk about it.

More secular or religiously liberal parents do not face this dilemma. They openly talk about sex and premarital sex. They don't have to justify their behavior to their children because they don't see the behavior as wrong or sinful. As a result, secular parents tend to give their children better sex education.[146]

Religious parents see honesty about normal human sexuality as too risky; therefore, they talk less to their children and give them less accurate information. This failure to communicate important, rational and emotional information leaves religious children more at risk than those raised in secular homes. The irony is that what religious parents most fear and preach against – premarital sex or unwanted pregnancy – is more likely to happen with their children than with secular kids. Guilt doesn't stop anyone, but it does inhibit clear thinking.

## Sex-Negative Messages to Girls

"Fathers, teach your daughters to say no until they get married. Mothers, teach your daughters how devastating premarital sex will be in their marriage." This is the message propagated by patriarchal religions the world over.

In religion, women are seen as the sexual gatekeepers, yet they are subordinate to their husbands. If a couple has sex before marriage, it is the woman's fault; she should have the moral power to say "no" and to save herself for her husband.

This message is present in Islam, Catholicism, Hinduism, Mormonism, Eastern Orthodoxy, Buddhism and many other religions. The notion that a woman's sexuality belongs only to the husband is a central tenet tied to the idea that a woman is the property of the father first, then the property of the husband. Incidentally, that is where Christians get the tradition of the father giving the bride away.

Messages to keep girls "chaste" are almost always accompanied by fear and guilt. Girls are taught sex is dirty and sinful; women are taught that it is their responsibility to control the sexual relationship. If they are given the message that sex is dirty and sinful, and women are the cause of the fall

---

146  See pp. 19-20 in Ray and Brown, "Sex and Secularism: What Happens When You Leave Religion." See IPCPress.com for the full report.

of man, it is no wonder many women go into marriage horrified of sex and unprepared, except to say no.

Here is an example of such married guilt:

> *I was an agnostic/atheist forced to convert to an extreme evangelical Christian faith in order to marry my wife, whom I recently separated from. She was a 30-year-old virgin when we married, and her prolonged abstinence wreaked havoc in the bedroom from the very beginning. We refrained from any kind of sexual activity while we were dating and engaged, and unfortunately we were unable to consummate our marriage on our wedding night. (When we were dating and engaged, and practicing "purity," I was promised and guaranteed that our sex life would be greatly rewarded by God, and I bought into it.) In fact, we didn't actually have what could be considered sex for over two weeks after we got married. When we did start having sex regularly, it was extremely awkward, and I could tell that the guilt and shame placed upon sex and normal human sexuality when my wife was growing up was holding her back from thoroughly enjoying life's greatest pleasure.*

The wife in this story was the victim of horrendous sexual programming by her Evangelical religion. With this kind of childhood religious programming, many religious marriages are sexually dead from the start.

### The Power of Oblique Communication

The major religions give powerful negative messages to women. The woman does most of the childrearing in patriarchal societies, so it is important for religion to infect her with guilt-inducing sexual ideas to ensure the children absorb the guilt as well. How are these messages conveyed to children, especially girls?

The messages are conveyed through oblique or indirect communication. Women's gossip within hearing of young girls is a particularly effective way of conveying such messages. Children love to listen to adults as they gossip and take in the stories they hear as lessons on how to live your life. What if a girl overheard a comment like this, "Mrs. X caught her daughter playing with herself; they are going to send her off to a special religious camp this summer so she will learn the fear of god." The eavesdropping child quickly picks up the meaning and tone of such communications and integrates it into her sexual map. It is hard to miss the message that masturbation can get you in serious trouble.

This kind of cloaked, gossipy talk often substitutes for the direct communication and information the child needs. Many parents and adults do this intentionally. Such quiet secretiveness, harsh judgment and often embarrassed tone communicates volumes to a child about the sinfulness of sex and the treatment you can expect if you are caught doing it. I have heard from dozens of women who were raised in deeply religious homes, and the pattern is remarkably similar.

Menstruation is another aspect of life that the religious label as shameful and dirty. Here is one woman's story, told as I was counseling her and her husband:

> *My mom never told me about menstruation. I knew she used tampons, and as a little girl I asked her about them. Her response was curt and clearly let me know it was not something I was to ask about again. I knew there was blood involved, and it scared me because I thought my mother was hurt. The most I could find out was that it had something to do with sex. When I realized what 'sex' was, that really freaked me out. I thought, "You mean I will bleed if I have sex?" I lived with this fear and uncertainty from as early as I can remember to about 10 years old. At that time, the older girls in my religious school started talking about things, and some were obviously breasts and talking about boys. I liked to listen, but I could never understand what was the truth and what were their own ideas. If I got up the courage to ask one of them, I got vague or conflicting answers.*
>
> *At about 12 years old, I remember playing with myself occasionally. It felt so good, but somehow I knew it was wrong. Touching myself gave me many sensations I had not felt before, but I always felt terrible afterwards. When I was about 12 ½, I was at school one day and suddenly got a really nauseous and creepy feeling. I excused myself to go to the restroom and discovered that I was bleeding. I went crazy, became hysterical and started crying in the stall. Someone heard me and tried to talk to me, but I was horrified that they would find out I was bleeding, horrified that I had done something terribly wrong and that someone would find out I had been playing with myself. When someone finally*

*got the door open and figured out what was happening with me, they laughed at me, then scolded me for trying to hide it and not knowing what it was.*

*When I got home that day, my mother already knew. She was derisive and cold. Her only comment was something like, "You should have known how to handle it. We talked about it years ago." I felt like a total loser. No one had told me anything; yet I was supposed to know everything. Now with my own daughter, I find it extremely embarrassing to talk about. I look back on my marriage of almost two decades and realize that my husband has suffered because I could never get hold of what sex should be for myself, let alone him. I am frozen when it comes to sex. I love my husband, but can't even imagine anything positive about sex with him or anyone. If we get divorced, I would understand.*

Among the most religious, there is an epidemic of sexual alienation and misinformation.

### Guilt in Religious Marriage

A married religious couple that is not having sex still has sexual energy. The sexual energy goes toward the church, the Sunday School, toward more vigorous prayer or teaching the children. It also goes into anger and frustration, expressed as depression or unhappiness, affairs, spousal abuse, child porn or molesting children. Even if one partner in a religious marriage is capable of turning off his or her sexual side, it is unlikely that the other is. The emotional satisfaction derived from good sex is sought in activities that are far less rewarding. As one person said about her previous religious life:

*We had sex as teenagers before we got married, I didn't ever want to feel that kind of guilt again, so I just avoided my husband and put all my attention on the children and teaching church school. The guilt got worst once we had children. He suffered and our marriage suffered until we left the church for good. Things are much better now, it [leaving the church] has renewed our entire relationship in ways I could never imagine when I was religious.*

**Women are both powerful and powerless in many religious marriages.** They are subordinate to their husbands but have the power and the obligation to control sex. Their sexual desire and gratification are seen as unimportant and maybe even evil. One minister preached, "The woman is a sacred vessel into which the soul of a new infant is formed. You should always keep that in mind when loving each other."

Such ideas create all kinds of barriers to sexual enjoyment and creativity, to say nothing of making a woman into an object to be used for religious propagation. With this idea, sex can never be just for enjoyment but must always be a threesome with some god. As one wag put it, "God is watching you while you have sex, and may be pleasuring himself as well."

From the beginning, religious girls are taught the sacredness of sex is in bearing children, *not* in having fun. This is, of course, totally backward since a woman may have thousands of sexual encounters and orgasms for every time she conceives. To claim that reproduction is the most important part of sex goes totally against our biology. For women who do not or cannot have children, this sends an even more insidious message – you are either selfish or barren. A selfish woman, in religious terms, puts her own pleasure above having children for god. A barren woman, in religious terms, is often seen as being punished by some god. Being barren may also be seen as a crime or a sin against her husband. In many parts of the world, a woman who chooses not or cannot have children is treated as second class. A woman who chooses not to get married is the most selfish of all.

## The Poisoning of Men and Boys

While there is little doubt that women suffer the greatest oppression and restriction from religion, men are victims as well. Much of what we discussed about guilt, shame and indirect communication applies to boys, too. Many religions start with the notion that the deity is male and that, therefore, males are superior to women. This irrational idea informs boys' sexual map as they grow into men and breeds ideas such as the following: women are subservient to men; men have control over women's bodies; and men are more intelligent and closer to their god.

This thinking, in turn, sets the stage for behavior that leads to abuse and conflict in relations between the sexes. For example, boys are seen as superior to adult women in many contexts. Many Baptist churches believe a woman should not be allowed to teach boys older than 12 years old. In Saudi Arabia, an adult woman must be accompanied by a male relative in public. Her 12-year-old son can accompany her – he is more adult than she is. These kinds of messages often lead boys to believe that they can act superior and intimidating toward girls.

At the same time, boys receive messages about masculinity that force them to deny their sexual urges. Most adolescent boys (and girls) masturbate, but religion says this is forbidden. Adults preach against it, and comments are made by peers and older adolescents telling the child it is wrong and a sin. Boys make fun of one another, calling anyone who masturbates a homosexual. "Real men don't masturbate."

With constant messages tying masturbation to homosexuality, boys learn to be ashamed of their sexual urges. They often take that shame and direct it toward anyone who they believe is homosexual. **I believe that most homophobia among adolescents is really intense shame about their own masturbatory behavior.**

Even if a boy is not necessarily religious or from a religious home, he is surrounded by a culture that perpetuates these ideas about women, masturbation and homosexuality. As a boy I was terrified of being called a homosexual. No one admitted to masturbating so I pretended I didn't either. I saw boys harassed unmercifully because they were somewhat effeminate. Most of all, I saw the source of these ideas coming from preachers, Sunday School teachers, church camp counselors and my grandfather, a country church minister. With the rise of Evangelical Christianity in the United States, Africa, South America and other places, these messages are probably stronger today than they were when I was an adolescent.

In a boys' locker room, it takes only one boy with foot fungus to infect a lot of others, if there are no preventive measures. In that same locker room, it only takes a few boys infected with religiously inspired ideas about masturbation, homosexuality and women's inferiority to infect many other boys. The prevention is a few well-educated, assertive and secular boys who can and will call out this behavior and stop its spread. A few students standing up to religious sexual intimidation can make a huge difference. That is why such initiatives as the "It Gets Better" campaign, started by Dan Savage, are so important, giving support to students to stand up and challenge sexual bullying.[147]

Wherever religious ideas are taught, there are higher levels of sex abuse, child abuse, divorce and spouse abuse. If we wish to address the problems

---

147    Dan Savage is the host of the nationally acclaimed Savage Love Podcast. Here is the pledge of the campaign: "Everyone deserves to be respected for who they are. I pledge to spread this message to my friends, family and neighbors. I'll speak up against hate and intolerance whenever I see it, at school and at work. I'll provide hope for lesbian, gay, bi, trans and other bullied teens by letting them know that 'It Gets Better.'" (See http://www.itgetsbetter.org/page/s/pledge/)

associated with sexual crime, abuse and harassment, the place to start is in solid, non-religious, sexual education of children and adolescents. This means that religious ideas about homosexuality, masturbation, male superiority, female purity, etc., must be directly challenged.

# CHAPTER 19:

# I DIDN'T RAISE HER THAT WAY!

*Why do some people catch religion and others don't? Why is my son religious when I didn't raise him that way?*

### Three Sources of Personality Influence

In earlier chapters we discussed genetic and epigenetic influences on sexuality. In this chapter we will narrow the discussion to the three main sources of influence on a child's personality. These can be labeled as genetics, shared environment and non-shared environment.

First genetics. With modern genetic research, there is little doubt that genes have a big influence on behavior. My son hated bananas from the day he first had a taste and never enjoyed playing with dolls. My daughter loved bananas, music and dolls from very early but did not take to baseball. A good deal of research in animals and humans over the past few decades shows that those kinds of interests are genetically influenced.

The second area of influence is the shared environment, which includes all the rules and preferences of the parents or adult guardians. My parents had a rule that every child in the family was to take two years of piano. In that shared environment all four boys in my family took two years of piano, even if kicking and screaming. My mother suffered as much or more than we did in enforcing that rule. In the end, my three brothers dropped piano as soon as they could and did nothing with music. I went on to do a minor amount of singing. Music just wasn't going to happen for us. We were much more intent on playing baseball and building forts, model cars and airplanes. The shared environment did not influence us much with respect to music, at least not the way my mother had hoped.

The third area of influence is the non-shared environment. While siblings may grow up in the same home, they actually live in very different environments. First, they are born into different times (except for twins). This means they have different peer groups, classes in school and opportunities, based on when they were born in the family. Second, their gender tends to create and attract a very different set of peers. Third, each child lives in a unique world mentally and physically.

When I was growing up, I shared a bedroom with one brother. We were born in the same family and shared a bedroom, but we chose very different peer groups and activities. I was always reading a book, doing scientific experiments or chumming with a limited number of friends. In contrast, my brother was always hanging around with friends and was into much more physical activities. My mother tried to force my brother to help me with my scientific experiments, but he had no interest unless it involved blowing something up. We chose very different types of friends and joined different groups and clubs. Within those groups and clubs we were exposed to many ideas and practices that had nothing to do with our parents or with each other. Our non-shared environments were as different as if we had lived in different homes, let alone the same bedroom.

## The 50-0-50

In 1997, Judith Rich Harris published an article that reviewed the literature on the influence of environment, genetics and parenting on human development, concluding that shared environment had almost no influence. Instead, she found that genetics and non-shared environment accounted for virtually all of personality development in the child. This has come to be called the 50-0-50 principle.[148] Simply put, it says that parents have little impact on the development of a child's personality. Genetics have about 50% and socialization apart from parents accounts for the other 50%. This controversial conclusion took the psychology world by storm. At first it was disputed and doubted, but it has since been corroborated in many ways and has become a central idea in personality development research. What she discovered and documented was that children have a mind and genes of their own. Parents' role is to provide a protective and enriched environment within which the child can experience and sample the world, but that is about all.

This conclusion violates many assumptions about childrearing, especially those of religionists who believe the Old Testament "spare the rod, spoil the child" philosophy of parenting. If parents have such little influence, why do so many think they hold such sway over their children? It is an illusion that is easily explained. If a parent loves playing baseball and her child turns out to love it, the parent tends to take credit for the interest. After all, she taught and supported the child in learning the sport. The truth is that the parent had genetically programmed athletic abilities and passed those genes on to the child. The same parent may have a second child who stubbornly refuses

---

148   See "The 50-0-50 rule: Why parenting has virtually no effect on children" available online at http://www.psychologytoday.com/blog/the-scientific-fundamentalist/200809/the-50-0-50- rule-why-parenting-has-virtually-no-effect-chi.

to play baseball and goes on to become a concert pianist. In this case, the parent may be disappointed in the child.

The parent did not "influence" the child to become a baseball player any more than she influenced the resistant child to become a concert pianist. Many parents fool themselves into thinking they were a key influence in a child's success but had no part in a child's "failure." The reverse can be true as well – some parents think they played a major role in their child's failure.

In reality, in both cases, the parent played a small role. Parents teach and expose their children to many different possible activities and interests including providing for and supporting their education. As children grow, they decide which interests are important to them. This does not mean that parents have no influence over their children, but that influence is not as direct and controlled as they would like to believe.

Parenting still has power, through key responsibilities like protection, age-appropriate education, boundary setting and environmental enrichment. That is, you may not be able to "influence" children, but you can discover what gets them excited and interested and foster and nurture those skills and talents.

### Religion and 50-0-50

Religiosity seems to have genetic predispositions in much the same way as piano playing and baseball.[149] In a groundbreaking 1990 study of identical and fraternal twins, Niles Waller et al. found that approximately 50% of the variance in religiosity was attributable to genetics. The rest was associated with the non-shared environment. Little or no influence came from the shared environment.

This is one of many studies that have found genetics to be a critical influence on religiosity and explains why two children raised in a religious home may go in entirely different directions as adults with respect to religion. One may continue in the parents' religion, the other may leave organized religion entirely. If they are religious, the religion they mostly likely gravitate to is their parents' religion or one very close to what they were exposed to as a child.

---

149   Waller, N. G., Kojetin, B. A., Bouchard, T. J., Lykken, D. T., & Tellegen, A. (1990). "Genetic and environmental influences on religious interests, attitudes and values: A study of twins reared apart and together." *Psychological Science*, 1, 138-142.

Some children are more susceptible to religious infection than others. If religion is in the home, those susceptible will get infected, others less so. The parental influence lies more in what religion a child adopts than in whether he or she gets religion. The same child raised in another home with a totally different religion, like Islam or Buddhism, may be just as susceptible to infection with that religion. Whatever is in the environment is what the child is most likely to catch, but only if he or she has a tendency toward religiosity.

As in our baseball and piano example, genetic influences are easily mistaken for parental influences. When the child grows up religious, the parent may claim credit for his religiosity. However, if another child resists "god's word," the parent may disavow her.

Religious parents desperately try to control the non-shared environment by sending their children to church, church camp, religious schools, etc. If children have no exposure to other religions or systems of belief, they can't choose those beliefs. If they are predisposed to religiosity, they too will become devout. If they do not have such a predisposition, they may rebel.

Finally, a study published in the *Journal of Personality* examined adult male identical twins (MZ) and fraternal (DZ) twins. The authors found that difference in religiosity in adolescents was influenced by both genes and environment, but during the transition from adolescence to adulthood, genetic factors increased in importance while shared environmental factors decreased. That is, environmental factors (parenting and family life) influence a child's religiosity, but the effects decline with the transition into adulthood. This study found that by adulthood, any influence from the shared environment largely disappeared. Genetics were far more important. Identical twins stayed about the same in religiosity over time while fraternal twins became more dissimilar.[150]

When two very religious parents have children, it is generally expected that their children will have a high probability of inheriting the genetic predisposition from both parents. As a result, highly religious parents are tempted to believe their religious teachings made their children faithful.

---

150   Koenig, L. B., McGue, M., Krueger, R. F., & Bouchard, T. J. (2005). "Genetic and environmental influences on religiousness: Findings for retrospective and current religiousness ratings." *Journal of Personality*, 73, 471–488. An even larger study by Kenneth S. Kendler et al. found strongly confirming evidence of genetic influence on religiosity. (Vance, T., Maes, H. H., Kendler, K. S. (2010). "Genetic and environmental influences on multiple dimensions of religiosity: a twin study." *Journal of Nervous and Mental Disease*, 198, 755-761).

By the same token, they are tempted to see a child who did not get the religious predisposition as rebellious and ungodly. Religious parents who adopt children are frequently disappointed that their children do not remain religious as adults.

Religious parents may be disappointed when children disavow their religion and secular parents may be puzzled when a child gets religion. Many a secular parent has told me, "I never took my children to church and I tried to teach them to think for themselves. Why did they become religious?" Just like some people catch a cold and others don't, it all depends on your natural vulnerabilities. Children who have a strong genetic predisposition toward religiosity may catch religion despite parental efforts to teach them critical thinking. As a parent, critical thinking skills are the best vaccine you can give your children, but it does not guarantee they won't get religion.

The best you can do as a parent is to expose your children to a wide range of religions. Rather than trying to "program them" to dislike religion, give them the tools to analyze it themselves. With the conceptual tools of critical thinking and skepticism, and adequate exposure to many religions, children are very likely eventually to conclude that all religion is crazy. Nevertheless, some children are susceptible to religious infection just like they are to a cold.

# CHAPTER 20:

# SEX ON A LEASH

*Human sexuality is incredibly flexible, but we all have unique tendencies and preferences. Knowing them puts us in control of our sexuality.*

## Sexual Flexibility

Now that we can see the relative effects of the three areas of potential influence, genetics, shared environment and non-shared environment, let's look at sex. Research over the last 20 years has shed light on the differences between men and women in terms of sexual attitudes. While we won't go into all the arguments within evolutionary biology and other disciplines, we can say with a good deal of certainty that women are more sensitive to social and cultural pressures than men in matters of sex. In a massive review of the literature on sex and sexuality, Roy Baumeister of Florida State University found that the effects of acculturation, education, politics, religion and family life on sexual attitudes and behaviors were all more potent among women than among men. He concluded that, "... men's sexuality revolves around physical factors, in which nature is predominant and the social and cultural dimension is secondary. For women, social and cultural factors play a much larger role."[151]

Other researchers have also noted the relative flexibility of women's sexuality. For example, in sexual preference surveys, women describe themselves as bisexual two to four times more often than men. Women also respond to a wider range of visual, tactile and auditory stimuli than men.

In practical terms, this means that a woman's sexual map is more influenced by the social environment than a man's. If the culture is sexually restrictive, a woman will adopt sexually restrictive attitudes and behaviors. If the environment is more open, she will be more open. While men can move from being more restrictive to more open when sexual restrictions are not present, they shift far less than women. In one of the largest studies to date, David P. Schmitt of Bradley University found strong evidence for the response of women to environment across 48 different cultures and 25 different languages. He concluded, "Overall, it appeared that when women gain more sociopolitical and relational freedom, sex differences between men and women shift from large magnitudes to more moderate magnitudes. In other words, women shift their sexual attitudes and behavior more toward that of men, though they never completely overlap."[152]

---

151    Baumeister, R. F. (2000). "Gender differences in erotic plasticity: The female sex drive as socially flexible and responsive." *Psychological Bulletin*, 126, 347-374.

152    Schmitt, D. P. (2005). "Sociosexuality from Argentina to Zimbabwe: A 48-nation study of sex, culture, and strategies of human mating." *Behavioral and Brain Sciences*, 28, 247-311.

This research shows that to a strong degree, sexual attitude and behavior are susceptible to social and cultural influence, especially in women. But sexual behavior also has a huge genetic component as can be seen in the behavior of almost every animal on the planet, including other primates and the other great apes. For example, Frans de Waal, in his book *Our Inner Ape*, observes that a bonobo raised among chimps is one miserable creature, given that chimps are genetically programmed toward aggression and power, whereas bonobos are genetically inclined toward matriarchy and highly sexualized interpersonal interactions.

While humans seem to have a wider, more fluid sexuality than chimps, bonobos or gorillas, there is ample evidence to suggest that our sexual behavior has genetic roots as well. For example, the urge to masturbate is genetic and present in infants and young children. Pleasuring oneself is common in all primates. The difference may be that we have more control over when and where we do it than other primates, but that is a learned behavior, as the parent of any small child will attest. Our brains are more tuned into social and cultural expectations, while apes are uninhibited in their masturbatory behavior.

## Sociosexual Orientation

While humans have a wide sexual spectrum, a given individual may be naturally more open or more conservative in his or her sexual tendencies. Just as some people are more introverted and others more extroverted, some people are sexually open while others are more closed. These tendencies have a strong genetic component independent of culture or training. We can measure the personality variables for introversion/extroversion and we can measure sexual tendencies as well.

In 1991, Simpson and Gangestad published an instrument called the Sociosexual Orientation Inventory (SOI), a seven-item (later revised to nine items) self-report questionnaire that assesses socio-sexual orientation (SSO) along a single dimension from "restricted" – indicating a tendency to have sex exclusively in emotionally closed and committed relationships – to "unrestricted" – indicating a tendency for sexual relationships with low commitment and investment, often after short periods of acquaintance and with changing partners.[153]

SSO is how you view sex. People who score low on the scale tend to be restricted in their sexual expression. That is, they are more love-oriented, begin sexual activities later in life and have fewer partners. Those scoring high engage in sex at an earlier point in their relationships, engage in sex with more than one partner at a time and are involved in sexual relationships characterized by less investment, commitment, love and dependency. SSO (like most personality traits) is relatively stable over a life time. While men tend to be more unrestricted in SSO than women, the variance within each gender is much greater than the variance between the sexes. The survey has been used in over 50 studies and proven useful in understanding the behavior of men and women within and across cultures as well as in demonstrating the genetic influence on human mating preferences.

J. Michael Bailey's[154] groundbreaking study of Australian twins found strong evidence that 49% of SSO is inherited. None is influenced by shared environment, and approximately 50% is accounted for by the non-shared environment. Here are some of the highlights of the findings.

- Those scoring high in SSO were more likely to divorce.
- One twin's score could predict the other twin's probability of divorce.
- Divorce was more closely linked to the individual's SSO than to whether his or her parents were divorced or not.
- Persons who had a low SSO were unlikely to get divorced even if their parents had divorced.

This shows the genetic component in our sexual map. A sexual style is not a product of either moral failure or moral rectitude but of a predisposition. Wherever a person falls on the SSO scale, he will not likely venture far from that point throughout his life. If he is sexually adventurous or conservative, that is probably what he will be at 20, 40 or 60. As the famous biologist E. O. Wilson once said, "genes hold culture on a leash."[155] Like walking a

---

153   It is a simple 9-item survey that can be taken and scored by yourself. (Penke's in-press version of the revision article is available at www.larspenke.eu/pdfs/Penke_in_press_-_SOI-R_chapter.pdf).

154   Bailey, J., Kirk, K. M., Zhu, G., Dunne, M. P., & Martin, N. G. (2000). "Do individual differences in sociosexuality represent genetic or environmentally contingent strategies? Evidence from the Australian twin registry." *Journal of Personality and Social Psychology*, 78, 537–545.

155   Wilson, E. O., "On Human Nature" reprinted in *The Biology and Psychology of Moral Agency*, (1998), p. 58.

dog, culture pulls in one direction or another, but our genetic makeup will tug us back to our "center" eventually.

## Sociosexual Orientation and Religion

Religion has a one-size-fits-all approach to sex and sexuality. The sexual rules of religion have nothing to do with biology or genetics. While SSO is the behavioral expression of your particular sexual map, religion may try to force a different map into your brain, but it rarely wins that battle. Think of how many "devout" ministers, priests or religious politicians get caught having sex with prostitutes, young boys or soliciting in bathrooms?[156] Religion does not stop the sex drive or the need for variety. If it did, the most devout would have the greatest control.

The research on SSO shows that humans score across the spectrum just as they do on other personality traits. We expect to see a spread of characteristics like introversion to extroversion, dominance to non-dominance, facility for math or languages or not. It is no surprise that sexual tendencies exhibit a similar spectrum. Yet, if we applied religious rules to SSO orientation, we would see that the only option for all the major religions is a restrictive SSO, especially for women.

As one might expect, SSO also correlates with other identifiable traits. For example, unrestricted individuals tend to be more extroverted, less agreeable, more erotophilic (they like erotica), more disinhibited, more impulsive, more likely to take risks and less strongly attached to a mate. Restricted individuals, on the other hand, tend to be more introverted, more agreeable, more erotophobic, more socially constrained, less impulsive, less likely to take risks and more securely attached.[157]

Both traits have their plusses and minuses. Would the world be better without risk takers? Would we find world harmony if everyone were introverted and socially constrained? Is it desirable that everyone be extroverted? That is essentially what religion insists when sex is involved. Religious sex

---

156   Louisiana senator David Vitner was involved with several prostitutes. He prayed and asked for forgiveness and was reelected senator. Ted Haggard, president of the National Association of Evangelicals, was caught with a male prostitute and doing methamphetamines. He was prayed over by a group of fundamentalist preachers and was declared "cured" of his homosexuality (but did they cure his meth addiction?). He now has a new and thriving church in Colorado Springs. Senator Larry Craig was arrested for soliciting in the men's bathroom in Minneapolis in 2007.

157   Schmitt, D. P. (2005). "Sociosexuality from Argentina to Zimbabwe: A 48-nation study of sex, culture, and strategies of human mating." *Behavioral and Brain Sciences*, 28, 247-311.

is by definition restricted. No sex before marriage, no porn, no sex outside of marriage, no masturbation, etc.

Where would Paul or Jesus fall on the SSO scale? Or, where would Solomon or David score? Where would some religious leaders have scored, such as Mohammed, Joseph Smith, Brigham Young, Jim Jones or David Koresh?[158] Adventurous, risk-taking leaders are often sexually unrestricted (think of John Kennedy or Newt Gingrich), and that is often the case for religious leaders as well.

There is a certain irony in sexually unrestricted, charismatic leaders telling their followers to be sexually restricted. On the other hand, it is just as unrealistic for sexually restricted priests or ministers to force their followers into a sexually restricted religious box. Their followers span the full spectrum of SSO. It is unlikely that an extroverted person could change to an introvert at a priest's command, and it is just as unlikely that a sexually unrestricted person could become restricted.

### Socio-Sexual Orientation and Relationships

Undoubtedly there are problems and dangers on both sides of the SSO line, but it is better to know what our tendencies are and deal with them openly than to hide them under the stifling dogma of religion. Some non-religious people are restricted in their SSO orientation whereas others can be more open with their sexuality and its expression. There is no reason why either side has to be right or wrong or better or worse; they just *are*! For those who are sexually unrestricted, there are dangers in how they handle their sexuality with respect to disease and dealing with emotional attachment. Having a predisposition toward an unrestricted sexuality is not a license to ignore good sexual practices with regard to both health and emotions. If you are a high SSO person, you still need to negotiate sexual relations responsibly. It does not take a religion to tell you that.

If your genetic predisposition is toward sexual restriction, this may skew your view of others, especially those who are not like you. Just because you do not need variety, sexual adventure or stimulation does not say anything about others. Those "others" could be your children, parents, friends or coworkers – even your spouse. Judging others because they are not like you

---

158   All these leaders had many wives or sex partners and gave religious justification for their behavior.

leads to broken relationships and a tendency to self-righteous behavior. A restricted parent may fail to understand and properly coach a child who is unrestricted. It is difficult, if not impossible, to teach or coach someone if she feels you condemn her for her natural tendencies.

In the general population, 10-20% are naturally restricted. They can easily follow the rules and strictures of their particular religion because that is their natural predisposition. The naturally restricted person may feel little need to masturbate and may find porn uninteresting. The restricted couple may find that sex once a month in missionary position is just fine. They see nothing wrong with it nor feel any pressure to do anything else, and they are correct with respect to their preferences.

Less restricted persons may feel sexually constrained occasionally and find that a good masturbatory session with some porn relieves the urge. They probably feel no need to find a paramour or to engage in flirtatious behavior at the office. A couple who is in the middle of restricted-unrestricted may feel the need to experiment occasionally, try a new toy or position or learn new sexual techniques. They also would understand the need for their mate to masturbate and fantasize about others occasionally.

More troublesome is the religious couple with one restricted and one much less restricted mate. With religion in the mix, the restricted mate not only brings his or her naturally restricted tendencies to the relationship but also the ammunition of religious guilt.

It is difficult for a naturally restricted individual to understand the needs and desires of the less restricted, who often express the attitude, "I don't need it so why should you?" Instead of supporting the spouse's desire and need that the other doesn't have, religion leads to devastating stress on the marriage that often disrupts the couple's sexual relationship and breaks up the marriage.

This is true for both men and women. While women tend to be more restrictive than men in our culture, a significant number of women want far more sex than they get from their husbands, but religious taboos prohibit them from discussing and negotiating openly with their partners.

Finally, unrestricted persons may feel guilty about their "sinful" desire but act on it anyway. Unrestricted religious people will behave according to their biology, but feel terribly guilty about it afterwards. This can lead to a cycle of out-of-control behavior, followed by a period of unremitting guilt and repentance, then back to the behavior. On the surface, it looks like an addiction, but in reality it is religious-induced mental illness. (Note that religions would have you believe it is an addiction, since that puts the spotlight on the behavior and not the ultimate cause, the religion.)

In light of religious teachings on sex, unrestricted people often feel they are fundamentally flawed. They are sinful and rebellious against god for having strong urges that go against the church's teachings. If the religious belief is deep enough, a person will not be able to look at his behavior rationally. The result can be a destructive cycle beginning with some religiously prohibited sexual behavior followed by repentance and prayer for a few weeks. Soon biological urges surface again, and he goes back to the behavior, followed by repentance once more. The process keeps him focused on guilt, not on rational ways to enjoy and express sexuality. Every time he goes through the cycle, it makes him feel less worthwhile. At the same time, the only way he can get relief is by going back to his religion.

The religious guilt cycle interferes with learning and change. Rather than learning who he is as a sexual being, he measures himself against an impossible religious sexual standard and always comes up short. Absent religion, many unrestricted people can deal with their behavior in a rational manner. Taking guilt out of the equation allows a person to see how he is hurting himself and others and what he can do about it. Eliminating guilt about sex allows a person to talk about needs and desires more honestly and negotiate with possible partners. If a person feels shame about his desires, he is unlikely to talk about it with anyone. As long as the cycle of guilt persists, harmful behavior will likely continue.

It is because of this pattern that I do not believe there is such a thing as sexual addiction. If there is, it is far less common than religious people would have us believe. The notion of sexual addiction, while not just an invention of the religious community, has certainly been taken up and championed by preachers and religious leaders in recent years. It fits within their guilt narrative and brings people back to the church that gave them the guilt in the first place.

# CHAPTER 21:

# "MY SEX DRIVE KEEPS ME FROM JESUS"

*Religion teaches us to ignore our nature and redirect the energy toward a god. As a result, people suffer emotional and psychological problems.*

## Unfaithful Pastors

Religious leaders are in the business of telling everyone how to behave sexually. If their message is correct, the evidence might be found in significantly more "moral" behavior than their followers. In a revealing 2005-2006 report by the arch-conservative Francis Schaeffer Institute, 1,050 pastors were surveyed about various behaviors and stressors in their jobs. Here are some of the results:[159]

- Of the 1,050 (100%) pastors surveyed, every one had a close associate or seminary buddy who had left the ministry because of burnout, conflict in their church or from a moral failure.
- 808 (77%) of the pastors surveyed felt they did not have a good marriage!
- 399 (38%) of the pastors said they were divorced or currently in a divorce process.
- 315 (30%) said they had either been in an ongoing affair or a one-time sexual encounter with a parishioner.
- Almost 40% said they had had an extramarital affair since beginning their ministry.
- 70% of pastors constantly fought depression.

Of the 13 findings in this report, the author says, "This is key" on three of them, all dealing with Bible study, personal devotions and teaching doctrine. The conclusion is that more Bible study would cure these pastors of their depression and make them happy.

Let's look at the dynamics of relationships within religious marriage and how it impacts mental health. It may give us a clue about what is going on with these pastors besides their poor Bible study habits.

## Religious Infection and Depression

A conservative minister has been clinically depressed for decades, taking medication and being in therapy off and on for years. He was pastor of the largest church in his community until he had an affair with one of the married women of the church, causing him to get fired. He and the woman divorced their respective spouses and married each other. He immediately found another less conservative church and became a pastor again. He went

159 "What is Going on with the Pastors in America?" by Dr. Richard J. Krejcir, Schaeffer Institute. Available online at http://www.intothyword.org/apps/articles/default.asp?articleid=36562.

right back into the depression pattern and within a few years acted out sexually again and got fired. In counseling he once stated, "My sex drive keeps me from Jesus."

When he left religion entirely, he found he was not depressed or sexually obsessed. His second wife was delighted when their sex life came back. Now he feels relaxed and in control of himself with no antidepressants. "Getting Jesus out of my life and bedroom was the best thing I could have done," he stated.

How do you tell a minister that religion is causing much of his depression and sexual obsession? The constant low-level pressure and stress of redirecting one's sexual energy causes emotional problems. Constant repression can lead to depression in one or both spouses. Treating depression often requires that a patient identifies and changes self-defeating thinking. Identifying religion as the problem is especially difficult, since people often retreat to religion to deal with their depression. In reality, however, while religion promises peace and fulfillment, it often creates more of what caused the depression in the first place.

Depression is not always caused by sexual repression or religious ideas, but these are often contributing factors. Remember the story of Rich and the Pentecostal church in Chapter 17, where all the women were sexually unavailable to their husbands? The guilt cycle and early religious training were very likely involved in those families. Moreover, using religion to treat depression often makes the problem worse. It's like treating a disease with more of the disease. It is effective in getting people to give time and money to the church, but it does not help the victim.

This pattern may go a long way in explaining high divorce rates among the more conservative religions in the United States, especially among the clergy.[160] Not only are clergy subject to the same irrational religious ideas as their followers, such as "prayer cures depression," they also see that their efforts don't seem to help. For a pastor who genuinely wishes to help people, the constant evidence that he is not helping may eventually take a toll on his mental health and undermine his religious marriage. In social-psychology research this is called social defeat stress.

---

160   Cullen, L. "Pastors' Wives Come Together," Time Magazine, 29 March 2007. Available online at http://www.time.com/time/magazine/article/0,9171,1604902,00.html.

## Dominance and Non-Dominance

Any relationship involves a power exchange. A free flow of power allows everybody involved to contribute and get their respective needs met. In a patriarchal religious marriage, power is hierarchical: men are dominant, and women are subservient, causing a serious disruption in the natural flow of power between the mates.

It is amusing to watch male religious leaders walk the tight rope of male dominance while trying to keep their assertive wives looking submissive. He must model the "head of the house," and she must appear "submissive" to him. The truth may be the opposite. She may be dominant and he submissive. Living such an act 24 hours a day is hard.

An example comes from a former minister's wife, married to a minister for over 20 years. "The hardest part of being a minister's wife was denying who I am," she told me. She could never show her dominant side, never take the lead sexually with her husband. He was a kind, gentle, soft-spoken, caring person who was sexually submissive, even passive. Their relationship was essentially sexless for the last 10 years of their marriage, a miserable existence for her. She resolved the conflict between her sexual desire and the restrictive religious map by leaving her husband and religion. She is now a successful businesswoman who doesn't seem to have a submissive bone in her body.

In the meantime, the minister had no idea how unhappy his wife was. "We focused on church and children for most of the marriage; sex was not a serious consideration," he told me. He didn't need a lot of sex, and as the years went by, he didn't seem to miss it. He fit neatly into a sexually restrictive SSO and had a very non-dominant personality. It was comfortable for him, and he assumed it was comfortable for her. In their religious paradigm, there was no way for her to communicate her needs.

Let's go back with this woman to a time before she got married. Imagine educating her in the concepts we are discussing here. We might ask:

- How dominant are you in your daily interactions?
- How much enjoyment do you receive from directing things?
- How much variety do you need in your sex life?
- How much do you enjoy being the sexual initiator?

Armed with answers to these questions, it is possible that she would not have married a non-dominant, sexually restricted minister. Similarly, educating her husband in the same concepts might have helped him understand the needs of a prospective mate and recognize how his restrictive SSO and non-dominant personality might conflict with her style.

Psychological concepts like SSO and dominance/non-dominance undermine religion's one-size-fits-all idea about sex roles. It is unlikely these concepts will be integrated into the premarital counseling sessions of priests or ministers. Couples will continue to get poor premarital advice, and ministers will continue to see their well-intentioned efforts come to naught, as they and their parishioners divorce as much or more than the less religious.

### Sexual Redirection and Thought Distortion

Redirecting sexual energy is often a good thing. We do it all the time. You may have a sexual thought about someone, but you don't act on it. You may want to make love with your partner but a work deadline looms, so you redirect your thoughts and energy into getting finished and then have a good romp in the hay. You may enjoy various fantasies that are impractical, so you don't act on them. Normal people redirect their sexual energy all the time, but religion takes that skill and hijacks it. Religion says, "No, you cannot do that, that is sinful. Direct that energy toward god."

Sexual desire does not disappear with increased religiosity and activity. Instead, it gets redirected but the thoughts and incoming stimulation continue. The result is constant distortion of the thought process. A person whose sexuality has been confined to a religious box will soon come to see people who are not restricted as immoral or evil. It is easy for the religious person to label others as sexual deviants, promiscuous, as somebody who cannot resist temptation or has no self-control. In its worst form, redirected sexual energy can lead to literal witch-hunts, persecution of gays and others whose practices are not in strict conformity to religious teachings.

### The Misbehaving Flock

We have seen how the religious sexual map hurts leaders' and ministers' wives. What about the followers?

As we discussed in previous chapters

- Baptists and Evangelicals in the United States have among the highest divorce rates.
- The best predictor of child abuse, after drugs or alcohol, is parents' religiosity.

- Sexual dysfunction is often related to religious guilt from childhood training.
- Teenage pregnancy is highest among the most religious.

Most religious people would deny that religion contributes to all these problems – that religion actually causes or contributes to the behavior it most abhors. Failure to identify religion as a cause allows it to stay hidden.

An elder was caught soliciting gay sex in a public park. Another elder's wife was caught in the baptistery having sex with the associate minister. The youth pastor and his wife were seen at a swingers' club. The chairman of the board was caught at a porn shop in another city. A deacon's teenage daughter is pregnant. No, this isn't a setup for a soap opera, these are real-life examples from a single church.

In the churches with which I was associated, there was always some kind of sexual scandal going on. Evidence of sex is everywhere in a church if you look or listen. Many church rumors may not be true, but what would members talk about if not other people's sexual sin? And it is sexual sin that gets the most attention. It seems to be a badge of honor among most religions to violate our very fundamental drives and then damn people and talk behind their backs when they can't conform to unrealistic sexual standards.

### Brainwashing Techniques for Evangelism

Many religions teach deprivation as a path to cleanliness and godliness. Fasting for Lent or Ramadan purifies your soul; sexual abstinence before marriage keeps you pure for your husband or wife; not having sex during menstruation keeps men from impurity. For thousands of years saints and leaders have taught deprivation as the path to god. From St. Benedict to Mahatma Gandhi, religious leaders have taught that deprivation is among the most direct paths to the deity. The trick is to convince people that their natural desires are unnatural and against some god's plan. Once this is achieved, people can be brought to believe that depriving themselves of things like sex and certain foods is a noble and godly thing to do. It is an incredible distortion that convinces people to redirect their energy and life toward the religion. People give up some of the most important parts of life in service of the god.

Deprivation or overstimulation, combined with fear and peer pressure, are the conversion tools of many religions. A loud Pentecostal service, an Evangelical revival, a fear-mongering sermon by an imam or a dark campfire service during a week of church camp are all designed to overwhelm the senses, confuse the mind and alter perceptions of reality.

The British psychiatrist William Sargant, in his book *Battle for the Mind: A Physiology of Conversion and Brainwashing*,[161] was among the first to document how humans can be convinced to believe religious or political dogma. Studying the torture techniques of Korea and China in the 1950s, Sargant demonstrated the power of these techniques to alter beliefs and behavior. But it does not take extreme conditions to transform someone. Sargant's analysis found that the religious revival methods of Charles Wesley (founder of Methodism) and other religious leaders bore strong similarities to Korean and Chinese methods.

Deprivation, overstimulation, denial and fear are ancient tools of religion, but how does sex play into this formula? Giving up or resisting a natural desire in the name of a god shows commitment to the god. Nuns and priests give up sex to be most like their god. Years of sexual deprivation goes against the biological map, and emotional and psychological distortion is often the result. Add to this repetitive rituals, readings, kneeling, praying and fasting, and the brain is under constant pressure to modify perceptions of reality in favor of an invisible deity that abhors sex.

Many religions create fear and disgust around sex for the followers. At best, sex is suspect and can keep you away from Jesus. These ideas can lead to trauma, even phobia of sex or certain aspects of sex. Infected persons may see avoidance of sex as critical to their salvation and attainment of eternal life and, therefore, engage in abstinence, celibacy or restricted sexual activity in the name of the deity.

## Two Steps to Delusion

How can a religion convince a person to give up so much? Many kinds of deprivation bring on altered states of consciousness. When denied nutrients, held in social isolation, denied sex, engaged in repetitive rituals, etc. our brains are affected, which can lead to confusion and disorientation. That is, the brain is put into disequilibrium or unbalance. In this state the brain is very susceptible to suggestion and reinterpretation of common experiences.

---

161   Sargant, W. (1957), *Battle for the mind: a physiology of conversion and brainwashing*. Sargant had a somewhat controversial life and career, but this book still stands as one of the most interesting analysis of religious conversion phenomenon.

Some states of deprivation or overstimulation lend themselves to altered states of consciousness – hallucinations, dreams, feelings of being in touch with a deity can all be evoked in these situations. You may have noticed in times of hunger, your mind tends to drift to food. If you love ice cream but are prohibited from eating it by your diet, you may dream of a chocolate-covered vanilla parfait.

Religion can use this same pathway to infect someone with a sense of the holy. It only takes two steps:

1.  Create sufficient deprivation, overstimulation or fear in the name of a god, leading to changes in brain chemistry. The brain begins thinking, dreaming and searching in an effort to understand and regain balance.

2.  Offer the brain a supernatural explanation for the feelings evoked by these chemical changes. For examples,

    *   The uncontrolled sobs you experienced means Jesus has forgiven you.

    *   When you spoke in tongues that proves the Holy Spirit lives in you.

    *   The vision you had shows that god talked to you.

Once a supernatural answer to these altered states is accepted, religious devotion drives even deeper, and the person comes back for more – having an answer for the feelings, even a supernatural one, is better than continuing to experience horrible guilt or fear. The resulting sense of relief can be immense and life changing. It often leads people to engage in behavior that serves the religion well, even if it destroys or harms them. In the meantime, the victims do not realize the manipulation. They don't see that the religion created the fear and deprivation in the first place.

Sexual deprivation follows the same pattern. Whether giving up sex for Lent or becoming a celibate priest, the function of the religious act is to eliminate sex as a competing activity in favor of greater religious infection. Distorted thinking comes out of deprivation as people begin to think of sex and sexuality as their "enemy." Sexual expression and behavior are seen as incompatible with devotion to a god. If somebody said, "I abstain from sex to please the ghost in my house," they would seem delusional, but to say, "I abstain from sex to please Jesus, (or Mary, or Allah or to follow the path of the Buddha)" is seen as admirable.

Sexual deprivation does not cleanse the soul, improve the mind or bring one close to Nirvana, Jesus or Allah. It is true that it focuses the mind on deeper religious infection, but at the same time it leads to a thought pattern that demonizes sex.

What is the consequence of this behavior? It probably reduces sexual pleasure and frequency between couples, while it increases guilt around one's sexuality. It generally distorts sex and sexual drive into an evil enemy that is designed to tempt you away from the god. You become alienated from your own body. How is it healthy to think of your natural drive and desire as an enemy?

Here is how one person summed up the sexual distortions that she experienced:

> While I was told that sexuality was a beautiful thing in the context of marriage, that was downplayed considerably in comparison to the evil of sexuality, fear of its power and the sin of lust outside of marriage. I also had the strong impression growing up that women were never supposed to have sexual desires. I've had sexual desire since I was a young teen, so by the time I was married, I had such a long history of feeling horrible about sexuality that I often can't be comfortable enjoying conventional sex with my husband.

This woman experienced sexual deprivation until she got married. No masturbation, and no sex outside of marriage. Damming up such powerful urges combined with the religious messages continue to impact her sexual enjoyment and development.

## Consequences for Future Generations

The guilt cycle leads religious people to have higher teen pregnancies and disease compared to youth who receive good, science-based sex education.[162,163] How do you negotiate condom use when you know you are not supposed to be having sex in the first place? The very act of negotiating or talking about birth control or condoms means you are intentionally planning to sin. With forethought and planning, you intend to violate god's law even as he

---

162    "US Abstinence Only Programs Do Not Work, New Study Shows," available online at http:// www.guttmacher. org/media/inthenews/2007/04/18/index.html.

163    Strayhorn, J.M., and Strayhorn, J.C. (2009). "Religiosity and teen birth rate in the United States." *Reproductive Health*, 2009, 6:14.

watches you. Better to simply ignore the reality of the situation and pretend that it was impulsive or accidental than admit you are a worthless sinner. If you get pregnant or catch a disease, it is not a big leap to believe it is god's punishment for your sinfulness. You deserved it. A baby conceived in such a situation is off to a poor start. Guilt and damnation will be associated with the pregnancy and child the rest of its life. Here is what one respondent from our on-line survey wrote:

> There was a large space of time between me becoming sexually active and becoming non-religious. During that time, I put myself at unnecessary risk of disease and pregnancy. While I was religious, guilt kept me from taking basic precautions like birth control or condom use. To me, using any sort of contraceptive was tantamount to admitting that I was planning for and, indeed, desirous of sexual activities. Deciding not to use contraception allowed me to convince myself that my pleasure was a side effect of fulfilling my boyfriend's desire for sexual activity.

We heard similar stories from hundreds of people in our research; stories of religious guilt leading people to take unnecessary risks while denying their sexual feelings and desires.

In my own family, the effects of religious distortion go back at least 80 years when my grandmother got pregnant under questionable circumstances, then divorced. She remarried a short time later. Her religious shame and guilt prevented her from admitting and dealing openly with the situation. She cut off contact with the father of her child and pretended she was never divorced. She was a harsh judge of anyone who divorced. No one else condemned her, but she condemned herself. She made many poor choices over her lifetime in the name of religion.

Within the church in which I grew up, virtually every family I knew suffered the consequences of religious choices as devastating as my grand-mother's. Were they told that the unwed pregnancies, affairs, divorces, sexual abuse and child abuse were often related to their religion, they would be offended. Guilt and shame blind entire communities to the devastating effects religion has on families and relationships.

The successful adaptation and evolution of our species is predicated on mating and bonding strategies going back hundreds of thousands of years. Religion throws a metaphorical monkey wrench into the works, then condemns us for behaving as normal human beings.

# SECTION V:

# PROGRAM YOURSELF FOR A CHANGE

## A Framework

If we don't want our biology to rule us, we must respect and acknowledge our biological leash. Ignoring or denying sexual urges and drives leads to disappointment and unhappiness. The religious view of monogamy is biologically irrelevant and often destructive. More marriages will last longer with more happiness by eliminating religious ideas of marriage, fidelity and monogamy and adopting ideas and behaviors that meet the real human needs in a relationship.

In this section I want to explore a framework for sex and sexuality. The information may help you make more informed and rational choices about who you are as a sexual being and how you want to relate to others. It may challenge your training and lead you to discover new ideas. You may decide to try new behaviors involving yourself or your partner. I am not advocating any particular course of action, lifestyle or marriage choice. I am advocating clear-headed, non-supernatural thinking in our relationship choices. My goal is to help you to build a more rational and less religiously-influenced sex life.

# CHAPTER 22:

# THE JESUS TRAP

*What makes people convert to the religion of their mate? What is the pattern that sometimes traps even atheists and other non-religious people?*

### The Jesus Trap Pattern

Getting involved with a religious person will sooner or later lead you to a guilt wall. You can have a lot of fun with guilt-ridden Catholics or Mormons, but the fun will come to an abrupt halt when their Jesus steps in – and he will. I call it the "Jesus trap," and millions of people have been suckered into it. When I give talks on the Jesus trap and ask how many have seen it in friends or family, about one third of the audience raises their hand.

It goes like this. Boy meets religious girl.[164] Infatuation and NRE[165] often overcome religious inhibitions, and sex begins. Because she has let go of her religious inhibitions, she can really enjoy herself. As long as the NRE remains strong, the sex will remain great.

Once the NRE wanes or an outside event opens the door, like someone at church finding out she is having sex, she will hit the guilt wall. At this point, she will insist on a "serious talk." During the talk, she will essentially say, "I can't continue this and stay faithful to my Jesus. Convert to my religion and we can go back to having fun again." If the man doesn't convert, the relationship may end.

If the man does convert, the next conversation will be, "I appreciate your converting, but I can't continue doing this unless we are married. Marry me and we can go back to having lots of fun." After marriage, the fun may resume for a while.

Within a few years, maybe just months, guilt over premarital sex or childhood training often creeps back in and the fun dies. You are now converted to a religion you never dreamed you would be in and married to a person who acts nothing like she did when you first met. Sexual ideas and behaviors that both of you enjoyed are now thought to be dirty or wrong. She loved oral or anal sex before, now it makes her feel guilty. She enjoyed role-playing and a porn film occasionally, now she says she cannot be a good mother and Sunday School teacher and still do those things.

You are in the Jesus trap. Getting out will be difficult and painful. Your whole life is now outlined by her religious agenda, and sex is not a very important part of it. When kids come along, she will begin infecting them with her religious sexual guilt. Your objections will mean nothing

---

164  As we noted earlier, it is usually the female who is more religious, but this story can and does go either way.

165  New Relationship Energy, as discussed in Chapter 17..

because the religion has activated the child infection program. The pattern is the same whether the religious mate is male or female, Baptist, Muslim or Catholic. You can try rational discussion, but once the religious program has been activated, reason is almost impossible.

This pattern is remarkably the same from person to person. Here is an example from a very successful scientist and businessman. Compare his experience to the pattern I described above.

### Bob's Story

*I was an atheist my whole life until I met this incredible woman in graduate school. I was 24 and she was 22. She was smart, intelligent and very sexy. We dated a few weeks. I learned that she was Mormon, but I knew nothing about Mormons so I ignored it. The sex was great, and we seemed to have so much in common. After a few months, she started talking about her Mormon beliefs and asking me to come with her to some services. I went along for the ride. At first, Mormonism looked as crazy as any other religion. But I really liked this woman and soon realized that I wasn't going to get anywhere with her unless I took Mormonism seriously. I dove in and didn't come up for air for 22 years.*

*In retrospect, it is hard to believe I was so easily sucked in, but I was in love. My two best friends even came to me and said, 'Have you lost your mind? You are acting like a religious fanatic.' I was offended by their comments. Within months, I had ended most of my old friendships and moved toward developing new relationships in the church.*

*Within a year, I had become a Mormon and we got married. I became very serious about it and rose to some very important positions. I taught a lot and studied constantly. We had five children, which was far more than I ever dreamed of having, but she was insistent that it was our duty to be fruitful. She would have had more if I had not simply refused.*

*I took my role as the spiritual head of the family very seriously. Twenty-two years later, I woke up early one morning in a cold sweat. I picked up the Book of Mormon and started reading from cover to cover as if I had never read it before. Then I picked up the Bible and did the same thing. This took me several weeks. The whole time I had a notebook by my side and I took notes on things that simply did not make sense.*

*In the end, I had a couple of notebooks full of contradictions and ideas that I realized were totally crazy. I began asking myself, "What enticed me into this religion? How did I totally ignore reason and common sense to believe this stuff? I have a master's degree in science for God's sake."*

*I was embarrassed and angry. I soon dropped my church work and made excuses to get out of teaching. I finally had to tell my wife that I had come to my senses. That night was the end of our marriage. She told me that she married a Mormon and would not stay married to a man who was not Mormon. We were soon divorced.*

*I look back and see how easily I was duped into one of the most insane religions on the planet – and I was an atheist! It pains me that I helped brainwash five innocent children into that cult. Needless to say, it has put a strain on my relationships with my children, but I am happy to report that two of them have left the church. The other three are even more religious than their mother.*

Why does the Jesus trap work so often? As we discussed in Chapter 17, during NRE the rational immune system is compromised. A person's emotional stability is off balance, and the pleasure hormones strongly affect perception and decision-making. Religion simply hops right into the non-infected person's mind, and conversion just seems like the right thing to do for someone you love.

The behavior is similar to the effect of the hairworm, a parasite that infects the brain of grasshoppers. Once inside the brain, it induces the grasshopper to jump into water so the parasite can exit the grasshopper and find a mate. The grasshopper dies. The parasite goes on to mate and have offspring. Many parasites and viruses are capable of taking over and controlling hosts so the parasite can reproduce. Religion acts much like the hairworm, taking control of the mind and directing the person to do whatever is necessary to infect new minds.

### Emotional Blackmail and the Jesus Trap

Just as we have a biological immune system that keeps pathogens out, critical thinking helps keep irrational ideas out of our heads. If one person is deeply infected with religion and the other person is sufficiently infatuated, religion is able to jump from one brain to the next and infect a new person. Many a Baptist has converted to Catholicism, and many a Hindu has converted to Islam as a result of this infection pattern.

While the pattern occasionally results in the woman converting, the fact that men start off less religious and women more so favors the conversion of the man. Rich Lyons, a former Pentecostal minister, tells how his denomination trained people in "friendship dating."[166] The object was to date a person for the purpose of introducing him or her to the Pentecostal church, not necessarily for marriage or a relationship. In Lyons' view, it was unquestionably manipulative and designed to take advantage of natural infatuations, leading the target into religion using the potential promise of relationship. He saw many people join and stay in the church even though the relationship did not last. This is the Jesus trap in action.

### The Jesus Trap and Raising Children

If you are involved in a potentially committed relationship with a religious person, open and detailed discussion of values and beliefs is critically important. The very act of discussing this will quickly reveal important differences, especially with respect to raising children. Honest discussion of these differences can be very uncomfortable and even threatening to the relationship, but once you are married, it is too late for rational discussion and decision making. Here is why.

If you choose to marry a religious person, the negotiation around religious behavior and childrearing practices will be difficult. If you can agree to raise the children in a religiously neutral manner, it is commendable, but unlikely to happen. When children actually come along, many agreements go out the window and the religious program kicks in. The religious spouse infects the children as strongly and quickly as possible as do religious grandparents and other family members. The non-religious parent is often powerless. If you choose to remind your spouse of the agreement, the response will often be anger and a myriad excuses as to why the agreement does not apply. Once the religious program fires off, it is almost impossible to get in the way or slow it down.

---

166 *Living After Faith* podcast, episode #38, available online at http://livingafterfaith.blogspot.com/.

This pattern holds for all but the most liberal religions. If you marry an Episcopalian or Unitarian, it probably won't be a problem. But keep in mind, when you marry someone, you also marry his or her religious parents and relatives. Even if your spouse is not religious, their family may be. She may have a difficult time telling her parents that they cannot take the children to their Evangelical Sunday School. Or the parents may offer to pay for tuition at a private religious school. Religious relatives can offer many temptations and inducements to infect grandchildren with religion. The fact that you are not bringing your children up religious makes them want to step in and do it for you.

### The Psychology Behind the Jesus Trap

The religiously infected person is not generally conscious of the strategy as it plays out. Their own hormones and biology (NRE) simply overwhelm religious guilt for the moment. They may experience guilt after the sex, but they can justify their behavior and reduce the cognitive dissonance in two ways:

1.   Ask forgiveness from their Jesus now or promise to ask for it later after they have converted their lover to Jesus.
2.   Work harder to convert their lover. God may overlook a little sexual indiscretion if it means a new soul for Jesus in the long run.

These justifications allow the religious person to engage in extremely uninhibited sex. Many victims of this strategy say that initial sex with the religiously infected person felt like a dam broke. One survey respondent wrote:

> *She was wild. I have had my share of lovers but never had anyone that fun and creative in bed. Of course, that promptly died when I told her I didn't care if she was religious – I was never going to become a Christian and if she kept pressing me, I was going to break it off.*

Religious persons are generally very interested in sex just like any normal person – and have an imagination and the energy for it. When constrained by the guilt cycle, however, they keep it under wraps. When guilt is temporarily removed, they can go to the other extreme. Many can remain in the uninhibited phase for weeks – months at most – then a wave of guilt overtakes them.

## Strategies for Dealing With the Jesus Trap

Dealing with the Jesus trap is difficult. She is probably not consciously thinking, "I will ignore my guilt for a while until I can trap him into accepting Jesus." He is not thinking, "I will go along with her religious stuff, but I'll be prepared in case she tries to convert me."

Here are some strategies to consider.

1.  Engage in open, direct and detailed discussion of religion to make the issues visible to both partners. It might take the form of, "I am having a great deal of fun with you and am really getting to like you a lot, but something puzzles me. Your religion says everything we are doing is sinful, how do you square that with what we are doing? Do you think you might start feeling guilty about it at some point? For my part, I don't see a problem, but I am concerned that the conflict between what we are doing and your religion may get in the way as we develop a stronger relationship."

    This strategy forces both of you to look directly at a major threat to the relationship. The downside in this approach is that it may evoke the guilt cycle and make it difficult for her to go back to having fun again. You may choose to enjoy the fun while it lasts. Just be aware, the fun will come to an end. The consolation is that the result will be the same whether you convert or not. A religious person simply cannot ignore the internal conflict forever.

2.  Honestly discuss your sexual attitudes. It may take the form of a discussion such as this: "I am really interested in you and think we may have something special between us. You have expressed interest in getting married and having children. I like that idea, but I also want to be sure that we are both on the same page when we do have children. I want my children to feel free and open about their sexuality. For example, many parents are shocked when they learn they have a gay child, when they catch their child using porn, or they learn that their child is discussing explicit sexual acts with a classmate. I'd like to discuss how we would approach these kinds of issues if we were parents. For my part, I would like our children to have

the same kind of free, open and creative kinds of sex we have been having since we began seeing each other. What are your views?"

This kind of discussion will quickly bring out the partner's religious sexual identity. You may soon experience his or her homophobia. He or she may also express their guilt over the kind of sex you've been having.

This kind of openness and honesty is not part of religious courtship. It brings out your values and challenges hers. Initiate the values discussion soon after you have decided to move the relationship to a more serious level. The more addicted you get to each other, the harder it will be to admit that the value differences are insurmountable.

The psychology behind the Jesus trap is simple if you understand the guilt cycle. In the course of dating, it is very likely that you will find a person who really seems to match you but is also religious. Hopefully, this discussion will give you the tools to think rationally about the relationship before making a commitment to someone who may try to convert you and infect your future children with religion without your agreement.

# CHAPTER 23:

# WHAT'S LOVE GOT TO DO WITH IT?

*People seek different levels of security and variety in relationships. One size does not fit all. But religious maps imprison us, blinding us to the problems the map itself causes.*

## You are a Walking Conflict

You are a walking conflict with regard to sex and relationships, as is every other person on the planet. On one hand, you want excitement, adventure, stimulation and being swept off your feet with the hottest, most attractive person in the world. On the other hand, you want to feel secure and stable, protected and supported by a solid partner. Most humans are a mix. Some want more security, others more adventure, but everyone wants some of both.

New relationship energy (NRE) helps fulfill the need for excitement and stimulation, but it does not fulfill the need for the stability and long-term support to rely on when the going gets tough. This is an entirely different kind of relationship. It is not the kind you read about in Harlequin novels or Shakespeare. It does not have flash, excitement and adventure, but what it offers is even more important. It offers a sense of security, of being loved, and loving and caring for someone.

We call both of these relationships love, but they are actually quite different at the biochemical level and at the social and psychological level. Long-term security relationship, or LTS, includes the feeling of safety and satisfaction you get when you can come home after a hard day and enjoy a quiet evening with your partner. Your body reacts to the security your partner offers and releases hormones that counteract the stress hormones generated throughout the day. This is a powerful experience and addictive in its own right, but it can take years of experience with a partner before you realize the positive results.

Now for the conflict. In Chapter 20 we discussed SSO (socio-sexual orientation). No matter where you fall on this spectrum, you probably want some level of excitement and some security. If you and your spouse are both high SSO, you crave the excitement and adventure that comes in NRE, but you also want the security of a solid partner. To meet those needs, you may seek out and enjoy adventurous activities together or separately. This might mean one partner runs marathons and the other has a boyfriend on the side. It might mean both of you enjoy sexual role-play or watching porn together occasionally.

If you are on the other end of the SSO scale, you crave the quiet sense of support and security that comes from a predictable routine and stable partner. Years of enjoying each other brings satisfaction, trust and well-being. A low level of sexual activity may be just fine. You would never dream of attending a fetish party, and the thought of sex outside of your own home has no interest for you.

Both of these styles can work. But there has to be a mutual understanding of each partner's excitement/security level. If the partners are too far apart on the SSO scale, they'll need much more understanding and communication. One partner will be interested in more adventurous sexual activities while the other sees no need. It can be a source of major misunderstanding, though not insurmountable.

Unfortunately, the religious culture around us values the low-SSO type of relationship. Low adventure, low excitement and low sexual activity provide a nice quiet place in which to infect children or grandchildren with negative religious sexual ideas. Religion needs this kind of environment to incubate.

## Monogamy Is Not the Default Position

The fact that humans, when given the opportunity, change partners occasionally helps us understand how we can love a partner but still want someone else – how a person can enjoy LTS with her partner but want NRE with someone new. These are not mutually exclusive emotional states. They can exist in the same person at the same time.

The famous CBS correspondent Charles Kuralt died in 1997. As the estate was being sorted out, a mistress surfaced and sued to maintain possession of the Montana property he had promised her. To most people's great surprise, it was then revealed that Kuralt had lived a double life for 29 years. But the Kuralt story may be more common than we realize. The aunt and uncle of a good friend of mine revealed that they had lived in an open relationship most of their married life. They dared not tell it to their family or friends, but they attributed the happiness they had experienced for over 50 years to their non-monogamy. Even a small amount of research on the Internet leads to many websites and organizations where people communicate and connect in non-monogamous lifestyes.

The ratio of men to women featured in the history books would lead one to believe that women did not even exist or played no part in our culture. Similarly, a reading of religious history over the last two centuries shows almost no atheists. One would think that atheists did not exist until Richard Dawkins wrote *The God Delusion* (2006), yet atheists have been present in significant number for centuries. In Utah, there are hundreds of polygamous Mormon compounds, but no one talked about them or even acknowledged they existed until Warren Jeffs was arrested for child abuse and molestation.[167] In the same way, there are many non-monogamists among us; they just don't advertise it.

Culture has a way of ignoring some kinds of people or making them so uncomfortable that they hide in plain sight. People will find ways to get their needs met, even if they have to hide it for 29 years. Warren Buffet, one of the two or three richest men in the world, was married for decades. When his wife moved to California to pursue a career, his mistress moved in with him with the full knowledge of his wife. The arrangement lasted for decades with his wife's full knowledge and approval. When his wife died, he married his mistress.[168] All this in Omaha, Nebraska!

How many famous people from FDR to Bertrand Russell, from Mark Twain to Simone de Beauvoir have led lives with multiple partners – whether openly or secretly? If it is common among famous people, it is happening among the less famous as well.

The shame in these stories is not in their non-monogamy, but in the secrecy with which those involved felt they had to live. Monogamy is not the default position for humans. Openly recognizing this would allow people to decide for themselves what types of relationships work for them. Religion and our religious culture dictates one approach to relationships, but as we saw in our review of other cultures and species, there are many possible relationship configurations. Even among different religions there are other configurations as we see in Islam, Hinduism and fundamentalist Mormonism. Of course, these religions are highly prejudicial against women, but they are different configurations from mainstream Christianity. Is it possible that there are relationship configurations that are friendly to women and men but not tied to traditional Christian marriage?

The challenge for those who want to throw off religious influence is to learn how to make rational choices about relationships and sexuality. Our Christian culture says monogamy is the only acceptable arrangement. Unless you are Christian, there is no reason to follow that particular dogma. Even the Christians do not adhere to Christian monogamy, despite their claims.

167   See, for example, http://www.dailymail.co.uk/news/article-2024150/Warren-Jeffs-trial-Paedophile-gets-life-sentence-50-brides-photo-emerges.html.

168   See http://feedlot.blogspot.com/2006/09/omaha-billionaire-warren-buffett.html.

Newt Gingrich has had three wives. He had affairs with two of them while married. That is not monogamy by any definition, yet he holds himself up as a devout monogamous Christian. I would estimate that well over half of the divorces in my home church were preceded by an affair on the part of one partner. That is not monogamy.

If people were taught to communicate openly about their sexuality, they would have wonderful opportunities to develop long-lasting, loving relationships that meet the needs of all parties and create safe spaces for children to grow up.

So what does love have to do with it? We would first need to determine what love looks like. Is love two men kissing after their wedding? Is it a Black man and white woman living happily married for 40 years? Is it two lovers having a 10-year relationship but never getting married? Is it a married couple getting all dressed up to go to a swingers' party? Is it a polyamorous woman with her husband and boyfriend? All of these forms of relationships are based on love and care, despite Christian, Muslim, Jewish, Mormon or Hindu scriptures. People within these relationships define love on their own terms, not in terms of scripture or the current religious interpretation. Love must be defined within the relationship, not by some outside criteria.

At the opposite end of the spectrum, a very religious couple I knew lived together for almost 45 years, hating each other most of the time and sleeping in separate bedrooms. Their children and grandchildren got an earful of complaints whenever they were alone with one of them. When the husband died, the minister praised the couple for their long happy marriage and for raising their children in the Lord. Yet, everyone knew this to be a lie, including the minister. But they were in church every Sunday and gave generously, so the charade was perpetuated.

Which of these relationship styles makes for greater happiness? Which allows people to grow and learn to communicate their aspirations and desires? Which is more honest? The religious couple lived a lie and their unhappiness impacted dozens of people inside and outside their family. Their religious values prevented them from divorcing or finding a different relationship arrangement, yet those same values did not help them learn how to be happy together.

## Imprisoned by the Religious Map

The need to lock in sexual monogamy for life is simply unrealistic for many people and may not even be emotionally or physically healthy. Recognition of this fact would go a long way toward making long-term relationships possible. If people communicated honestly on these issues, other relationship approaches might work for a wide range of people. Of the 50% in our culture who divorce, how many might remain married if other relationship options were seen as viable?[169] How many who stay in miserable marriages would find renewed happiness and commitment to one another?

Most people simply inherit the sexual map of their religious training and never examine it. So when they repeatedly get in relationship trouble, they never think to examine their map to ensure it is accurate. A very religious former coworker of mine was married three times over several decades and had children by two wives. A few minutes of discussion over lunch one day easily revealed why. He believed strongly that the man is the head of the house, and his attitudes about sex were prudish at best. It would never occur to him that his map of marriage, sex and relationships was the primary reason for so much unhappiness and disappointment in his life. He was imprisoned by his map.

Changing our childhood map can be difficult, but it can be liberating. Here is what two of our survey respondents wrote in response to the question, "How has your sex life changed since leaving religion?"

- *(It is) more liberating; less guilt; less fear about supporting people of other sexual orientations; more loving relationships; more freedom of expression physically; I feel healthier physically and mentally.*
- *I now feel like I can explore sex more. There is no God that is judging me or overlooking what I do. I can do what I want, and feel good about it because I know that I'm doing it for both my partner's pleasure and my pleasure.*

As part of our research, we have received hundreds of similar comments from people who decided to change their maps.[170]

---

169    A brief article on this is available at http://www.telegraph.co.uk/news/worldnews/northamerica/usa/2095967/Why-having-an- affair-could-save-your-marriage.html.

170    Ray and Brown, "Sex and Secularism: What Happens When You Leave Religion." See IPCPress.com for the full report.

Religion creates an unnecessary layer of complexity. It is difficult enough to make clear-headed decisions about your relationships without including a voyeuristic god in your bedroom.

## Marriage: One Size Does Not Fit All

Religion has a spotty record with respect to marriage. For centuries the church was mostly concerned with the marriages of the rich and powerful and showed little interest in the marriages of the peasant class. Local culture often dictated how and why a person got married. For a thousand years or more, church weddings were rare in Europe. The church issued no marriage licenses (neither did the state). Many people "married" by simply moving in together. The first time the church might officially know of a marriage was when two people appeared at the church to get their baby christened.[171]

With the Reformation, marriage became more important for both Protestant and Catholics, primarily because the respective churches wanted to have clear claim to the children. Marriage in the church ensured membership by the children as well. For the last two hundred years, marriage in the West has been a one-size-fits-all model based on the assumption that marriage is forever and divorce is not an option.

Considering the 50% that divorce and the 25% or more who remain in unhappy marriages for life, this model only works for about a quarter of marriages. Remove religion from the equation, and there are no compelling reasons to perpetuate this model.

## Rethinking Marriage

Why do people get married? Love is a part of it, but if love is based on NRE, then we know it will end relatively soon. If a true partnership is the goal, then both parties need to look beyond NRE. They need to make decisions about children and their religious or non-religious training. Couples need to talk openly about how to negotiate future changes to the relationship, including thinking rationally about how the marriage might be dissolved, if that time comes. This is all very unromantic stuff, but when contemplating a long-term partnership, romance must take a back seat.

---

171  Coontz provides a look at this in *Marriage, a History: How Love Conquered Marriage* (2005).

### Don't Let the Pope (or Any Clergy) Define Your Relationships

Relationship experts and activists have been exploring alternatives for years. From gay marriage to limited contract marriages, even governments are rethinking marriage. In 2011, Mexico City, noting that the city has a divorce rate of 50% and most marriages end in two years, introduced legislation for a two-year marriage contract. The contract could be renewed but would automatically end after two years. The Catholic church complained. "This reform is absurd. It contradicts the nature of marriage," said Hugo Valdemar, spokesman for the Mexican archdiocese. "It's another one of these electoral theatrics the assembly tends to do that are irresponsible and immoral."[172] The statement should have said, *"It contradicts the nature of Catholic marriage."* The church has no right to define marriage except for those inside the church. The church made the same complaint when Mexico City legalized gay marriage in 2009.

Dr. Deborah Anapohl's groundbreaking book *Love Without Limits* (1988)[173] was one of the first books to explore alternative relationship models like polyamory. Since its publication, dozens of other books have looked at ways people can develop committed relationships outside of traditional religious models. Further, the non-profit organization Loving More was established in 1991 to promote awareness of polyamory, and the movement has grown immensely since then. It is interesting to note that the polyamory movement has far more women leaders than men, and many of the best-selling books on the subject are by women.

Susan Pease Gadoua, author and marriage therapist, has proposed that marriages be contractual for specific purposes and time periods.[174] As part of the process, she asks, "Why do people want to get married?" The answer to the question helps determine the marriage contract. If people want to get married for financial security, without children, that would frame one approach to a marriage contract. If marriage is for purposes of raising children, that creates a different set of expectations and obligations. If the

---

172    "'Til 2013 do us part? Mexico mulls 2-year marriage," available online at http://www.reuters.com/article/2011/09/29/us-mexico-marriage-idUSTRE78S6TX20110929.

173    Recently updated as *Polyamory in the 21st Century: Love and Intimacy with Multiple Partners* (2010).

174    Gadoua has published two books on the topic: *Contemplating Divorce, A Step-by-Step Guide to Deciding Whether to Stay or Go* (2008), and *Stronger Day by Day: Reflections for Healing and Rebuilding After Divorce* (2010).

marriage brings children from previous relationships, that is yet another important consideration. Gadoua advocates negotiations about marriage expectations and clear-headed contemplation of how to dissolve it, in a civilized and respectful manner.

Within the BDSM[175] community, a form of relationship contract has been in use for decades – a framework for defining the limits and expectations of a relationship. While not legally binding, the contract facilitates genuine discussion about relationship expectations and forces people to clarify expectations, examine hidden assumptions and enter into agreements that are satisfactory to all parties. In addition, contracts are limited and subject to renegotiation every six months or so. It is a dynamic approach to relationships that recognizes nothing is static.

The purpose here is not to endorse any particular style or approach to relationships but to show that there are many options and creative ways to define relationships. There may be Catholic, Muslim, Baptist or Mormon marriage, but there is no universal right of religion to define marriage outside the walls of its church. On the other hand, we have the power to define relationships in ways that fit our needs and the needs of those we love.

---

175  BDSM: Behavior-Discipline-Sado-Masochism. See this site for a comprehensive overview of contracts, http://www.leathernroses.com/generalbdsm/generalbdsm.htm#contracts.

# CHAPTER 24:

# JEALOUSY: THE ANTI-LOVE POTION

*Sexual jealousy is an emotion that originates in ideas about sex and ownership.*

*"A jealous husband doesn't doubt his wife, but himself."*
**-Honore De Balzac**

*"Jealousy is nothing more than a fear of abandonment."*
**-Arab Proverb**

*"Jealousy is all the fun you think they had."*
**-Erica Jong**

*"A competent and self-confident person is incapable of jealousy in anything. Jealousy is invariably a symptom of neurotic insecurity."*
**-Robert A. Heinlein**

*"Jealousy is not so much the love of another as the love of ourselves."*
**-Francois de La Rochefoucauld**

*"Jealousy, that dragon which slays love under the pretence of keeping it alive. "*
**-Henry Ellis**

### Our Jealous Culture

The idea and expression of sexual jealousy varies widely from one culture to the next. Margaret Meade famously claimed it was nonexistent in Samoan culture, though some have disputed that.[176] Further, Bronislaw Malinowski found minimal cause for sexual jealousy in the matrilineal Trobriand Islands,[177] nor does it seem to be a problem among the matriarchal Na of China. Many human cultures seem to be relatively free of it.

Despite claims by evolutionary psychologists like Steven Pinker,[178] the evidence for an evolutionary or genetic basis for jealousy is not convincing. Evolutionary psychologists tend to ignore cross-cultural and cross-species data, in favor of data that are affected by universal religions.[179] Finally, they generally ignore the fact that sex is rarely procreative in humans but is used far more for recreation and bonding. The human tendency to jealousy appears to be largely cultural, but let's examine the evidence.

Conflict over mates is characteristic of many species. Chimps and gorillas have major conflicts and rivalries over mates. One might say that a silverback gorilla guards his females jealously, putting on aggressive displays to discourage possible rivals. Chimps and gorillas treat sex like a precious commodity to be guarded and protected. On the other hand, jealousy seems to be largely missing among the female-led bonobos, for whom sex is not a precious commodity, so no need to defend mates or attack others. As we have seen in previous chapters, humans are very flexible in their sexuality and have the capacity to act like gorillas, chimps or bonobos. It is our culture that seems to push us one way or another.

With property ownership comes possessiveness. If women are property, they are guarded jealously. Once women break free of their property status and gain economic autonomy, male jealousy begins to look like what it truly is – the need to own and control females.

---

176   Margaret Mead's *Coming of Age in Samoa: A Psychological Study of Primitive Youth for Western Civilization* was first published in 1929.

177   Malinowski's *The Sexual Life of Savages* was originally published 1929.

178   Steven Pinker in *How the Mind Works* (1997), as well as Tooby, J. and Cosmides, L. "Toward Mapping the Evolved Functional Organization of the Mind and Brain," in M. S. Gazzaniga (Ed.), *The New Cognitive Neuro-sciences* (2000, second ed., pp. 1167–1178).

179   See, for example, "Jealousy and Violence: A Skeptical Look at Evolutionary Psychology," by David J. Buller. Available online at http://www.skeptic.com/reading_room/sex-jealousy-and-violence/.

On the female side, jealousy is related to control of resources in the interest of the woman and her young. A woman may show jealousy toward another female who is draining off a male's resources, thus depriving her and her young. If, as with the Na culture (discussed in Chapter 11), the father's resources are not involved in raising the child, there is less reason for women to express jealousy of other women. If, as in the case of the Hadza culture, the child is raised as much by the clan as by the parents, there is also less need for female jealousy. The father's resources are important, but not critical.

With feminine economic autonomy, the idea of owning or controlling women is diminished. Men are less able to guard their mates, so other ways of relating to women are necessary. Also, with female autonomy, a woman is less threatened by other women taking resources because she controls her resources. The notion of owning or controlling a man's resources diminishes, so other ways of relating to men are necessary as well. For example, most cultures focus on the man's social and economic status. Women were taught and even required to marry men who have the most resources and then jealously guard those resources for her children.

The model may have been functional in the past, but is it functional now? If a woman is financially independent and does not want children, the "marry a high-status male" model may be counterproductive in finding a compatible mate. Many women earn as much as or more than the men they might marry. If the only model is to marry high-status men, then the pool of candidates is vanishingly small for higher income women.

### Learning to Be Jealous

No one has found a jealousy gene, but many people believe we are born jealous or are genetically predisposed to jealousy. We certainly have a predisposition to protect things we need for survival and reproduction, as does any species. In many ways, our culture defines what is important and sets the criteria for becoming jealous. If the culture says, "Protecting and controlling your women is important," then most men and women will play their parts in that scheme. If, on the other hand, the culture does not place great value on controlling women, then there will be less jealousy.

This can be illustrated with the following examples. In our culture, it is not normal to kill your wife when you learn that she is having an affair. In Saudi Arabia or areas of Pakistan and other Muslim countries, however, killing one's wife and her lover would be viewed as an honor killing. Even if it is against the law, few are prosecuted for doing it and families support the husband. This level of jealous behavior is learned and even encouraged by the culture. To an Arab man, the murderous rage he feels is a normal emotion – normal, in the sense that it is expected and understood by people in that culture. Even women may see this as justifiable homicide in a Muslim culture.[180]

In our own culture, English court cases in the 17th and 18th centuries show that judges and juries let men off with minimal punishment for the crime of wife beating and even killing if the wife was known to be unfaithful. The famous English jurist William Blackstone noted in 1783 that killings provoked by infidelity were "of the lowest degree of manslaughter … for there could not be a greater provocation."[181]

In the 19th and early 20th centuries, all male juries in England and the United Staes might find the murderous husband "not guilty by reason of temporary insanity" or call it manslaughter rather than murder. That level of jealous behavior was understood as justifiable by the male-dominated culture of the time.[182]

While Paul says in Corinthians 13:4 that "love is not jealous," the idea and practice of jealousy is deeply rooted in religion. Deuteronomy and Leviticus spell this out starkly.

> **Deuteronomy 22:20-21, NAB,** But if this charge is true (that she wasn't a virgin on her wedding night), and evidence of the girl's virginity is not found, they shall bring the girl to the entrance of her father's house and there her townsmen shall stone her to death, because she committed a crime against Israel by her unchasteness in her father's house. Thus shall you purge the evil from your midst.

> **Leviticus 21:9, NAB,** A priest's daughter who loses her honor by committing fornication and thereby dishonors her father also, shall be burned to death.

180   The international organization StopHonorKillings.com tracks honor killings throughout the world. Though there is more than jealousy involved in this crime, it is rarely prosecuted in many countries regardless of the motivation – jealousy or not. Men and families are thought to have the right to kill a wayward girl or woman.

181   Blackstone, E. (1783). *Blackstone's Commentaries.*

182   Mullen, P. (1995). "Jealousy and Violence," *Hong Kong Journal of Psychiatry* 5, 18-24.

You might ask, are these verses dealing with jealousy? It is wife guarding. With the threat of death, the assumption is that she will remain faithful. If a wife is not faithful, then her children may not be yours and your property may go to someone else's progeny. The logic is based on cultural ideas about property rights, but it looks like jealous behavior. Most important for our discussion, this behavior, whether you call it jealousy or something else, is learned; it is not genetic. As a result, it can be unlearned or modified as we can see by the change in our culture over the last few centuries.

Today, there is no excuse for spousal murder based on jealousy or property rights. Many men and women who, in times past, might have gone into a jealous rage today control their emotions, talk through the issues, go to a marriage counselor or file for divorce. We have seen a remarkable decrease in the type of behavior in the last 150 years, far too fast for an inborn or genetic trait to change.

### The Decline of Jealousy

What has caused this change? It was precipitated by general and emotional education that opened up options. With few options, emotional frustration takes over and becomes behavior we identify as jealous. Non-religious professionals and organizations are ready to educate and intervene when emotions get out of control. Mental health services are available and general education is better. We also have resources that work in favor of learning self-control. Police can be called quickly, and investigative tools make it easier to find the culprit. Finally, increased economic independence makes women less controllable. If a man wants a mate, jealous, controlling behavior isn't an effective way of getting and keeping her.

As mentioned, if jealousy is learned, it can be unlearned. Our entire culture has unlearned some of the jealous habit over the last two centuries, but we still have a way to go. Unfortunately, jealousy is still actively taught and encouraged in our culture, often with the collusion or support of religion.

### Adolescent Jealousy

Girls and boys are taught from very young that they "should" be jealous of anyone who might take their boyfriend or girlfriend. The list of teenage love songs that include mention of jealousy is enormous. Unfortunately, teens learn a knee-jerk response to sexual tension or conflict rather than a reasoned and rational response to relationship building.

Listen to any number of songs, and the words "my girl," "my guy," "my love," "mine forever" and "yours forever" are everywhere. In novels, plays, self-help books and poems, the focus on owning someone is the main theme. It is a lot simpler to claim ownership than to build a relationship.

Possessiveness and jealousy begin when two adolescents first experience the power of NRE. The opiates produced in their brains are literally addictive. The problem comes when NRE gets mixed in with ideas of "love is forever" or "sex means commitment" or dependency issues like "I need you" or "I can't live without you." These messages seem harmless, except that people actually believe them when in the throes of NRE, especially if they have never been taught otherwise.

At the same time, our culture, and religion particularly, pushes the idea that love is forever and sex means commitment. What is an adolescent to do when the hormones are raging, first love has hit hard and all these feelings are psychologically paired with irrational messages that promote unrealistic expectations and dependency?

Without proper emotional and conceptual tools, adolescents are at the mercy of pop songs and religious teachings. Much of the chaos of adolescence in the United States could be tempered with sound sex and relationship education. Sound sex education doesn't just talk about sex, it discusses and provides opportunities to practice responses to emotionally charged situations that most people face sooner or later. It teaches about the full range of options available and how to set priorities in life. As with most other things in life, people who are educated make better decisions and achieve their goals more often than those who are not. Sex is no different.

Unfortunately, most religions are against such honest and up-front education. From teen pregnancies and STIs to teen suicide, the root causes of these problems often arise in religious training and resistance to healthy sex and relationship education.

How does this relate to jealousy? The crazy ideas that teens imbibe carry forward into marriage and parenthood. When someone believes, "I can't live without you" or "You are mine forever, no matter what," they often do things that drive their spouse away. These kinds of beliefs lead to possessiveness and dependency, not mature adult behavior. They certainly don't promote good communication skills.

## Jealousy Says More About the Jealous Person

Jealousy says a lot about a person's sexual map. A jealous person is making a statement about his or her ownership or control of another person. It's a dangerous idea, one that belongs in the dustbin of history.

People who believe they have a right to judge, evaluate and control others' sex lives are often emotionally uneducated and have a sexual map based on religious notions of sexual purity and women's roles in society. The belief that a man or a woman has a right to judge and control others leads to parental and spousal behavior that is emotionally and physically damaging. Not only are women subject to abuse and control, so are husbands and children. If the child's sexual orientation or sexual interests conflict with the religious ideas of the parents, abuse is likely. Whether we call this jealousy or not, the behavior of a man guarding his "wayward" wife or daughter looks a lot like it. If a woman believes she owns her husband, her jealously controlling behavior can be stifling.

Ideas and beliefs cause the behavior we label jealousy. Ideas that lead to jealous behavior are irrational. For example, a jealous woman might have the belief that "I must control my husband or he may stray to someone else just like my father did." Her belief does not come from her husband's behavior but from her insecurities and childhood experience. This is the most common reason for jealous behavior: the jealous person is insecure and has an excessive fear of loss or abandonment. Jealousy is not a single emotion but the coming together of many emotions based on certain beliefs. To understand jealousy, we must unpack it.

## Unpacking Jealousy

Jealousy that comes from fear of loss or abandonment is a relationship killer. These self-defeating ideas need to be systematically discarded and replaced by ideas based on reality, not on emotions experienced in childhood. Only then can a person begin to learn the important skills of relationship building and effective communication.

If a person has hidden beliefs that "All men cheat" or "All women are gold diggers," it will influence his or her behavior, maybe into a form we might identify as jealousy. Most people will not admit these beliefs. They will deny they are jealous but behave in ways that appear controlling and jealous. Here is how it works:

**Belief:**  "All men cheat, so I have to keep close track of my husband."

**Behavior**: Constant tracking of husband's whereabouts, who he talks to, who he calls or emails.

**Belief**: "Keeping close track of my man will keep him married to me and make me feel secure."

**Behavior**: Constant focus on his whereabouts. Most people, whether man or woman, would be driven away by this kind of behavior.

Identifying hidden beliefs allows us to see the fallacies in thinking that lead to self-defeating behavior. Identifying and changing these can make a huge positive difference in the development of a relationship. There is far more to learn about dealing with this kind of irrational thinking than we can discuss here. If you would like to learn more about self-defeating thinking, consult some of the resources in the bibliography. For now, I want to deal with some specific irrational ideas that are bound up with religion.

## Sex Is a Precious Commodity

Our culture has a good deal of influence over what we value. If something is deemed important enough we may even be willing to die for it. Some people will die for their country. Others will die for their religion. Both of these are culturally defined.

Religion says that following the sexual laws of Jesus or Mohammed is so critical that you could die and burn in eternal hell for violating them. This is a great excuse to get into other people's sexual lives. "If you are gay, I am going to save you from hell." "If you want to have premarital sex, I am going to help you understand what eternal suffering is like." In any case, the logic is air tight – by abusing or controlling you in this life, the religious person is saving you from hell in the next. The same logic was used by the Spanish Inquisition.

These religious ideas define what people can and cannot do with regard to sex. First, religion defines sex as precious and limited. You can only have sex with one person per lifetime and that sex must conform to specific guidelines – or you will burn! When something so essential is severely limited, that really raises its value. If sex is a precious commodity, you must protect it at all costs. If you violate it, the price to restore yourself to sanctity will be high. Women, protect your virginity. Men, jealously guard your wives and daughters to keep them from falling into Satan's sexual trap. Never masturbate and practice abstinence only.

Jealousy is only functional if you believe that sex is a limited commodity to be guarded like gold. If sex is not a limited commodity, then religion has lost its most effective tool for infection.

The idea of defending your mate against sexual competition is rampant throughout our culture and is deeply rooted in the major religions. If you believe that sex is primarily for reproduction, men must control women to ensure the progeny are theirs. If you believe that sex is primarily for bonding, the reasons for jealousy are less compelling. That is not to say your lover or spouse is not important. If you have a good relationship, it is reasonable and rational to do things that will keep your partner interested and attracted to you. But maintaining and enjoying a relationship is not the same as jealously guarding it. Jealousy is the opposite of maintaining and growing in a relationship. Jealousy includes elements of fear, anger, suspicion and control that have no place in a mature relationship.

A person who is hungry will do desperate, need-based things to get food. By the same token, a person who defines his love as necessary for life will behave in equally need-based ways. The desire for someone is a want, not a need, but our brains easily confuse the ideas. A boy in love may act as though he cannot live without his girl. The behavior is based in our biology and the opiates in our brains, manufactured when we are in the throes of New Relationship Energy – in love. The effect lovers have on one another is similar to a chemical addiction. Fortunately, teaching people about this aspect of our biology can help them anticipate and govern their behavior more rationally when the time comes. It is emotional education, and it works to help children, youth, and even adults negotiate their social world more effectively.[183,184]

Using these kinds of tools, we help people change their need-based sexual map to a want-based map. Want-based thinking is not prone to jealous behavior. It explores options for mutual satisfaction. It sees the wants and desires of the other as equal. Want-based thinking does not see sex as a

183   Diekstra, R. F. W. (2008). "Effectiveness of school based social and emotional education programmes worldwide." Available online at http://educacion.fundacionmbotin.org/index.php?a=educacion_responsable_evaluacion.

184   Payton, J, Weissberg, R. P., et al. (2008). "Positive Impact of Social and Emotional Learning for Kindergarten to Eighth Grade Students: findings from three scientific reviews." CASEL. Available online at http://casel.org/publications/positive-impact-of-social-and-emotional-learning-for-kindergarten-to-eighth-grade-students-findings-from-three-scientific-reviews-executive-summary/.

precious commodity to be hoarded and protected, but as something to be shared, learned and enjoyed.

When you unpack jealousy, there isn't much there except some crazy ideas on a very flawed map. It is a map that is strongly reinforced by religion's ideas about fidelity, monogamy, eternal love and things like committing your marriage to god.

### American Sex

If you were raised in American culture, you are surrounded by the religious idea that sex is a limited commodity. It influences the way you date, who you date, how you relate to the opposite sex, even how you have sex. At every phase of the dating and sexual relationship process, this idea injects itself and often causes jealousy. The entire culture holds this belief. Millions of people go without sex because religions say it is limited.

You probably have visions of a million-person orgy right now. That wouldn't be what I am suggesting. I am suggesting that notions of fidelity, ownership and jealousy all interfere with people enjoying one another. Think back to the cultures we examined where there were no religious restrictions. The Na do not believe sex is a limited commodity. The Mangaians don't get jealous. No one owns the sexuality of a woman in the Hadza culture. We impose these cultural concepts on ourselves. If you are non-religious, you can discard these ideas and write your own rules (which we will explore in the next chapter).

### Frubble or Compersion

In the last few years new language has developed around relationships in the polyamory and BDSM communities. Since multiple relationships are so common in these communities, they have learned to deal positively with jealousy. The result is language and ideas that turn jealousy on its head. For example, compersion (also called frubble) is defined as "A state of empathetic happiness and joy experienced when an individual's current or former romantic partner experiences happiness and joy through an outside source, including, but not limited to, another romantic interest."[185] We have a choice in how we treat situations. We can fall back on jealousy or we can experience the joy of our partner.

---

185   See http://en.wikipedia.org/wiki/Compersion.

The point is that jealousy is culturally learned and, therefore, can be unlearned. The poly community has been able to reframe it. Are there jealous people in the poly community? Of course. The difference is that they have tools for dealing with it more rationally than other groups. In the poly community, jealousy is generally exposed and discussed so the person can look inside and understand how jealousy hurts himself and his relationships.[186]

As the great science fiction writer Robert Heinlein (an early pioneer in polyamory) said, "Jealousy is a disease, love is a healthy condition. The immature mind often mistakes one for the other, or assumes that the greater the love, the greater the jealousy – in fact, they're almost incompatible; one emotion hardly leaves room for the other. Both at once can produce unbearable turmoil ...."[187]

There is little to be learned from religious approaches to sex and relationships. Religious values do not foster emotional maturity and rational approaches to relationships. Indeed, religion places a third party in the equation – a god. Religion does foster jealousy, control of women and the ever-present voyeuristic god in the bedroom. The Old Testament god says, "I, the LORD your God, am a jealous God"(Exodus 20:4-5). From his obsession with people's sex lives, we might conclude he is jealous of all the sex everyone else is getting.

Now let's look at three big ideas that anyone can use to create fulfilling and satisfying relationships, relationships that meet your needs even as you meet those of others.

---

186 The long-running podcast "Polyamory Weekly" has discussed jealousy from many angles over the years. It is most interesting to hear that sexually monogamous people listen to it and find the advice and discussions even help them in their relationships. Online at http://polyweekly.com/.

187 Heinlein, R. (1991). *Stranger in a strange land*. The book was originally published in 1961 but with 27% cut by the publisher, who claimed it was objectionable. In 1991 Heinlein's widow retrieved all the excised material and republished the book uncut. The result was a much more complete and interesting work that included characters who were polyamorous, though the word had not yet been invented at the time.

# CHAPTER 25:

# WHAT'S THE BIG IDEA?

*Sooner or later monogamous marriage hits the end of the biological leash. If you eliminate religious marriage ideas, how do you develop relationships?*

*"You have to let go of who you should be in order to be who you are."*
**-Brene Brown in a TED lecture**

## The Tyranny of the "Shoulds"

Religion tells you who you should be, not who you are. If you were raised in a religion or a religious culture, you were given a host of sexual "shoulds" designed to induce guilt and keep you coming back to the religion for forgiveness. Many sexual shoulds sneak into our self-identity early in life. Shoulds say more about a religion's infection strategy than they say about you.

Many religious people are the sum of all the shoulds they absorbed in their early training. Because their shoulds define them, they never learn who they are. They are too busy being who their minister, parents, spouse, church or Sunday School teacher says they should be. People who rely on shoulds to make life decisions often make poor choices. For example, reasoning, "I should marry a nice Christian boy/girl," instead of, "It would be best to marry someone who is compatible with me in many ways and has no guilt around sex."

The great psychotherapist Dr. Albert Ellis called this the "tyranny of the shoulds." He often said in his workshops, "Shouldhood leads to shithood. Don't should on yourself, and don't should on others – it stinks."[188]

Eliminating shoulds will enhance your life in many ways, not only in sex. Change ideas from, "I shouldn't be angry with my parents for making me feel so guilty about sex" to, "My parents did the best they could with the tools they had. It is irrational to be angry with them for trying to raise me in the way they thought best."

Many people spend years getting over sexual hang-ups they learned in their religious training. I won't deny this can be difficult to overcome, but much of the difficulty can be changed by learning new ways of thinking – changing your sexual map. If you continue to be angry with parents or religion, it is a sign that you are still using old thought patterns. Change the thought pattern and the emotion often changes as well.

## The Mating of Souls

New Age religions have brought into the popular love language the idea of "soul mate." It seems a benign idea at first glance but warrants closer examination. If soul mate just means someone you get along with, have lots of common interests and strong emotional connection with,  it's not

---

188   Ellis, A. (1975). *A New Guide to Rational Living.*

particularly harmful. What can be harmful are people who take this notion seriously and make important decisions based upon their determination of how their "soul" matches up against that of their lover or partner.

Whether you are into New Age or not, many religionists espouse similar ideas. If you and your religion believe you possess a soul, that is the beginning of a delusion that will inevitably disappoint you and lead to disappointment with your partner. I have heard many married Christians claim that their god brought them together. Many a (now divorced) Baptist minister has claimed from the pulpit that god gave him his wife.

Many people feel they are more than their physical being. That a soul exists outside their body – outside of time and space – something that lives on, despite overwhelming evidence to the contrary. The most immediate consequence of soul belief is that it creates an invisible and, by definition, nebulous intermediary between you and your partner. How does one know what a soul likes and doesn't like? How does one mingle one's soul with another's to see if they match? How does one distinguish between soul com-munication and physical communication? What is the difference between effective communication and observation skills and communicating with the soul?

The feelings one gets when communicating well with another person can be incredibly rewarding and gratifying, but it says nothing about a soul. Everything needed to establish a strong and loving relationship with another human being can be done with skills that are learned or taught. Good communication skills make for highly satisfying relationships, no soul required. Here is a short list of skills:

1.  Active listening skills: the ability to not only hear what the other person is saying but to understand and explore some of the underlying concerns and emotions so that you feel you are able to articulate your partner's issues and concerns in a way that makes him or her feel heard and cared for.

2.  Anticipation skills: the ability to understand someone well enough so you can anticipate some of their needs and concerns and take appropriate action. For example, you know a friend likes flowers or a certain kind of food, so you arrange to provide those on occasions when it would make her feel loved and cared for.

3.  Ability to subsume your needs and desires when needed: When

a partner is sick, emotionally distraught, under pressure at work, upset with a child, etc., you put your needs on the back burner and support her emotionally.

4. Ability to identify and avoid unhealthy levels of need or dependency: A good partner knows when to call you on your "baggage." It may be as simple as saying, "I will not participate in your pity party. Let's get to work and see what you can do to get back on track." This is a difficult skill to learn and perform because it means putting the other person's well-being ahead of the relationship. It is delicate because it has the potential to disrupt a friendship, as it does any relationship. If you are misreading the situation, it can come across as cruel and unfeeling. If you are correct, but the other person is not willing to take responsibility for his behavior, it can make him withdraw. Ultimately, it is the most caring thing you can do as a friend, lover or partner, but it requires deep trust and skill.

We could list many more. The question is, "Where in this list of skills is a soul required?" Any of these skills and behaviors can evoke feelings of deep care, compassion, love and support. They are skills a mother or father may show to a child, a lover to a partner. Continual practice of them leads to levels of trust that make us feel deeply connected to another person.

On a less romantic level, this kind of interaction probably prompts our brain to release a dose of oxytocin – the bonding and trust hormone. Oxytocin has been shown to be important in mother-child bonding as well as sexual bonding for both men and women and trust between people working together on a common project. At a chemical level, you feel close to someone because they can evoke a release of oxytocin and other chemicals in your brain. If you were to take an oxytocin-blocking drug, chances are you would feel less close to them.[189]

It is not very romantic, but reality is a better basis for building a relationship than fantasizing about a soul mate or counting on a god to find you a partner.

---

189    "To Trust or Not to Trust: Ask Oxytocin," by Mauricio Delgado in *Scientific American.* Available online at http://www.scientificamerican.com/article.cfm?id=to-trust-or-not-to-trust.

## Your Cheatin' Heart – Escaping the Conceptual Prison

Religion puts a set of moral rules around sex and sexual relationships. These rules are so far from our nature as to be cruel and fundamentally unrealistic. As we have seen, the proof is in the fact that religious people behave in almost the same way as non-religious people do. The main difference is that they feel quite guilty, whereas the non-religious feel much less guilty. The biggest problem with religious sex is that there appears to be no way out. You either follow the church's moral strictures or you are unsaved and unclean.

The result of this conceptual prison is that people step outside anyway but try to hide it. So-called "cheating" is the reason for 17-25% of divorces, according to some researchers, and that number may be a low estimate. Other research indicates that nearly 70% of all married men and 60% of married women have had affairs. That's two out of every three marriages.[190] With divorce highest among the most religious states and zip codes, we can probably assume that religious people are having their share of affairs.

Cheating is ethically wrong, whether you are religious or not. It is a violation of a promise. That may sound harsh, but there is far more to this notion of cheating than current pop culture knows. From my experience, people who cheat have two conflicting goals, First, they often want to stay married to their partner – or they would leave; and second, they desperately want something that is not present in their marriage. The genetic map pushes them toward variety and they have reached a sexual satiation point with their spouse.

Pop culture notions of monogamy are strongly based on religion. Whether country music or rock, opera or Harlequin novels, stories and songs mix ideas of temptation, evil, god, angels, fallen women, sin and much more. Religious monogamy has no way to understand satiation or need for variety. Religion puts a leash on our sexuality and expects to keep us on the straight and narrow.

What happens when you decide to slip the leash and leave religion? You must develop your own ethical guidelines. God won't punish you if you have an affair, but your life may become miserable if your spouse finds out. People who cheat always have a dozen excuses: she never wanted sex; he

---

190  Hein, H. (2001) *Sexual Detours: The Startling Truth Behind Love, Lust, and Infidelity.*

never listened to me; she hated my friends; he treats my family terribly. The underlying reason is simple – humans get tired of each other and want variety. Once we recognize these simple facts, we can explore new options.

## It's Not All About the Sex

It is important to develop an ethical approach to issues of sexuality, one that respects the needs of both parties and allows for reexamination or renegotiation. What if one or both partners want to stay married but is no longer stimulated in the marriage? How could that be handled? How can a couple explore these issues without feeling inadequate or blamed?

We know that humans like variety, are extremely sexual and that ignoring an urge doesn't make it go away. Because one partner wants new stimulation, it does not mean the other is inadequate or somehow at fault. These are old notions based on shoulds, oughts and musts from religious training.

If we live our relationships on shoulds, oughts and musts, we are missing wonderful opportunities to share and learn from the most important people in our lives. We don't have to live by guilt and shame-inducing rules. We can step outside of the conceptual prison and learn to be adults who treat our mates as full partners and make mutual decisions that enhance and enrich life. We can remain together for as long as we like, even a lifetime, while ensuring that both are emotionally and sexually fulfilled.

Here are three things I call Big Ideas that, I believe, can enhance the opportunity for happiness in relationships and reduce the need for divorce. Test them for yourself.

## Big Idea Number One: Challenge Hidden Assumptions

The first Big Idea is the most revolutionary. Recognize and celebrate your natural human tendencies and work out a way to satisfy your desires without blaming each other or getting divorced. This means examining the hidden assumptions baked into every relationship, especially marriage. Ideas like the following:

- He/she should be attracted to me no matter what.
- Marriage is forever, with or without sex.
- The children come first.
- We can be married only if we are sexually monogamous.
- To want sex with someone else means he/she doesn't love me.
- I should be happy with one sex partner for the rest of my life.

These are irrational assumptions that strongly influence thinking and behavior. They often remain unspoken and unexamined. Let's take a brief look and understand why they are irrational.

**He/she should be attracted to me no matter what.** One can easily imagine situations where attraction would die. She gains 200 lbs. He becomes physically abusive. She starts a crack cocaine addiction. He stops bathing. Most people would quickly find these unattractive even if the person was Mr. or Ms. America when they married. The question then becomes, "What are the boundaries of attraction?" "What responsibility do you have to remain attractive as a marriage partner?"

**Marriage is forever, with or without sex.** Sex was probably an important part of the initial attraction. To expect that your partner's sex drive will stop just because yours has is probably delusional. Marriage lasts as long as the two of you decide it does. There is no way to force someone to remain married. If you don't want sex but she does, you had better reexamine your assumptions if you want to stay married.

**The children come first.** The marriage came first; if you don't take care of the marriage, the children suffer. A loving marriage provides a safe place for children to thrive. Parents who don't have time for each other while they are raising the kids are often on the fast track for divorce.

**We can be married only if we are sexually monogamous.** This idea causes more divorces than all others combined. There are millions of people throughout the world who have happy, thriving marriages while enjoying lovers outside the marriage. The French have made an art form of it for centuries. This is not to say it is always a good idea, but it is an option that would save a lot of otherwise good marriages.

**To want sex with someone else means he/she doesn't love me.** We love multiple people all the time. Why is it when sex gets involved, people suddenly think they own the other person's sexuality? (See the Chapter 24 on jealousy.)

**I should be happy with one sex partner for the rest of my life.** Sexual monogamy is an unrealistic expectation for 50-70% of the population. Indeed, sexual monogamy is among the rarest of sexual preferences in nature. Sex is a strong human appetite. Accepting this fact allows for more rational ways to handle marriage.

### Big Idea Number Two: Be Honest With Yourself

The second Big idea is to learn how to be honest with yourself so that you can be honest with your partner. When someone is dissatisfied, they generally blame their spouse or partner. The cold hard truth is that the dissatisfaction is inside *you*. If you are dissatisfied, admit it and talk with your spouse openly and honestly. This is frightening, even terrifying, for most people and for good reason. Talking about the ideas listed above can be extremely threatening. Panic, anger, blame and upset come quickly. Honesty requires courage, but it also requires love, tact and an understanding of the other person.

While long-term sexual monogamy is not natural to humans, modern society thrives on social monogamy. Families benefit greatly from long-term stable marriages. Individuals benefit emotionally, financially and psychologically. I am very much in favor of social monogamy.

In their excellent book *The Myth of Monogamy*, David Barash, Ph.D., and Judith Lipton, M.D., explore how common it is among many species to be socially mated to one "spouse" but to have sex with others. For example, the myth that swans are monogamous was disproved when DNA testing found that 17-20% of the eggs belonged to a different father. Swans also "divorce" far more often than once thought.[191] They are not sexually monogamous but they are socially monogamous – mated for long periods of time.

In the West, we practice social monogamy but not necessarily sexual monogamy. Cheating is a non-monogamous choice made without the partner's knowledge or permission. When we believe all the religious ideas about marriage, we cannot see a way to live a sexually non-monogamous life without destroying our socially monogamous lives. But non-monogamy is a radical proposal. So let's look at the options when one or both partners are dissatisfied:

1.   Remain together in misery with the ever-present possibility of cheating.
2.   Divorce and seriously disrupt the family and social network.
3.   Explore ways to rejuvenate the marriage from within.
4.   Practice sexual non-monogamy and social monogamy.

191   Barash, D. P., & Lipton, J. (2001). *The Myth of Monogamy: Fidelity and Infidelity in Animals and People.*

**Option one: Remain together in misery with the ever-present possibility of cheating.** This is very common. A significant number of marriages that never end up in divorce choose this option. Maybe as much as 25-30% of marriages become more like brother and sister living together. If both can turn off their sex drives, this option may be a permanent solution; if not, it can be miserable. If one or the other feels trapped and helpless, the celibacy can lead to depression and other medical problems. Unhappy people do not take care of themselves physically or emotionally. They gain weight, don't exercise, self-medicate with alcohol or prescription drugs and fundamentally fail to recognize the source of their problems – a marriage that is not satisfying their emotional and sexual needs.

**Option two: Divorce, and seriously disrupt the family and social network.** Divorce is emotionally devastating to everyone involved, but it is made worse by the false assumptions people have about marriage. Ideas like "Til death do us part" or "We will get the kids raised, then we will be happier." When the break does happen, people often blame and vilify their spouses rather than admitting their fundamental assumptions were wrong in the first place.

Blame and recrimination create more emotional turmoil. In most cases, a marriage was in trouble for years before the divorce. The couple assumed that by ignoring problems they could keep the marriage going on automatic pilot. When a spouse's genetic leash yanks her back to her biological roots, she feels a strong urge to break out of the monogamy trap. Years of ignoring sexual or relationship needs often takes one or both of partners by surprise. Clients have said, "I thought we had a good marriage, then I got the divorce papers," or "I thought we were happy until I discovered she was having an affair."

**Option three: Explore ways to rejuvenate the marriage from within.** Rejuvenation is difficult, but not impossible. Couples do find ways to revitalize their relationships and live happily for decades. The task is daunting because it requires a fundamental reassessment of the marriage. In some ways, it is like creating a new marriage. For some, the process feels like walking a tight rope between two tall buildings. The tension, questioning, rethinking and trying of new ideas and new behavior can be exhausting. You can fall off the tight rope. But couples who have successfully made it to the new marriage say it was worth the risk and effort. Some even say they are as happy in their rejuvenated marriage as they were the first few years of marriage.

**Option four: Practice sexual non-monogamy and social monogamy.** The option of sexual non-monogamy and social monogamy respects our biology but is furthest from religious ideas about marriage. This area is far too large for us to discuss here. I would recommend reading some of the great resources available on this topic in the bibliography.

Many people have successfully integrated sexual non-monogamy (polyamory)[192] into their socially monogamous marriages. I recently attended a conference with about 300 secular college students. A speaker asked, "How many people are 'poly friendly'?" Ninety percent of the hands went up. Most religious college students don't know what the word means, let alone feel open to the possibility. It is an idea that secularists can explore but it is unavailable to religionists. Whether this is a good option or not, only you and your partner can decide. It may be a good option if it allows a couple to stay married and finish raising children. It may be a bad option if issues of security and jealousy cannot be managed.

Regardless of the options you choose, the most important thing is to choose consciously. Don't let ancient religious programming dictate your emotional and intellectual responses. You are a biological and social creature living in a biological and social world. Recognizing this gives you the power to make more rational decisions about how you want to enjoy the only life you have.

### Big Idea Number Three: You Are Normal

The realm of "normal" in human sexuality is vast. If you want to masturbate several times a day – that is normal. If you want to have sex with your partner several times a day – that is normal. If you want to be spanked before you have sex – that is normal. If you want to have oral sex frequently – that is normal. If you want to have a threesome – that is normal. If you like to dress up in the clothes of the opposite sex – that is normal. If you get off by watching naked men popping balloons – that is normal. If you want a husband and a lover on the side – that is normal.

There is nothing wrong with you if you have normal ideas, urges and drives. If your sexual behavior is consensual among adults and hurts no one else, it is fine. In the BDSM world, it's called "safe, sane and consensual," a

192 Polyamory: based on the Latin for many loves. The practice, desire or acceptance of having more than one intimate relationship at a time with the knowledge and consent of everyone involved.

good way to sum it up. No church has the right to get into your bedroom and tell you what is normal.

What is abnormal are priests, nuns and popes, an uptight Baptist minister's wife, a fire-breathing misogynistic imam. These are all far from the mainstream of human sexuality. They have a perfect right to be and believe what they like; unfortunately, they have political and social power to make life miserable for millions of people with their guilt and shame-based sexualities.

These three Big Ideas will help you identify hidden assumptions and religious programming. They will also help you redraw your map of what sex and relationships mean to you and your partner.

The ultimate goal is for you to learn to live happily with your sexuality and develop long-term, productive relationships based on realistic expectations.

# CHAPTER 26:

# THE END OF RELIGION AS WE KNOW IT

*Religion is evolving to survive but is losing the battle in many regions, largely because of the Internet. Sexual information is far more available now, which interferes with religion's ability to use sexual guilt to perpetuate.*

## The Evolving Church

As I explored in *The God Virus*,[193] religions mutate and evolve, just like any organism. Churches are adjusting and changing their sexual ideas but are always a few steps behind the culture. Here is the evidence:

- The Catholic church is giving annulments at unprecedented rates in the United States to prevent a hemorrhaging of members. You can't excommunicate all the Catholics who are divorcing, or few members will be left to contribute to the church.

- Virtually all Catholics in the Western world use birth control and many have had abortions. The church continues to condemn both. It has tried (but with little success) to excommunicate Catholic politicians who supported birth control and abortion.

- Baptists and non-denominationals are experiencing among the highest divorce rates in the United States. Divorced people used to be shunned and forced out of the church. You cannot eliminate all divorced people or half the church will soon be gone. As a result, these churches are trying to support divorced people even as they soft-pedal the message that divorce is immoral.

- Despite the teachings of conservative churches, the rates of premarital sex are equally common between the religious and non-religious. Churches turn a blind eye to those who live together or are in non-marital sexual relationships.

- Some Evangelical churches that condemned masturbation just a few years ago are now soft-pedaling their barbaric approaches to it. Kids can read on the Internet that masturbation is perfectly normal. It makes it much more difficult to infect them with guilt messages when it is clear that the religious teachers and preachers don't know what they are talking about.

- Some churches are coming to terms with homosexuality and openly welcoming gays. By marginalizing gays, they alienated the parents, brothers, sisters, aunts and uncles of gays. You may be able to kick the gays out, but you can't afford to kick their relatives out as well.

---

193   Ray, D. (2009). *The God Virus: How Religion Infects Our Lives and Culture.*

• People born into a world using the Internet will be much more difficult to infect with crazy ideas about sex. The churches are trying desperately to adjust to this reality.

## Almost Everyone Is Doing It

What is the future of religion and sex? A recent article in the conservative magazine *RELEVANT* called "Almost Everyone Is Doing It" found that 80% of single Evangelicals have had sex outside of marriage while 76% say it is wrong. It also found that 88% of secular singles have had premarital sex. As we have noted earlier, there isn't much difference between the two groups. The article examines all aspects of the "problem" trying to understand why young Christian people are having sex when they believe it to be wrong.[194] Nowhere do they examine the obvious – biology happens. It is like they assume humans are not biological but spiritual.

Josh McDowell, one of the key leaders of Campus Crusade for Christ (now rebranded with the name Cru), said it best in a speech, "Unshakable Truth, Relevant Faith," at the Billy Graham Center in Asheville, N.C.[195] He warned that sexual immorality through the Internet is "marginalizing the maturity of the witness of Christ ... all over the world. It's an invasive, intruding immorality ... that is all just one click away," adding that the majority of questions young people ask him are about sex, mainly "oral sex."

This is a Christian leader's analysis, and I would agree with him in many ways. Religions throughout the world are losing control of sex. Ironically, the result is greater joy and satisfaction, less disease, and fewer unplanned pregnancies and less traumatic guilt around normal sexual behavior.

McDowell had little to offer his listeners. Yet he proposed three ways to deal with the problem of children learning from the Internet. "First, we have to model the truth ... Second, we have to build relationships ... and third, We have to use knowledge ... You better arm yourselves to answer your children's and grandchildren's questions ... no matter what the question is ... without being judgmental. Kids' greatest defense," he said, "was the knowledge of truth." He may as well say, *"Access to truth, reality and reliable information is the greatest threat to religion."*

---

194   Available online at http://www.relevantmagazine. com/digital-issue/53?page=66.

195   Reported by Anugrah Kumar in *The Christian Post*, available online at http://www.christianpost. com/news/apologist-josh-mcdowell-internet-the-greatest-threat-to-christians-52382/.

Unfortunately for religion, modeling the truth, building honest relationships and gaining knowledge will not keep people infected with religious sexuality. Open and honest discussion of these topics will help children resist the crazy ideas religion teaches about sex and, as a result, make better decisions. Modeling the truth will undermine the sexual foundations of Christianity, Islam, Hinduism, Buddhism, Mormonism and any other religion that seeks to control human sexuality.

## Sex, Religion and the Planet

There are seven billion people on the planet, projected to become nine billion by 2040. In every industrialized country, when a certain level of wealth and education is reached, the population tends to decrease the rate of reproduction. The most secular societies have the lowest reproduction rates. Educated, secular people are choosing to have far fewer children than in the past. Indeed, a large segment are choosing not to have any children.

What does this mean for sex and sexuality? For thousands of years, religion has kept humanity focused on reproducing in the interest of propagating the religion. Policies around birth control have been opposed by religion and continue to be opposed. Evangelicals and Catholics are preaching vociferously against condoms in Africa and the United States. Mormons still oppose masturbation. Southern Baptists are against abortion and birth control for teens.

This has serious implications for sex in our culture and world culture. As we have seen throughout this book, sex is largely for bonding and recreational purposes with 1,000 to 10,000 sex acts for every live birth. With far lower birthrates, improved birth control and in-vitro fertilization (test tube babies), sex plays a decreasing role in reproduction. This means that old religiously-based taboos and superstitions about sex and sexuality no longer have meaning in the context of reproduction. "Be fruitful and multiply" simply falls on deaf ears.

These facts call for a close examination and rethinking about the role of sex in society and relationships. As more countries increase the education and economic level of their populations, it appears that the role of religion will continue to fade and with it guilt and shame. Whether through birth control or ecological collapse, disease or resource constriction, there will be less human reproduction in the future. The era of unrestricted human reproduction is coming to an end. Religions will have to find other means of propagating or die. With more highly educated populations that have access to vast amounts of information, it will be more difficult for religions to mentally trap people and teach their distorted views of sexuality. The result will be less distortion in our understanding and pursuit of sexual pleasure and relationship building. We will be able to act like the sophisticated social primates that we are.

## A New ~~Commandment~~ Suggestion I Give You

Go ye therefore and enjoy deity-free sex – have fun!

Ali, Ayaan Hirsi. (2007). *Infidel.* New York: Free Press.

Ali, Ayaan Hirsi. (2010). *Nomad: From Islam to America, A Personal Journey Through the Clash of Civilizations.* New York: Free Press.

Anapol, Deborah M. (2010). *Polyamory in the 21st Century: Love and Intimacy with Multiple Partners.* Lanham, MD: Rowman & Littlefield Publishers.

Baker, Robin. (2006). *Sperm Wars: Infidelity, Sexual Conflict and other Bedroom Battles.* New York: Basic Books.

Barash, David P., & Lipton, Judith. (2001). *The Myth of Monogamy: Fidelity and Infidelity in Animals and People.* New York : W. H. Freeman and Co.

Baumeister, R. F. (2000). "Gender differences in erotic plasticity: The female sex drive as socially flexible and responsive." *Psychological Bulletin,* 126:347-374.

Berg, Amy (Director), Donner, Frank (Producer), et al. (2006). *Deliver Us From Evil.* Santa Monica, CA: Lionsgate.

Buller, D. J. (2005). "Sex, Jealousy and Violence: A Skeptical Look at Evolutionary Psychology." *Skeptic,* 12(1). Available online at http://www.skeptic.com/reading_room/sex- jealousy-and-violence./

Carrier, Richard. (2009). *Not the Impossible Faith: Why Christianity didn't need a miracle to succeed.* [United States]: Lulu.com.

Comfort, Alex. (1972). *The Joy of Sex: A Gourmet Guide to Lovemaking.* New York: Simon and Schuster.

Coontz, Stephanie. (2005). *Marriage, a history: from obedience to intimacy or how love conquered marriage.* New York: Viking.

Dawkins, R. (2006). *The God Delusion.* Boston: Houghton Mifflin.

Delgado, M. (15 July 2008). "To Trust or Not to Trust: Ask Oxytocin." *Scientific American*. Available online at http://www.scientificamerican. com/article.cfm?id=to-trust-or-not-to-trust.

Diamond, Jared M. (2005). *Guns, Germs and Steel: The Fates of Human Societies*. New York: Norton.

Diamond, Jared M. (2006). *The Third Chimpanzee: The Evolution and Future of the Human Animal*. New York: HarperPerennial.

Diekstra, R. F. W. (2008). "Effectiveness of school based social and emotional education programmes worldwide - part one, a review of meta-analytic literature." In *Social and emotional education: an international analysis*. Santander: Fundacion Marcelino Botin. Available online at http://educacion.fundacionmbotin.org/index.php?a=educacion_responsable_evaluacion.

Easton, Dossie, & Hardy, Janet W. (2009). *The Ethical Slut: A Practical Guide to Polyamory, Open Relationships & Other Adventures*. Berkeley, CA: Celestial Arts.

Edelman, B. (Winter 2009). "Red Light States: Who Buys Online Adult Entertainment?" *Journal of Economic Perspectives*, 23(1), 209-230.

Ellis, Albert. (1975). *A New Guide to Rational Living*. Englewood Cliffs, NJ: Prentice-Hall.

Ellis, Albert. (2003). *Sex Without Guilt in the 21st Century*. Fort Lee, NJ: Barricade.

Fisher, Helen E. (1992). *Anatomy of Love: The Natural History of Monogamy, Adultery, and Divorce*. New York: Norton.

Gadoua, Susan Pease. (2010). *Stronger Day by Day: Reflections for Healing and Rebuilding After Divorce*. Oakland, CA: New Harbinger Publications.

Goodall, Jane. (1971). *In the Shadow of Man.* Boston: Houghton Mifflin.

Heinlein, Robert A. (1991, 1961). *Stranger in a strange land.* New York: Putnam.

Hein, Holly. (2001). *Sexual Detours: The Startling Truth Behind Love, Lust, and Infidelity.* New York: St Martin's Griffin.

Hitchens, Christopher. (2010). *Hitch-22: A Memoir.* New York: Twelve.

Hutchinson, Sikivu. (2011). *Moral Combat: Black Atheists, Gender Politics, and the Values Wars.* Los Angeles, CA: Infidel Books.

Kinsey, Alfred C. (1948). *Sexual Behavior in the Human Male.* Philadelphia: W.B. Saunders.

Kinsey, Alfred C. (1953). *Sexual Behavior in the Human Female.* Philadelphia: Saunders.

Marshall, Donald S. & Suggs, Robert C. (Eds.) (1971). *Human Sexual Behavior: Variations in the Ethnographic Spectrum.* New York: Basic Books.

Malinowski, Bronislaw. (1987, 1929). *The sexual life of savages in Northwestern Melanesia: an ethnographic account of courtship, marriage, and family life among the natives of the Trobriand Islands, British New Guinea.* Boston: Beacon Press.

Marlowe, Frank. (2002). "Why the Hadza are Still Hunter-Gatherers." In Sue Kent (Ed.), *Ethnicity, Hunter-Gatherers, and the "Other": Association or Assimilation in Africa.* Washington: Smithsonian Institution Press.

Miller, Geoffrey F. (2001). *The Mating Mind: How Sexual Choice Shaped the Evolution of Human Nature.* New York: Anchor Books.

Ogas, Ogi, & Gaddam, Sai. (2011). *A Billion Wicked Thoughts: What the world's largest experiment reveals about human desire.* New York: Dutton.

Payton, J., Weissberg, R. P., et al. (2008). "Positive Impact of Social and Emotional Learning for Kindergarten to Eighth Grade Students: findings from three scientific reviews." CASEL. Available online at http://casel. org/publications/positive-impact-of-social-and-emotional-learning-for-kindergarten-to-eighth-grade-students-findings-from-three-scientific-reviews-executive-summary/.

Pinker, Steven. (1997). *How the Mind Works*. New York: Norton.

Ray, Darrel W. (2009). *The God Virus: How Religion Infects Our Lives and Culture*. Bonner Springs, KS: IPC Press.

Ray, Darrel W., & Brown, Amanda. (2011). "Sex and Secularism: What Happens When You Leave Religion." See IPCPress.com for the full report.

Regnerus, Mark. (2007). *Forbidden Fruit: Sex and Religion in the Lives of American Teenagers*. Oxford; New York: Oxford University Press.

Richardson, Kim Michele. (2010). *The Unbreakable Child*. Lake Forest, CA: Behler Publications.

Robertson, R. G. (2001). *Rotting face: Smallpox and the American Indian*. Caldwell, ID: Caxton Press.

Ryan, Christopher, & Jetha, Cacilda. (2010). *Sex at Dawn: The Prehistoric Origins of Modern Sexuality*. New York: Harper. Note: a 2011 edition was titled, *Sex at Dawn: How We Mate, Why We Stray, and What It Means for Modern Relationships*.

Sapolsky, Robert M. (14 November 2010). "This is Your Brain on Metaphors." *New York Times*. Available online at http://opinionator. blogs.nytimes.com/2010/11/14/this-is-your-brain-on-metaphors/.

Sapolsky, Robert M. (2002), *A Primate's Memoir: A Neuroscientist's Unconventional Life Among the Baboons*. New York: Scriber.

Sargant, William Walters. (1957). *Battle for the mind: a physiology of conversion and brainwashing*. Garden City, NY: Doubleday.

Schmitt, D. P. (2005). "Sociosexuality from Argentina to Zimbabwe: A 48-nation study of sex, culture, and strategies of human mating." *Behavioral and Brain Sciences*, 28:247-311.

Symons, Donald. (1981). *The Evolution of Human Sexuality*. Oxford; New York: Oxford University Press.

Thomas, Gary. (2000). *Sacred Marriage: What If God Designed Marriage to Make Us Holy More Than to Make Us Happy?* Grand Rapids, MI: Zondervan Pub. House.

Waal, F. B. M. de. (2005). *Our Inner Ape: A Leading Primatologist Explains Why We Are Who We Are*. New York: Riverhead Books.

Waller, N. G., Kojetin, B. A., Bouchard, T. J., Lykken, D. T., & Tellegen, A. (1990). "Genetic and environmental influences on religious interests, attitudes and values: A study of twins reared apart and together." *Psychological Science*, 1, 138-142.

White, Wrath. (28 May 2008). "The Invisibility of the Black Atheist." Available online at http://wordsof- wrath.blogspot.com/2008/05/ invisibility-of-black-atheist.html.

Wilson, E. O. "On Human Nature," in William A. Rottschaefer (Ed.), (1998). *The Biology and Psychology of Moral Agency*. Cambridge; New York: Cambridge University Press.

Worell, Judith. (2002). *Encyclopedia of Women and Gender: sex similarities and differences*. San Diego, CA: Academic Press.

ducks
    penises, 100–102
    reproduction, 101
    sexual behavior, 100–102
duplicity, 20–22, 24–25, 148

**E**
Earl Paulk, 47
education, sex, 168–169, 181, 198
egalitarian culture, 135
Ellis, Albert, 264
Emma Smith, 53
emotion, gender differences, 75
empathy, 260
England, Victorian, 40
environment
    attraction, 121
    group membership, 163–165
    jealousy, 252–255
    learning, 119
    marriage, 192
    personality, 208–209
    religiosity, 210–212
    sexuality, 127–128
epigenetics, 117–118
ethics, 87
eunuchs, 59
Eve and Adam, 44, 96, 162
explorers, introducing disease,
    159–160
external effects, 117–118

**F**
family, 63
fantasies, 183
Father of Latin Christianity, 53, 152

father of modern biological classifica-
    tion, 100
fear, 26, 199–200
fear of death, 161–162
female circumcision, 165–166
Francis Schaeffer Institute, 222
Frans de Waal, 105–106, 215

**G**
Gadoua, Susan, Pease 248
Gangestad, 215–216
Gary Thomas, 37, 48
gender differences, 75–76
genetic programming, 116
genetics, 208, 209, 210–213, 253
genitals, ritual marking, 163–166
Gingrich, Newt, 47, 245
girls, 199
goal of religion, 23, 39, 191
gods, Greek religion, 142
Goodall, Jane, 104
Gorham, Candace, 81–83
gorillas
    jealousy, 252
    penises, 103
    sex organs, 103
    sexual behavior, 103
Gospel of Mary, 52
Gospel of Phillip, 52
Gospel of Pistis Sophia, 52
Graham, Billy, 51
Greek culture
    boys, 143
    class, 141
    prostitution, 141
    shame, 63
    women, 141–142

## About the Author

Darrel Ray has been a student of religion since college. With an undergraduate degree in Sociology and Anthropology from Friends University in Wichita, Kansas, he went on to Scarritt College for Christian workers in Nashville, Tennes, where he received a MA in Church and Community in 1974. Originally thinking he might go into the ministry, he soon realized that he believed very little of what he had been taught about religion. He changed focus to psychology and took a Doctor of Education degree from Peabody College of Vanderbilt University in 1978.

He continued to participate in several churches including teaching and preaching and serving a tenor soloist in several choirs. He also trained army and civilian chaplains and ministers in counseling techniques and consulted with several religious organizations until 1990 when he left religion altogether. Since that time he has turned his attention to the study of religion as a human phenomenon.

With the publication of his best-selling book, *The God Virus: How Religion Infects Our Lives and Culture*, Dr. Ray has been in great demand as a speaker throughout the United States and Europe. His talks are entertaining and informative, illustrating the psychology of religion and its negative impact on many aspects of life including sexuality, educational achievement, child development and marriage.

He is one of the few psychologists who directly challenges religion as a impediment to healthy human sexual and relationship development. Visit IPCPress.com for more information or to contact Dr. Ray.